TWENTIETH CENTURY VIEWS

The aim of this series is to present the best in contemporary critical opinion on major authors, providing a twentieth century perspective on their changing status in an era of profound revaluation.

Maynard Mack, *Series Editor*
Yale University

JOHN UPDIKE

A COLLECTION OF CRITICAL ESSAYS

Edited by
David Thorburn and Howard Eiland

Prentice-Hall, Inc. A SPECTRUM BOOK *Englewood Cliffs, N.J.*

813.54

Library of Congress Cataloging in Publication Data

MAIN ENTRY UNDER TITLE:

JOHN UPDIKE: a collection of critical essays.

(Twentieth century views)   (A Spectrum Book)
Bibliography: p.
Includes index.
1. Updike, John—Criticism and interpretation—
Addresses, essays, lectures.   I. Thorburn, David.
II. Eiland, Howard.
PS3571.P4Z74   813'.5'4   79-1481
ISBN 0-13-937607-0
ISBN 0-13-937599-6 pbk.

Editorial/production supervision by Eric Newman
Cover illustration by Stanley Wyatt
Manufacturing buyer: Cathie Lenard

10   9   8   7   6   5   4   3   2   1

PRENTICE-HALL INTERNATIONAL, INC. *(London)*
PRENTICE-HALL OF AUSTRALIA PTY. LIMITED *(Sydney)*
PRENTICE-HALL OF CANADA, LTD. *(Toronto)*
PRENTICE-HALL OF INDIA PRIVATE LIMITED *(New Delhi)*
PRENTICE-HALL OF JAPAN, INC. *(Tokyo)*
PRENTICE-HALL OF SOUTHEAST ASIA PTE. LTD. *(Singapore)*
WHITEHALL BOOKS LIMITED *(Wellington, New Zealand)*

NEBF
7.12

Contents

OLINGER NOVELS

THE COUP

THE SHORT STORIES

Acknowledgments

The editors wish to thank Professor George Hunt, S.J., of Le Moyne College for helpful advice during the early stages of their work. We are grateful, too, to John Updike, who cheerfully answered many questions and helped to ensure the accuracy of the biographical chronology.

For permission to quote from copyrighted material, we wish to thank the following: the Macmillan Publishing Company, Inc., for excerpts from "Crazy Jane on God" from *Collected Poems* of William Butler Yeats, copyright 1933 by Macmillan Publishing Co., Inc., renewed 1961 by Bertha Georgie Yeats, reprinted also by permission of A.P. Watt Ltd., M. B. Yeats, and Miss Anne Yeats; Farrar, Straus & Giroux, Inc., for excerpts from *The Tenants* by Bernard Malamud, copyright 1971.

For permission to quote from *The Poorhouse Fair* by John Updike we thank Alfred A. Knopf, Inc., and Victor Gollancz Ltd. Grateful acknowledgment is also made to Alfred A. Knopf, Inc., and to Andre Deutsch Ltd. for permission to quote from the following copyrighted works of John Updike: *A Month of Sundays; Picked-Up Pieces; Rabbit, Run; Rabbit Redux; Marry Me; Pigeon Feathers and Other Stories; Bech: A Book; The Centaur; Couples; Of the Farm; Olinger Stories; Assorted Prose; The Same Door; The Music School;* and *Museums, Women and Other Stories.*

JOHN UPDIKE

Introduction: "Alive in a Place and Time"

by David Thorburn

It is said of Sinclair Lewis that having yielded to an invitation to address a writing class in an Ivy League college he began by asking how many in his large audience wished to become writers. A forest of hands filled the air, and Lewis responded with the shortest and arguably the wisest academic lecture ever given on this subject: "Well, Goddamn it! Go home and write."

It is one of John Updike's chief distinctions, though he is rarely honored for it, to have offered us during the two decades of his prolific career a definition by example of the writer's vocation that respects Lewis's wise tautology: a writer is one who writes. Systematically resisting the blandishments of the media and the easy pleasures of the cocktail and lecture circuit, Updike has always chosen to live at a distance from the centers of literary influence, insisting that he be known by his published work and not by his performances as a literary celebrity. Not counting four children's books and a collection of stories selected from several earlier volumes, Updike has given us twenty-three books since 1958: nine novels, seven collections of short fiction, four books of poetry, a play, and two collections of essays.

This unmannerly fertility—so unlike the irregular, flamboyantly advertised appearances we have been schooled to expect from American writers—has surely damaged Updike's reputation among reviewers and intellectuals, but it has also liberated him from the tyrannies of literary fashion. His steady productiveness has brought him a substantial and international audience, whose loyalty has nourished his faith in the traditional literary genres, and especially his belief in the power of realistic fiction to illuminate contemporary life.

Although he is scarcely the naively old-fashioned writer many reviewers persist in describing, Updike *is* a thoroughly conservative figure, whose moderate, rational, and unromantic conception of his craft directly challenges reigning ideas of the artist as an adversary genius and moral prophet. Particularly suspicious of the apocalyptic and self-advertising clamor rising from the pages of so many American books in recent decades, Updike has held to a quieter, more disciplined idea of his work. He inherits, and richly extends, the modernist project of sexual candor and psychological investigation, but he decisively resists the aggrandizing, irrationalist, and morally imperial tendencies in modern and contemporary art. *Think Big* is the working title of Henry Bech's never-to-be-completed third novel, intended as his magnum opus, and Updike's brilliant stories about this blocked, eerily representative American genius are a comically potent judgment on the crippling pretensions of school-text modernism.[1] When writers think big as prescribed in the modernist syllabus, Updike says, when they embrace the secretly boastful assumption, at once arrogant and sentimental, that our modern experience is uniquely degraded, they "do reality a disservice," substituting facile abstractions—the world as wasteland, life as an absurdist or surreal nightmare—for the press and smell and muddle of actuality. What is truly momentous in the example of the founding modernists, Updike has argued with increasing authority in his essays, is not their apocalyptic fervor, which the scholars (following T. S. Eliot) have emphasized excessively, nor their intimidating formal experiments, also overvalued by the academic explainers, but their radical empiricism, their respect for the minute, apparently inconsequential particulars in experience: "the kind of timid reverence toward what exists that Cézanne shows when he grapples for the shape and shade of a fruit through a mist of delicate stabs." "Let us not take it for granted," writes Virginia Woolf in her seminal essay on modern

---

[1] The first seven Bech stories, along with a bibliography of his faltering career that wittily satirizes the American literary establishment, are accessible in *Bech: A Book* (1970). Bech's later adventures continue to appear in the magazines. The quotations in the following sentences in this paragraph are from Updike's novel *A Month of Sundays* (Knopf, 1975), p. 203, and from Updike's speech, reprinted in *Picked-Up Pieces,* accepting the National Book Award for *The Centaur* (1963).

fiction in *The Common Reader,* "that life exists more fully in what is commonly thought big than in what is commonly thought small." This might be the motto for Updike's work, its enabling principle.

"Don't you love your wife?" an old girlfriend asks her would-be seducer in an early Updike story, characteristically recounting a transitory encounter in a doctor's waiting room. "Incredibly much," he answers honestly, and kisses the girlfriend's neck. Disclosing her own willingness by the form her resistance takes, she protests again: "I thought you were successful. I thought you had beautiful children. Aren't you happy?" His baffled response—"so purely inspired its utterance only grazed his lips"—crystallizes the discontent that perplexes and ambiguously nourishes all the groping adulterers in Updike's fiction: "I am, I am—but happiness isn't everything."

Updike is more articulate than most of his characters, though his best work always respects their confusions, and the title of the gently comic story from which I've quoted names his mastering theme: "The Persistence of Desire." His characters move through their lives as through some too-familiar watery element; habit and chance and material comfort govern their experience. They are not pierced by subversive intensities of dissatisfaction like, say, the people in D. H. Lawrence. They are, like most of us, incapable of decisive altering acts of choice or will, and their lives are wrenched or radically changed only from without, by the stumbling actions of others, and rarely permanently. But they are troubled or distracted by a recurring intuition of partialness or incompletion.

The chief outward sign of this dis-ease is sexual unrest, but Updike has consistently associated the marital transgressions of his characters with metaphysical or religious longings, as if to suggest that adulterous cravings in our affluent rootless era are the confused expression of an instinct for freedom itself, a rebellion against the confinements of age and circumstance. *Rabbit, Run* (1960) begins with an epigraph from Pascal, offers in a supporting character (the well-intentioned Reverend Eccles) a vivid emblem of the frailty of conventional religious counsel in these secular times, and ends, as Rabbit runs from his gathered family in the final pages of the novel, with the hero glancing toward "what once consoled him": a church window, symbolically "un-lit" and thus merely "a dark circle in a stone façade."

Endemic in Updike's stories and novels, such religious allusions declare openly—and, in his early work, too facilely—what the full texture of his fiction indicates more obliquely and also more rich-ly: that his subject is always some variation on the spiritual and communal enfeeblement of contemporary American society, particularly among the suburban middle class. "We in America need ceremonies, is I suppose the point of what I have written," he says in the last sentence of the last story in *Pigeon Feathers* (1962). But the qualifying "I suppose" is crucial. For even in his earliest fiction, though more fully and more coherently in his later work, Updike's keen sense of the pain and loss and narrow-ness in middle-class life has been tempered by his awareness of "something gritty, practical, mortised, functional in our lives, something olfactory and mute" that wars against all summarizing and "eludes our minds' binomial formulations."[2] Increasingly since the first Rabbit book, he has recorded the filial and sexual entanglements of his characters with an attentiveness that com-plicates his pessimism by the very thoroughness of its respect for ordinary living, for "the flux, the blurring, the endless innuendo of experience as we feel it." It is perhaps misleading to think of Updike as a straightforward realist; he himself would claim that Vermeer's light-suffused interiors, those miracles of accurate rendering that yet sacralize or transfigure what is ordinary, are closer to his mimetic ideal. But Updike's fiction is deeply in-formed by a kind of moral realism that deserves to be called Joy-cean: a realism or common-sensicalness that is 'rooted in an understanding of the *dailiness* of life, its inconclusive discrete-ness, the principle of drift.

Rabbit Redux (1971) was thus an essential book for Updike to write, despite the massive risks to which this sequel to his best-known novel committed him, because the earlier book ends in an uncertainty that offends against Updike's deeply antiapocalyp-tic sense of things. *Redux* is not a retraction, but it is a clarifica-tion, for it brings Rabbit back, nearly a decade older, and

---

[2]*A Month of Sundays,* p. 203. The quoted phrase in the next sentence is from the National Book Award speech, cited earlier.

immersed of course in the middle-class life from which he flees on the last page of *Rabbit, Run*. The younger Rabbit's clear ancestor is Huck Finn, a figure of intuitive or natural decency whose best qualities are thwarted by the moral conventions and institutions of "civilized" America. But Huck was a child, and anyhow lived in an older and rural world: there were territories he could light out for at the end of his story. Rabbit, the sequel acknowledges, has no place to run. The older Rabbit's literary ancestor is not an asexual child orphaned into the limitless promise of the wilderness frontier but a husband and father of early middle age, the presiding figure of modern literature: Joyce's Leopold Bloom. Bereaved of one child and cuckolded just as Rabbit is, Bloom is an ordinary, city-dwelling man whose experiences will not yield to heroic or romantic paradigms.

Updike addresses his hero in the title of the first Rabbit book, urging him to a heroic repudiation of the imprisonments of his undistinguished life. But as his novels and stories of the next decade all show, this counsel is mere wishfulness, true to his character's yearnings but not to the muddled unsimple reality of our life as it is. And so in the later book an older Updike addresses not his character but his readers, asking in the daring final paragraph (whose terms and syntax complexly echo his own earlier ending as well as that of *Ulysses* itself) if they are unsentimental enough to accept, if they are generous enough even to respect, the undramatic and wearily imperfect reunion of Rabbit and his adulterous wife:

> ...his hand...comes upon the familiar dip of her waist, rib to hip bone, where no bones are, soft as flight, fat's inward curve, slack, his babies from her belly. He finds this inward curve and slips along it, sleeps. He. She. Sleeps. O.K.?

Joyce has always been the locus of what Harold Bloom would call Updike's anxiety of influence, as *The Centaur*'s elaborate shaky mythological structure indicates. But the Joyce who comes increasingly to matter for Updike is not the technician and intricate pattern-maker of so many scholarly handbooks but the patient chronicler of domestic life, the poet of carnal experience. "There is a line from Joyce," says the narrator in "Wife-Wooing," one of the stories in *Pigeon Feathers*. "Smackwarm. That was the

crucial word. Smacked smackwarm on her smackable warm
woman's thigh. ... A splendid man, to feel that."[3]

The self-revising ambitions so boldly realized in *Rabbit Redux*
have always exerted a definitive pressure on Updike's fiction,
which engages and reengages the themes of adultery and family
relations with a meticulous intelligence that many reviewers,
especially of his recent works, have shockingly underestimated.
It is essential to distinguish this disciplined self-awareness from
the clever or smug "self-referentiality" that American graduate
students are nowadays taught to find in every text. The hermetic
self-consciousness of the later Nabokov, for example; the riddled
labyrinth-making of Borges—these have little in common with
the stubborn thoughtfulness that compels Updike to return again
and again to scenes of primal intimacy: to those moments and
places in real life where we declare our feelings and dangerously
touch the lives of others.

Marry Me (1976), for example, reexamines the central moral
and domestic drama of *Couples* (1968) but is purged of the earlier
book's subsidiary marriage stories and its vast sociological ambitions. The later book closes like a merciless tight camera on a
couple very like Piet and Angela Hanema, the dissolution of
whose marriage is at the heart of *Couples*. But in renaming them
plain Jerry and Ruth, Updike signals his reluctance to impose
an abstract religious symbolism on their fiercely ambiguous behavior. Updike's religious preoccupations survive in *Marry Me,*
but here—as in *A Month of Sundays,* published a year earlier—
they are assigned fully to his protagonist: no *a priori* symbolism
of names, no allegorical turning of the plot (such as the church-
burning near the end of *Couples*) offers sanction to the hero's
conception of himself as one of the last God-fearing men. The
result is that the protagonist's Kierkegaardian dread, his stargazing and intermittent yowling insomnia, even his conscience-
stricken tenderness toward the wife he betrays and humiliates
but cannot bring himself finally to leave—all are exposed as
projections of his ego, as unconscious stratagems for eliciting sympathy and mothering care from his wife and his mistress. These

---

[3]The passage, slightly misremembered, is from the Sirens episode of *Ulysses:*
"Smack. She let free sudden in rebound her nipped elastic garter smackwarm

women and the hero's male rival—an emotionally wounded businessman who in some ways reincarnates Freddy Thorne of *Couples,* the reverend Eccles of *Rabbit, Run,* and other Updike pharisees—are presented with a sympathy and psychological fullness that further clarify the hero's destructive indecisiveness. The novel does not question the genuineness of his groaning fear of death, his need to believe in God, his distracted guilty passion for a woman not his wife. But these attributes, nearly always the badge of Updike's heroes, are seen with a new stringency because they are granted no reinforcement in the metaphoric texture of the novel or in the arrangements of its plot. The passivity and histrionic narcissism that were always latent in the tender, yielding lovers who populate Updike's fiction are brought fully to the surface in *Marry Me,* and our understanding of the psychological and ethical problems dramatized in his earlier work is thus deepened and enriched. "Men don't like to make decisions," vacillating Jerry tells his wife late in the novel, "they want God or women to make them." And she replies grimly, in correction: "Some men."

This movement toward a more stringent and self-judging comedy—Updike's fiction is always essentially comic, even when his characters suffer most intensely—is no doubt linked to his personal history. His marriage of twenty-three years ended in divorce in 1976, when the youngest of his four children was sixteen, and there is an arresting mixture of nostalgia and self-contempt not only in *Marry Me* and *The Coup* (1978) but also in the austere, shapely stories of separation and divorce that Updike published in *The New Yorker* during the 1970s and collected in *Problems and Other Stories* (1979). In these recent stories Updike's powers of observation and description are deployed with a master's conciseness, the fruit of twenty years at the steady practice of his craft. Snatches of conversation intended as neutral civilities, and rendered with a perfect fidelity to the rhythms of actual speech, put us in touch with tides of resentment and pain and intimate longing which the speakers themselves would prefer to

---

against her smackable woman's warmhosed thigh" (p. 266 in the 1961 Random House edition).

suppress or from which they had imagined themselves to be free. The most ordinary spaces and objects, catalogued with unflamboyant accuracy, are seen to be full of meaning, mute totems of the humanly significant.

> The dogs barked, then at his scolding voice came running to greet him. They thought he still owned them. ... Domestic life funnels through certain centers of congestion; the back door was one, where the dogs, the lilacs, and the trash cans converged, all but blocking the steps to the back porch, which was cluttered with skis and snow shovels and last summer's flowerpots and rusted garden tools. The door opened between the washer and the dryer, in a side portion of the kitchen. A previous owner had built an unhandy set of shelves over the radiator; on the lowest shelf a cat napped on a nest of drying mittens and gloves. Jean was at the sink, the other cat rubbing around her ankles. She looked over in mock astonishment. "Well, look who's here!"
>
> "Where's everybody?" Fraser asked, keeping his distance. It had been relatively easy to wean himself from kissing her in greeting. Living together, they had seldom kissed; the kissing had come along as part of their separation, when they were still unused to saying hello and goodbye.
>
> "Get *away,*" Jean said, to the cat, and with a flip of her foot sent the animal skidding across the linoleum. "Nancy's spent the night with the Harrisons after a dance, and Kenny's out testing his new driver's license. The other two are at college—but you know that, don't you?"
>
> "I pay their bills," Fraser said. "Kenny passed? That's great. Isn't it?"
>
> "It is if he doesn't kill himself. All he talks about is 'cruisin'.' He wants to drive you back into Boston tonight. I told him certainly not."
>
> "Why do you think I'm going back to Boston?"
>
> "My God, haven't you had *enough* of her? Why don't you just move *in?*"
>
> "We thought you couldn't stand it."
>
> "That's right. I couldn't. How smart of you both."[4]

In a recent essay on the English novelist Henry Green, whom he describes as a "saint of the mundane," Updike speaks of Green's

---

[4]"Domestic Life in America," *The New Yorker,* Dec. 13, 1976, p. 43. The essay on Green quoted in the next paragraph appeared in *The New York Review of Books,* May 18, 1978.

ambition to render human experience in its irreducible complex minuteness, "with its weave of misapprehension, petty confusions, fitful and skewed communications, and passing but authentic revelations." Of course this describes Updike's enterprise as well. And we must value his achievement as he values that of the older writer: for its rare and artful witness to "what can be seen and heard by a man alive in a place and time."

THE RABBIT NOVELS

We have writers willing to be mayor but not many excited to be citizens. We have writers as confessors, shackled to their personal lives, and writers as researchers, hanging their sheets of information from a bloodless story line. But of writers immersed in their material, and enabled to draw tales from a community of neighbors, Faulkner was our last great example. An instinctive, respectful identification with the people of one's own locale comes hard now, in the menacing cities or disposable suburbs, yet without it a genuine belief in the significance of humanity, in humane significances, comes not at all.

UPDIKE
Picked-Up Pieces

An Image of Precarious Life

by Richard Gilman

I remember how surprised I was when I discovered, after having written a highly enthusiastic review of John Updike's first novel *The Poorhouse Fair,* that a number of other commentators had found the book a failure, deficient in some central qualities that are supposed to be the hallmarks of important fiction. Weight, ideas, resolution! Oh, a good style, a poet if you like, but no heft, no thought, and not the ghost of a wrap-up, a firmly tied knot that we can't break, which is what we pay novelists to give us.

The Poorhouse Fair was a novel of great imaginative accuracy, a delicate ranging of the immediately felt and experienced against abstraction, ideology and mechanical orderings of existence, and inconclusiveness was precisely what it depended on for the truth of its vision. Humility of this kind is apparently so rare in fiction these days that certain critics, the kind who keep their eyes peeled and blessings ready for doctors, saviors or corroborators, were baffled and disgruntled by Updike's refusal to do more than keep a fertile space open.

I think the times are against them. We are in a necessary period of non-solution in the novel, of anti-literature, which is essentially a resistance to tying neat knots, offering explanations, coming up with big solid counterweights to the miseries of life, providing alternative existences such as have come more and more to be demanded of fiction, that is to say, heroes to whom the reader can latch on and be carried right out of his mean, stifling *non-literary* days and years. Updike, like the new French *alittérateurs,*

Original title: "A Distinguished Image of Precarious Life," by Richard Gilman. From *Commonweal,* 73 (October 28, 1960), 128-29. Copyright © 1960 by Commonweal Publishing Co., Inc. Reprinted with permission.

doesn't want the novel to perpetuate itself as a compensation, a branch of philosophy or a rival of science, a *way out.*

Not that he is particularly conscious of all this. *Rabbit, Run* gives off little of the air of implementing a plan which mars some of the work of Alain Robbe-Grillet or Nathalie Sarraute, for example. But it is all there, or at least nothing else is there, no tying together of loose threads, no conclusion you can put on a shelf, no road-maps, no reinforcement of attitudes or beliefs. Only a distinguished balancing-act over a void, a major image of precarious life being true to itself. And that is certainly going to make those critics mutter all over again.

The protagonist of the novel is Harry Angstrom, known as Rabbit from his days as a fleet loose-jointed high-school basketball star. He is twenty-six, has a job demonstrating something called the MagiPeel kitchen peeler in the department stores of his birthplace, a small city in Pennsylvania, is married to a high-school girl friend who is "dumb...she's really stupid," and has a two-and-a-half-year-old son.

One day he returns home after work, having stopped to participate in a pickup basketball game with twelve-year-olds, during which he felt a return of the old power, the one-time skill in his hands. His wife, pregnant with their second child, is sitting before the television set watching a children's program and drinking Old-fashioneds. He notices that two short wrinkles have appeared at the corners of her mouth, giving it a greedy look, and that her hair is beginning to thin. They quarrel, caress one another, recoil, in a sterile blind dance as of unwilling cell-mates.

And then something snaps. Rabbit goes to pick up their son at his mother's, but keeps driving instead, out of the city and far into the night, until at a certain point, because the vast country is so uniform, because the map has "so many red lines and blue lines, long names, little towns, squares, circles and stars," he turns around and heads back to Brewer, not home.

He has thought of his old basketball coach, a man who made him feel "a natural," and goes to him for sanctuary. Through the coach he meets a woman, a semi-prostitute on whom his ache for love descends. He lives with her, gets a job as gardener to an old woman, loving the work of putting seeds in the ground "...the simplicity. Getting rid of something by giving it. God Himself folded into the tiny adamant structure." He is in a clearing; the air is breathable.

But then a struggle begins for his soul. A Protestant minister named Eccles, a man his own age, arid, no true believer but tense with an itch to effect sociological cures, takes charge of the "case," attempting to bring the couple together. Through him Rabbit feels the tide coming in again: guilt, remorse, the pressure of a vague religion, morality, the known.

When his wife enters labor he rejoins her, abandoning his mistress, who unknown to him has also become pregnant. For a time he makes a go of it, his parents and in-laws circling like motorcycle cops ready to blow the whistle. But the walls close in again and one night he leaves the house after his wife has rejected his body (throughout the novel, sexuality functions as both area of true life and image of the agonies of human separation), and seeks his mistress.

Before he can find her, Eccles reaches him with the news that his wife, having worked herself into a drunken state, has accidentally allowed their infant daughter to drown in the bathtub. Once more Rabbit comes back, and for a moment their common tragedy unites him to his wife. But at the cemetery he bolts again, since nothing has really changed, the trap is waiting, baited this time with pity, his wife is not his true life, he cannot be held by abstract appeals, Eccles' religion or his parents' sad eyes, he cannot give up his hunger for authenticity.

He goes to his mistress and is confronted with her pregnancy and an ultimatum: either she or me, work it out. "He doesn't know, what to do, where to go, what will happen, the thought that he doesn't know seems to make him infinitely small and impossible to capture. ... It's like when they heard you were great and put two men on you and no matter which way you turned you bumped into one of them and the only thing to do was pass. So you passed and the ball belonged to the others and your hands were empty and the men on you looked foolish because in effect there was nobody there."

On one level *Rabbit, Run* is a grotesque allegory of American life, with its myth of happiness and success, its dangerous innocence and crippling antagonism between value and fact. But much more significantly it is a minor epic of the spirit thirsting for room to discover and *be* itself, ducking, dodging, staying out of reach of everything that will pin it down and impale it on fixed, immutable laws that are not of its own making and do not consider its integrity.

This constitutes, if you will, a rebellion against the nature of existence, but it is a rebellion we are all involved in, with greater or lesser consciousness. "Harry has no taste for the dark, tangled, visceral aspect of Christianity, the *going through* quality of it, the passage into death and suffering that redeems and inverts these things, like an umbrella blowing inside out. He lacks the mindful will to walk the straight line of a paradox. His eyes turn toward the light however it glances into his retina."

Which is to say that Harry is not an admirable character; fiction that has repudiated a teaching or confirming role has no "admirable" characters. But moralists needn't fear that Updike is preaching that we should all leave our wives and responsibilities. He is simply presenting us with a vision of what persists beneath the adjustments we have made to necessity: the dream of freedom, in which truth finally has no other test than its coherence with our deepest desires, and nothing is so that we have not made so. That seems to me to be a theme with which literature, in all its authentic occasions, has in one way or another concerned itself.

Rabbit Angstrom's Unseen World

by Dean Doner

According to one reviewer, John Updike's fine novel *Rabbit, Run* is in part successful because the protagonist is symbolic of us all. If Rabbit Angstrom is not Everyman, the reviewer claims, he is at least Everyman *circa* 1961. In him the reader may see himself, and at the close of the book, "We too are running for cover."

I do not mean to suggest that this response is voluntary. Identification between himself and fictional characters is, these days, an absolute requirement of the competent and sophisticated reader. To fail to recognize oneself in the protagonist of a novel or a play is supposedly to fail to understand or appreciate the work at all. And since Rabbit Angstrom, like many contemporary literary figures, is a remarkably unpleasant person in a number of ways, the implication is clear: failure to see oneself mirrored in Rabbit's character is an admission of willful blindness, cowardice, or simple naïveté. The modern reader is not expected to open a book and look upon life. He is challenged to see himself in everything he reads. Every novel, drama, or short story is an exercise, for the reader, in self-analysis.

The reviewer of Updike's novel was under the spell of a dogma so pervasive in modern thought as to be inescapable, so sacred as to be almost beyond question. "No man is an *Iland*, intire of it selfe." When Western man no longer primarily identified himself and his fellow men as sons of God, it became necessary to proclaim the unity of Man in secular terms—liberty, equality, fraternity, for example. In our time all the important forces—literary,

"Rabbit Angstrom's Unseen World," by Dean Doner. From *New World Writing 20* (Philadelphia: J. B. Lippincott Co., 1962), pp. 63-75. Reprinted by permission of the author.

political, humanitarian—have rallied around Donne's famous words, for Donne's analogy permits modern man the chance to proclaim his faith in Unity without appearing to make an act of Faith at all. By simple reason it is seen that "if a *Clod* bee washed away by the *Sea, Europe* is the lesse." Similarly, each man's death diminishes me. Donne's analogy is an example of a concept which a culture grasps at almost all levels. Yet it is exactly that concept which *Rabbit, Run,* as well as Updike's earlier work, examines with a critical eye.

Harry "Rabbit" Angstrom is fleeing from a great number of things, many of them the usual pressures, the usual traps, of contemporary life. Few novels delineate more clearly than this one the claustrophobic nature of our institutions: an economy which traps a man into mean, petty, lying hucksterism; tenement-apartment housing which traps a man and his family into close, airless, nerve-shattering "togetherness"; unimaginative, dirty cities which offer no release for the spirit; the ugly voices of advertising and television; the middle-class morality which wars with man's nature. These are the common villains, although they are exceptionally well presented by Updike and given fresh illumination and fresh horror. But behind all these forces, as though they were mere façades, lies the real net which snares this Rabbit, the real crowding which he consistently fears. That net is essentially the total implications of Humanism, the denial of the Unseen, the insistence upon shared life and therefore shared guilt—in short, those concepts which have produced the quintessence of modern feeling, Angst.

Humanism and humanists have consistently been the villains of Updike's work. In the early story, "Lifeguard," reprinted in *Pigeon Feathers* (1962), Updike portrays a divinity student who, as a summer lifeguard, broods over the scene below him—the sprawling flesh, sand, and sea—as a God-Christ figure. Christ as a lifeguard is a happy choice for Updike, and his divinity student is specific in his charges:

> That the sea, with its multiform and mysterious hosts, its savage and senseless rages, no longer comfortably serves as a divine metaphor indicates how severely humanism has corrupted the apples of our creed.

In his first novel, *The Poorhouse Fair* (1958), Updike's villain is a humanist named Conner, the prefect of the poorhouse. His predecessor was a man named Mendelssohṅ. From Conner's point of view there is almost nothing good to be said for Mendelssohn. He was a notorious drinker. He left the prefect's office "bare, drab, dirty, unordered: a hole where a tramp napped." The poorhouse was not efficient. "Half the county home acres were lying fallow, waste. The outbuildings were crammed with refuse and filth. The west wing was a death trap." Had there been a fire, the inmates would have burned to death; had one of the old people eaten an unwashed peach, he would have died.

Nonetheless, Conner feels in competition with the inmates' memories of Mendelssohn—not without reason, for the older inmates remember Mendelssohn with a fondness which Conner, for all his efficiency, cannot compel.

> "Can't you picture Mendelssohn now?" Amy Mortis asked at another table. "How he'd have us all singing and shouting prayers and telling us how we all must die? Ah wasn't he the man?"
> "Yet we'll see him again," the woman beside her reminded.
> They were seeing him now. A great many eyes had lifted from their food and were directed by common impulse toward the vacant dais where the prefect had had his table before Conner came and deemed it arrogant to eat elevated above the inmates. ... As the songs grew more religious the rims of Mendelssohn's eyes grew redder, and he was dabbing at his cheeks with the huge handkerchief he always carried and was saying, in the splendid calm voice that carried to the farthest corner and to the dullest ear, how here they all lived close to death...here they lived with Death at their sides, the third participant in every conversation, the other guest at every meal.　[Rpt. New York: Fawcett World Library, pp. 56-57]

That they now have only food where once they had hymns and prayer, that it is in a sense God who has gone from the vacant dais is made clear in the novel. Looking at Mendelssohn in his coffin, Conner concludes that his predecessor had "in part thought of himself as God." Conner, on the other hand, thinks of "no one as God."

> He had lost all sense of omen. ... Young for the importance of his position, devout in the service of humanity, Conner was unpre-

possessing: the agony, unworthy of him, he underwent in the presence of unsympathetic people was sensed by them, and they
disliked him for it. ... Conner felt not a shred of awe, though, ortho-
dox in the way of popular humanist orators, he claimed he did. ...
The sculptor has his rock and the saint the silence of his Lord, but a
man like Conner who has vowed to bring order and beauty out of
human substance has no third factor; he is a slave, at first, to
gratitude.   [pp. 12-14]

He is a slave also to appearances and to impressions. Within
his simple humanistic world in which the elimination of pain produces good with rigid mathematical certainty, Conner has to
believe that good intentions must produce good results. "He won-
dered what kind of impression this made and did not see how it
could be other than good. His intentions were wholly good."

Thus, when all his concern for efficiency, hygiene, and physical improvements to the poorhouse result in the inmates' stoning
him, Conner can only cry, from his baffled heart, *"Unjust"* and
fight within his soul the impulse to crush ingratitude.

True to his creed, throughout the novel Conner takes appearances for fact, and he assumes that the ninety-four-year-old Hook,
who towers above the other inmates, has directed the attack
against him. Hook is Conner's natural antagonist. From the first
of the novel, looking out of his tower-office on to the grounds
below, Conner has felt that Hook was "capturing the domain,"
and he has been jealous of the old man. The novel is essentially
the story of the antagonism between these two men, for Hook
serves as a spokesman for orthodoxy as opposed to Conner's
Humanism. Updike has resisted the contemporary temptation
to make his character a blatant Christ-symbol, but it would be
fair to say that Hook invokes Christ. His life is "empty of material
purpose," and his message is absolutely anti-Humanist: "Virtue,"
Hook said, "I understand as obedience to the commands of God."

Hook is much concerned with the shoddy carpentry which
passes for satisfactory work in his time—the novel is set in 1973.
"Depend upon it," he says, "there are no workmen now as there
were in my day." And later: "Looking back I perceive a mar-velous
fitting together of right and wrong, like the joints the old-time
carpenters used to make, before everything was manufactured
metal and plastic."

Conner scoffs at the idea that "a young carpenter in Syria two thousand years ago" could have been a God. "As to being a carpenter," Hook answers, "it has often struck me that there is no pro-fession so native to holy and constructive emotions, or so appropriate for God to make flesh assume." And though he reveals in his remarks a basic contradiction of Humanism, Conner declares that "The truth is, Mr. Hook, that if the universe was made, it was made by an idiot, and an idiot crueler than Nero. There are no laws. Atoms and animals alike do only what they can't help doing."

The antagonism between Hook and Conner is joined in the parlor after lunch. The inmates, who had been preparing the grounds for their annual fair, have been driven inside by a shower. Conner joins them, and the discussion turns to the nature of Heaven. For Conner, Heaven will come on earth when there is ultimately no disease, for pain *is* evil, he declares. In this earthly paradise, there will be no "oppression, political or economic, because the administration of power will be in the hands of those who have no hunger for power, but who are, rather, dedicated to the cause of all humanity." And though of all the characters in the novel Conner perhaps knows himself least well, he concludes with his belief that "Each man will know himself—without delusions, without muddle, and within the limits of that self-knowledge will construct a sane and useful life."

Hook is not wholly adequate to sharp debate, though he was once a fine debater. His attention wanders, and he does not hear well. Nonetheless, he states his position explicitly: "It is an error now to believe that the absence of evil will follow from the elimination of pain." And he pronounces two precise judgments upon Conner: "Your bitterness is the willful work of your own heart," and "There is no goodness without belief. There is nothing but busy-ness."

The argument between the men ends with the arrival of the orchestra, which is persuaded, since it is raining, to play for the inmates in the parlor. "Like many humanists," Updike remarks, "Conner was deeply responsive to music. In the language of melody speeches about man's aspirations and eventual victory could be made that explicit language would embarrass." Music permits Conner to daydream:

> Man was good. There was a destination. Health could be bought. ...
> He envisioned grown men and women, lightly clad, playing, on
> the brilliant sand of a seashore, children's games. ...A man threw a
> golden ball, his tunic slowly swirling with the exertion; a girl
> caught it. No fear here, no dread of time. Another man caught the
> girl by the waist. She had a wide belt. He held her above his head;
> she bent way back. ...The man was Conner. [He visualized] a world
> which worshipped him.   [p. 87]

Late in the day we leave Conner, bitter because he has been
mocked, but stubbornly retaining "the conviction that he was
the hope of the world." Hook goes to bed and then later awakens
to stand motionless in the moonlight which floods his room,
"groping after the fitful shadow of the advice he must impart to
Conner, as a bond between them and a testament to endure his
dying in the world. What was it?"

On that question the book ends. What is the advice Hook might
give to the humanist Conner; or to the world where the dais is
vacant; or to the world in which adolescents swear, not on the
Bible, but "on a stack of telephone directories" that they will not
touch their girls if the girls will but consent to parade naked in
front of the car's headlights?

The spokesmen of *The Poorhouse Fair* are relatively conventional figures: the old man bound to traditional ways and judgments, the young atheist illusioned and unaware that the world
is both more complex and more real than his system compre-
hends. In his second novel, *Rabbit, Run* (1960), Updike has been
successful in portraying, not spokesmen for his ideas, but characters whose lives illuminate their convictions, whose actions
define their understanding of human possibilities and the nature
of reality. The humanist in *Rabbit, Run* is an Episcopalian minister, Reverend Jack Eccles. Though Reverend Eccles partially
defines his position in one or two places, it is what Eccles does
and not what he says that is important. And instead of presenting
an articulate and simple spokesman against Humanism, Updike
portrays in Rabbit Angstrom a man suffering the total implications of Humanism, a man fleeing the "crowding" and the shared
life and shared guilt of Humanism. Rabbit runs, but he remains
baffled, unable to say clearly what it is he runs from or runs

toward. Only twice in the novel does he even catch a glimpse of the unseen world, and in each case he is unable to express his joy or his wonder in a way which would impel others to believe in its existence. He is not a spokesman for, but like all other characters in the book, a product of Western Humanism. "He lacks the mindful will to walk the straight line of a paradox." He has no taste for the *"going through"* quality of Christianity. "His eyes turn toward the light however it glances into his retina." Paradoxical though those remarks are, we can yet say that Rabbit is the only character in the novel (except for a minor character, the Lutheran minister Fritz Kruppenbach) who knows that an unseen world exists.

In *Rabbit, Run* it is the structure of the novel itself which shows Humanism to be a net thrown down across this Rabbit's life, a net so immense that it is inescapable and so like a veil that the unseen world behind it can be glimpsed only in the briefest moments—or can, as its name implies, not be glimpsed at all but only felt, only intuited. "His feeling that there is an unseen world is instinctive, and more of his actions than anyone suspects constitute transactions with it." For all other characters in the novel (save Reverend Kruppenbach) the net of Humanism is, for all they know, the sky itself beneath which they live their unexamined lives. Because there is no unseen world for them, they have only one another; thus they may justify their interference in each other's lives.

The germ of *Rabbit, Run* is found in Updike's short story "Ace in the Hole," first published in *The New Yorker* and reprinted in *The Same Door* (1959). The protagonist of this story, Ace Anderson, is an ex-high school basketball star, as is Rabbit Angstrom. Ace drives home from work—he has just been fired—picks up his daughter at his mother's house, and goes home to his small apartment. When his wife returns home from work, they have a nagging, inconsequential quarrel. Rather than continue the quarrel, Ace picks up his wife and dances with her. "The music ate through his skin and mixed with the nerves and small veins; he seemed to be great again, and all the other kids were around them, in a ring, clapping time."

In the short story, as in the novel, the ex-basketball star strives to shut out the unpleasantness of the present by recreating the greatness of his past. Before his wife comes home, Ace wonders if

"he should have married her, and doubting that made him feel
crowded." During their quarrel, his wife says to him, "Well,
please listen to this, Mr. Six-Foot-Five-and-a-Half: I'm fed up.
I'm ready as Christ to let you run."[1]

The setting of *Rabbit, Run* is Brewer, Pennsylvania, and its
suburb Mt. Judge (presumably Reading and Shillington). The
novel opens with Rabbit Angstrom walking home from work. He
stops to watch some boys playing basketball. Immediately the
major theme of the book is sounded: "He stands there thinking,
the kids keep coming, they keep crowding you up." The sexual
imagery which pervades the novel begins immediately, also, for
Harry Angstrom, as one reviewer remarked, does indeed breathe
sex as lesser men breathe air. Rabbit enters the game, and he
recaptures a pale image of the excitement and glory that were
once his.

> You climb up through the little grades and then get to the top and
> everybody cheers; with the sweat in your eyebrows you can't see
> very well and the noise swirls around you and lifts you up, and
> then you're out, not forgotten, at first, just out, and it feels good
> and cool and free.   [Rpt. New York: Fawcett World Library, p. 9]

The theme of going upward, going "out," to some good place is
reinforced, for Rabbit soon leaves the game and begins to run, up
the alley and then uphill. He runs often in the novel, and he tries
often to impel himself and others upward.

Arriving home, the claustrophobia of his life settles upon him.
There are the little things: the closet door bangs the television
set; his wife, Janice Springer, is bleary-eyed from too many old-
fashioneds and too much television—she is watching the Mickey
Mouse Club at the moment. The apartment is dirty and cluttered.

> The kid's toys here and there broken and stuck and jammed, a leg
> off a doll and a piece of bent cardboard that went with some break-
> fast-box cutout, the rolls of fuzz under the radiators, the continual
> crisscrossing mess—clings to his back like a tightening net. ...[He]
> senses that he is in a trap.   [pp. 16-17]

[1]In addition to these similarities, there are numerous others. In both the story
and the novel keys are always described as "scratching" at doors. Both Ace's
mother and Rabbit's mother side with their sons against their daughters-in-law.
Both Ace and Rabbit work for used-car dealers. There are other similarities of
action. The changes which have been made tend to make Rabbit more sympathetic than Ace and Rabbit's wife less sympathetic than Ace's wife.

He goes to pick up his son, Nelson, who is being taken care of by Rabbit's mother. Instead of going into his parent's house, however, Rabbit stands in the back yard and watches a scene through the kitchen window. His mother is feeding Nelson, his sister is dressed and painted to go out, his father sits "tired and grizzled." Rabbit leaves without his son, gets his car from in front of the Springers' house, and heads for Texas. He was stationed in Texas during his army service, and he goes vaguely toward the sun-drenched Gulf and the girls he remembers there. His attempts to follow a road map confuse him, however, and by midnight he is still in northern West Virginia. Significantly, he ends up on a road that grows narrower and narrower as it climbs steadily upward. It ends in a lovers' lane of parked cars. The map has lost all sense for him, and he feels it to be "a net, all those red lines and blue lines and stars, a net he is somewhere caught in." An old man who filled his car with gas had told Rabbit that he must first decide where it was he wanted to go, and then go there. As he sits in the "petting park," tearing the map into little pieces, Rabbit thinks again of that advice.

> Decide where you want to go and then go: it missed the whole point and yet there is always the chance that, little as it is, it is everything. At any rate Rabbit feels if he'd trusted to instinct he'd be in South Carolina. [p. 34]

This opening sequence is the whole novel in miniature, for Rabbit's story is a series of encounters from which he runs, intuitively upward, following a "light" which he knows must exist but which he can never truly see and never finds. It is possible to say that Rabbit never does decide where he wants to go — it may be impossible for anyone to say that — but there are moments when he almost glimpses his destination. His attempts to communicate this intuition, however, are never successful, and his failure draws the net always closer around him and increases the sense of "crowding" which he fears. The road map — the way laid out for him by other people — always leads Rabbit further into the net. And since he never reaches his destination — never even gets as far as "South Carolina" — there is no way for him to demonstrate his conviction that he'd travel best by following his instinct.

Frustrated in his attempt to flee, Rabbit returns to Brewer, though not to his pregnant wife. He looks up his old high school basketball coach, Marty Tothero, probably because Tothero's coaching had consisted simply of always letting Rabbit run. Furthermore, next to his mother, Rabbit feels that Tothero had the most *force*. But Tothero has long since fallen on evil days. He introduces Rabbit to Ruth Leonard, a prostitute. Uninvited, Rabbit simply moves in with Ruth.

Rabbit brings her both love and dismay. Updike handles well the ambiguous, puzzled feelings Rabbit rouses in Ruth. Rabbit despises the paraphernalia of contraception, for example, but he won't seem to acknowledge what he is asking of Ruth, who is naturally hesitant to trust this strange man who suddenly insists on being, not her lover, but her husband. Ruth is wholly experienced, yet she cannot understand this stranger who appears in her life, bringing love and long walks up Mt. Judge. She knows she will lose him to the wife, but she cannot resist his gift, whatever it is.

The morning after the first night they make love again, while across the street people are going to church. For the first time we find out that Rabbit believes in God. Lying on the bed, watching out the window, Rabbit says a silent and sad little prayer. When Ruth asks him if he believes, he says, "Well, yeah. I think so," and wonders if he is lying. "If he is, he is hung in the middle of nowhere, and the thought hollows him, makes his heart tremble."

> Across the street a few people in their best clothes walk on the pavement past the rows of worn brick homes; are they walking on air? Their clothes, they put on their best clothes: he clings to the thought giddily; it seems a visual proof of the unseen world.   [p. 77]

Later the thought returns:

> He hates all the people on the street in dirty everyday clothes, advertising their belief that the world arches over a pit, that death is final, that the wandering thread of his feelings leads nowhere. Correspondingly he loves the ones dressed for church; the pressed business suits of portly men give substance and respectability to his furtive sensations of the invisible...the beauty of belief, he could kiss their feet in gratitude; they release him from fear.   [p. 196]

When he goes back to his apartment to pick up his clothes, Rabbit meets Reverend Eccles, who has been waiting for him. Eccles is the Springers' minister, and his job throughout the novel is to try to patch up the marriage. His conception of the ministry is sociological or psychological: he plays golf with people so that he can get to know their troubles on a palsy basis; he spends a good deal of his time drinking Cokes at the corner drugstore so that he can know the teenagers and thus "reach" them.

Updike's writing is always extremely tight. Every scene evokes the major imagery, every scene sounds the true rhythm and beat of the whole. Walking down the street, Rabbit feels Eccles' car approaching him from the rear.

> He feels the green car crawling behind him; he thinks of throwing the clothes away and really running. ...As a shark nudges silent creases of water ahead of it the green fender makes ripples of air that break against the back of Rabbit's knees. The faster he walks, the harder these ripples break. ...He feels caught. ...He feels tenacity in his captor. [pp. 85-86]

Immediately Eccles steps out of the car and asks for a match, but Rabbit has given up smoking. "'You're a better man than I am.' He pauses and thinks, then looks at Harry [Rabbit] with startled, arched eyebrows."

Rabbit accepts the offer of a ride, and the net is thrown down across him. When Rabbit had not returned with Nelson, Janice notified his parents. Then at two in the morning she had called her parents, who had called Eccles. The circles extend, spread. Rabbit had intended only to leave his wife, but he is now guilty of disturbing at least five people, one a complete stranger to him.

> "Gee, I'm sorry. I didn't mean to get you out of bed."
> The minister shakes his head irritably. "That's not to be considered."
> "Well, I feel terrible about this."
> "Do you? That's hopeful." [p. 88]

But of course it is exactly the fact that he has disturbed all these people that is important to Eccles, for the minister controls people by throwing the net of shared guilt about them, by showing them the uttermost consequences of their every act—consequences not to their souls, but to the earthly happiness of others. "With my church, I believe that we are all responsible beings, responsible for ourselves and for each other."

Rabbit plays golf with Eccles, who uses the game to question Rabbit. What is it Rabbit wants? He cannot explain. He can only say, "There is something that wants me to find it." If Eccles' imagery is all horizontal—people responsible for people—Rabbit's imagery is vertical: "It seems plain, standing here, that if there is this floor there is a ceiling, that the true space in which we live is upward space."

Eccles keeps nagging Harry about this "thing" that he is trying to find: "'What thing? Have you ever seen it? Are you sure it exists?... What *is* it? Is it hard or soft? Harry. Is it blue? Is it red? Does it have polka dots?'"

The first of Rabbit's two attempts to say what this "thing" is comes in this scene. He finally succeeds in lifting a golf ball correctly:

> It recedes along a line straight as a ruler-edge. Stricken; sphere, star, speck. It hesitates, and Rabbit thinks it will die, but he's fooled, for the ball makes this hesitation the ground of a final leap: with a kind of visible sob takes a last bite of space before vanishing in falling. "That's it!" he cries and, turning to Eccles with a smile of aggrandizement, repeats, "That's it."   [pp. 112-13]

When Janice has her baby, Rabbit returns to her. They take up their life again, Rabbit having meekly swallowed as best he can the vast spread of guilt which he had spilled. But he leaves Janice again, and this time—if it was not clear before—with no justification or at least none with which the reader can sympathize. Janice, still recuperating from the birth, rejects his sexual advances, and Rabbit flounces out of bed and leaves. Janice sits by the window, watching the dawn and drinking in order to dull the knowledge that Rabbit has left her again and that her mother will blame her for not being able to hold him. Rabbit goes to Ruth's apartment, but Ruth is gone. Feeling cramped and hopeless and closed in, he calls Eccles, only to discover that Janice, while drunk, has accidentally drowned the baby.

He returns again, and they prepare for the funeral. At the funeral parlor Rabbit experiences a sense of "liberation": it comes when his mother blurts out, "Hassy, what have they done to you?" This liberation is completed at the graveside.

> "I am the resurrection and the life, saith the Lord: he that believeth in me, though he were dead, yet shall he live: and whosoever liveth and believeth in me, shall never die."

> The angular words walk in Harry's head like clumsy blackbirds; he feels their possibility. Eccles doesn't; his face is humorless and taut. His voice is false. All these people are false: except his dead daughter. ...
>
> "He shall feed his flock like a shepherd: he shall gather the lambs with his arms, and carry them in his bosom.". ...
>
> "The Lord is my shepherd; therefore can I lack nothing."
>
> Eccles' voice made fragile by the outdoors. ... Rabbit's chest vibrates with excitement and strength; he is sure his girl has ascended to Heaven. ...
>
> Yes. That is how it is. He feels them all, the heads as still around him as tombstones, he feels them all one, all one with the grass, with the hothouse flowers... all gathered into one here to give his unbaptized baby force to leap to Heaven.
>
> "Casting every care on thee." He has done that; he feels full of strength. The sky greets him. It is as if he has been crawling in a cave and now at last beyond the dark recession of crowding rocks he has seen a patch of light.   [pp. 242-44]

It is this strength and this belief which prompts him, standing above the filling grave, to turn to all the mourners and say, "Don't look at *me* ... I didn't kill her."

> This comes out of his mouth clearly, in tune with the simplicity he feels now in everything. Heads talking softly snap around at a voice so sudden and so cruel.
>
> They misunderstand. He just wants this straight. He explains to the heads, "You all keep acting as if *I* did it. I wasn't anywhere near. *She's* the one." He turns to her, and in her face, slack as if slapped, sees that she too is a victim, that everyone is; the baby is gone, is all he's saying, he had a baby and his wife drowned it. "Hey it's O.K.," he tells her. "You didn't mean to." He tries to take her hand but she snatches it back like from a trap.
>
> His face burns; forgiveness had been big in his heart and now it's hate. He hates her dumb face. She doesn't *see*. She had a chance to join him in truth, just the simplest factual truth, and turned away in horror. He sees that among the heads even his own mother's is horrified, blank with shock, a wall against him; she asks him what have they done to him and then she does it too. A suffocating sense of injustice blinds him. He turns and runs.   [p. 244]

He runs uphill, then along the wooded ridge of Mt. Judge, and eventually finds himself working downhill again—which is the only way "he can be returned to the others."

He obscurely feels lit by a great spark, the spark whereby the blind tumble of matter recognized itself, a spark struck in the collision of two opposed realms, an encounter a terrible God willed. His stomach slides; his ears seem suddenly open to the sound of a voice. He scrambles back uphill, thrashing noisily in the deepening darkness to drown out the voice that wants to cry out to him from a source that flits from tree to tree in the shadows. He runs always against the rise of land, chasing it in treacherous light.   [p. 247]

Eventually he telephones Eccles, but Mrs. Eccles hangs up on him. He goes to Ruth's apartment and learns that she is pregnant with his child. Then, in the street, he feels indeed caught in the "middle of a dense net" and "he runs. Ah: runs. Runs."

It is likely that a reader's first response to this novel is that Rabbit is in a net of his own making; that he is a weak, vicious, perverted man who has left an astonishing trail of disaster in his wake; that he is attempting to escape from nothing more than his just responsibilities; and that his one great instinct leads him not toward God, but toward sex in almost any form and at almost any time.

But this reaction is part of Updike's effect. Perhaps no novel has described so explicitly the actual performance of various sexual acts. In addition, the drowning of the baby is a scene of real horror, handled as it is so that the reader sees clearly what is coming. Finally, Rabbit's cruel remarks at the graveside are exactly as they are described—as brutal as a slap in the face.

The book is intentionally shocking. Furthermore, with a sure sense of what he is about, Updike has avoided the easy shock achieved by most such novels: his language is never "dirty." The shock of this book is real, is involved in Updike's vision, is—if I may so describe it—theological. Brutal as Rabbit's remarks are, the real impact and the real significance of the scene at the graveside comes when we realize that, of all those gathered there, only Rabbit believes in God. There is not one good word to be said for him, yet he alone perceives the Unseen.

"So severely has humanism corrupted the apples of our creed" that it is only against the shock of Rabbit's gross sexuality and his breaking of our humanistic world's most sacred laws of responsibility that Updike can achieve his effect. Take the scene on the golf course between Eccles and Rabbit. The shock which this book carries is conveyed when the minister taunts Rabbit for believing in the Unseen. For Eccles and all other characters in the novel except Rabbit, only the tangible is real. Not unless a thing is "red" or "blue" or "has polka dots" can even a minister believe in it.

> [Rabbit] wants to believe in the sky as the source of all things. ... "I mean"—he's never before felt *pleading* with Eccles—"remember that thing we used to talk about? The thing behind everything."
> "Harry, you know I don't think that thing exists in the way you think it does." [pp. 233-34]

Reverend Kruppenbach underlines this notion when he sternly lectures Eccles on the proper duties of a minister:

> Do you think this is your job, to meddle in these people's lives? I know what they teach you at seminary now: this psychology and that. But I don't agree with it. You think now your job is to be an unpaid doctor, to run around and plug up holes and make everything smooth. ... I was listening to what [your story] said about you. What I heard was this: the story of a minister of God selling his message for a few scraps of gossip and a few games of golf. What do you think now it looks like to God, one childish husband leaving one childish wife? Do you ever think any more what God sees? ... It seems to you our role is to be cops, cops without handcuffs, without guns, without anything but our human good nature. ... Well, I say that's a Devil's idea. [pp. 142-43]

Were this the only opposition to Eccles' attempts to patch up the damage Rabbit strews in his wake, we would not be justified in saying that Eccles' humanism is shown wanting. But the structure of the story itself argues against Eccles. Mrs. Eccles is right: if Rabbit and Janice had not been brought back together, the baby would not have been drowned. Furthermore, where is Eccles' chief duty in smoothing the wayfarers through life? He attempts to patch up the Angstroms' life and neglects his own family. Nor does he have, being human, enough love to help everyone. He happens to like Harry. But there are people he does not particularly like; therefore he must pick and choose where he will meddle; he must judge or play God. Ultimately, the novel itself says clearly that no man understands enough to take it upon himself to repair the world, no man reads responsibility accurately enough to know where justice lies or how it is to be manipulated.

What is Rabbit, then? Do we have in him a kind of impotent Christ figure of the kind Faulkner portrays? Perhaps, in a way, we have. Several times in the novel he is spoken of as having a gift—often, though not always, in sexual terms—which he feels compelled to give. "He loves folding the hoed ridge of crumbs of soil over the seeds. Sealed, they cease to be his. The simplicity. Getting rid of something by giving it. God Himself folded into the tiny adamant structure." More specifically, his gift is defined by Mrs. Smith, an old woman for whom he works while living with Ruth: "That's what you have, Harry: life. It's a strange gift and I don't know how we're supposed to use it but I know it's the only gift we get and it's a good one." Only once, though jokingly, does Rabbit analyze his gift. "I am a mystic," he says. "I give people faith."

But if he is a kind of Christ-figure, he is also the opposite. Updike works in paradoxes, and he did not name his protagonist Harry without reason. Rabbit is also Satan, specifically called by Eccles "a son of the morning." This combination of Christ-Satan is not new, of course. Updike is using the old concept that it is only the extremes—only the angels and the devils—who know of the existence of Heaven and Hell, who know that our true space is upward space. Only he who knows there is a floor is able to infer, as Rabbit does, that there must also be a ceiling. The other characters tread the middle ground, as cut off from Heaven as they are from Hell.

Thus, at the graveside, the real shock is Updike's illumination of the true nature of Humanism. Like the characters gathered about the grave, we are totally disgusted with Rabbit's behavior. When he turns and denies his guilt and accuses his wife, we—like the others—are shocked. How can even Rabbit Angstrom be so brutal, we ask, as to accuse his wife of being solely guilty at the very moment when she needs most help and most understanding? It is in answering that question that we understand the true impact of this novel. It is not because he is lascivious and irresponsible that Rabbit brutally accuses his wife and denies his guilt. It is because he alone, of all the characters gathered about the grave, believes in God. For Rabbit the words "I am the resurrection and the life" have meaning; for the other characters they are an empty formula. When one believes in God, one may assign guilt, for there is a help: "casting every care on Thee." For the other characters, stricken beneath the net of Humanism, there is no help beyond themselves. How then are they to bear the burden of their lives if they do not share this guilt? Lacking any belief in God, they must cast their cares on one another, must spread the stain of their guilt as widely as possible.

In his story "Lifeguard" Updike also unites opposites. He has his divinity student-lifeguard say,

> Are you offended that a divinity student lusts? What prigs the un-churched are! Are not our assaults on the supernatural lascivious, a kind of indecency? If only you knew what de Sadean degradations, what frightful psychological spelunking, our gentle transcendental-ist professors set us to, as preparation for our work, which is to shine in the darkness.

When Rabbit returns to Ruth after the funeral, she is certain what his gift is: "Boy, you really have the touch of death, don't you? ... I see you very clearly all of a sudden. You're Mr. Death himself."

It would seem best, however, to allow this dual symbolism— Rabbit as Christ-life and Satan-death—to strike a kind of balance. In Rabbit Angstrom Updike has portrayed a man who is himself "the encounter a terrible God willed: the collision of two opposed realms." A man of mammoth lust, he is nonetheless a man sus-tained when he can believe in the Unseen and lost when he cannot.

> Momentarily drained of lust, he stares at the remembered con-tortions to which it has driven him. His life seems a sequence of grotesque poses assumed to no purpose, a magic dance empty of belief. *There is no God; Janice can die:* the two thoughts come at once, in one slow wave. [p. 165]

After he has returned to Janice the first time, and while Janice and the baby are still in the hospital, Rabbit takes Nelson to the playground.

> He feels the truth: the thing that had left his life had left irrevoca-bly; no search would recover it. No flight would reach it. It was here, beneath the town, in these smells and these voices, forever

behind him. The best he can do is submit to the system and give
Nelson the chance to pass, as he did, unthinkingly through it.

[p. 188]

He is wrong, of course, for it had not left irrevocably: he cannot exist without it.

Rabbit's Progress

by Richard Locke

What distinguishes *Rabbit, Run* from all of Updike's other works (until the appearance of its sequel) is its dynamic balance between description and narrative energy: as Rabbit escapes from one enclosing situation to another, the pace never flags and yet the physical and psychological details have never been more sharply in focus. The minutiae of the Eisenhower age—the paradigmatic Mickey Mouse TV show, the religious revival, the all-American glamor of high-school heroes, the cramped apartments of small town sweethearts who married too young, the hallowed authority of athletic coaches and parents—all are perfectly there.

But the verisimilitude is. more than skin deep. Updike meticulously conveys the longings and frustrations of family life, the interplay of love, tenderness, aggression and lust with self-esteem, the differences of feeling and speech from class to class and generation to generation. The prose speeds along with grace and strength; the present tense has given it dramatic immediacy and yet permitted a rapid flow of psychological nuance. Rabbit's wife, his mistress, the disapproving parents, his old coach, an all-too-modern Episcopal priest and his wife, the two young children all are brilliantly drawn. Rabbit is caught in the center—a kind of anti-Job who won't abandon the pleasure principle, or a male Madame Bovary who instead of killing himself simply runs away.

Thus, the essential theme of *Rabbit, Run* is civilization and its discontents: the opposing claims of self and society, the sacrifices of energy and individuality that civilization demands. In *Rabbit,*

Original title: "Rabbit Redux" by Richard Locke. From *The New York Times Book Review,* 76 (November 7, 1971), pp. 1-2ff. Copyright © 1971 by The New York Times Company. Reprinted by permission.

Run, Updike pulled against the 1950's, defending the claims of the libidinous presocial self against the smothering complacencies of small town white America. Now in *Rabbit Redux* (that is, Rabbit "returns") he pulls against the 1960's and defends his hero's new commitment to civilization, his longing for social and personal continuity in an age where both are hard to come by.

In the new book Rabbit has greatly changed; it's been ten years since he last ran away. At 36 he's no longer a bounder, but plugs away, like his father, as a linotypist in a local print shop. He sticks to his responsibilities and lives by the old American rules which it cost him so much to learn: family loyalty, hard work, sexual compromise. But in the 1960's such rules no longer seem to apply. "Everybody's the way I used to be," he says.

Rabbit's wife, Janice, has also changed. She is restless, no longer the gloomy stay-at-home. Now she bustles out to work at her father's new Toyota agency, while Rabbit is stuck in his dwindling blue collar trade and is finally laid off as obsolete. Janice, not Rabbit, is the one who has an affair and runs away from home—for much the same reason as he once did. This time he is left behind, the town cuckold, caring for his teen-age son.

Lonely, adrift, Rabbit takes an 18-year-old runaway girl into his house; he becomes her lover and father. The family expands when she brings home another stray: a black Vietnam veteran on the run, who styles himself an agent of apocalypse—and indirectly brings down fire and brimstone on the house. Rabbit returns to his parents' home. Once again he sleeps in his old room, regresses into adolescent fantasies. But in the end his wife decides to let her lover go and comes back to her family. A more complex health and order are achieved.

The action takes place in the summer of 1969, and the Apollo moon shot is used as the organizing image of the book. As Rabbit and his father sit drinking in a bar and he first learns that his wife may be unfaithful, the astronauts are taking off. As Rabbit's life falls apart, Armstrong sets foot on the moon. Everything in the middle sections is in free fall as Rabbit spins around the dark side of the moon. In the end Rabbit and his wife home in like space capsules and, of course, like rabbits in a hutch. The lunar wasteland of contemporary America is everywhere. The tacky houses of the suburban development where Rabbit lives blister the landscape like craters on the moon. Downtown there are deserted lots and empty stores. Desolate shopping centers are lit by burger joints where the drinks all taste like chemical sludge and Luna specials (two cheeseburgers with an American flag on top) are sold. The endless electronic buzz of television fills the air with news reports of rocket launchings and racial turmoil. The young trip out on pot and heroin; their sexual license is bombed out, arid, frozen. All these elements are subtly brought together in the controlling image of space exploration, a journey out into a void and then back to earth.

In *Rabbit Redux,* for the first time in his career, Updike deals in a large way with public subjects: violence, the Vietnam war, black revolution, drug addiction, middle American anger and frustration, hippie life-styles, the moon shot. With great narrative facility he has integrated these volatile elements within a realistic novel of suburban life in 1969. In outline, the book may seem populated with clichés, but on the page they are redeemed by Updike's accurate evocation of people's voices and feelings as well as his description of physical details. Updike has always written about the inner surface of banal experiences; in *Rabbit Redux* he shows highly familiar subjects in all their human particularity.

For example, Rabbit has a series of violent political arguments with his two sexual rivals: his wife's lover and the young black. In *Bech: A Book,* Updike wrote that "even in an age of science and unbelief our ideas are dreams, styles, superstitions, mere animal noises intended to repel or attract." In the give and take of these debates it is nearly impossible to detach the ideas and political opinions from their psychological, novelistic base. Rabbit gets wild about Vietnam when he feels personally and sexually threatened; he overcomes his fear and dislike of blacks when he himself is an outcast and a cuckold.

The wide range of tones and rhythms in black speech has never been so well reproduced in contemporary white writing. (The apposite comparison is Ralph Ellison's *Invisible Man.*) Bernard Malamud's stereotyped black novelist in *The Tenants* and Saul Bellow's wordless menacing black pickpocket in *Mr. Sammler's Planet* come nowhere near the depth and accuracy of Updike's black characters: a printer, a lowlife singer, the young Vietnam veteran. Although symbolically Rabbit is clearly the "suffering servant" and father, and this young black is clearly the Antichrist —preaching sermons that mix Afro-American history and religious nihilism and administering the sacraments of drugs and sex—this black is portrayed with enormous sympathy and force and is anything but an allegorical cut-out.

In *Rabbit, Run* the hero confronted an essentially static social situation and dove into his inner spaces to avoid it. In *Rabbit Redux* he confronts an unnervingly dynamic social situation that plunges him into outer space—beyond his family, his class, his race and his normal earthbound feelings and behavior. *Rabbit, Run* was a major book about the fifties; *Rabbit Redux* is, like Mailer's *Armies of the Night,* a major book about the sixties—the period when the struggles of the private self became political events and political events broke in on private lives.

Of the writers who are working in a professional way to help us come to some unsteady and evolving understanding of our human and cultural predicament as we slide into the seventies, two in recent years are complementary—Norman Mailer and John Updike. A metaphor might help us here. Mailer is a mountain-climber; Updike a miner. Mailer is heroically scaling the heights—of himself, of ideas, of urban life, of the future, of the sky, the outer spaces. He is aggressive, public, ostentatiously political, outrageously daring, unsparing of himself. Updike is an underground worker, chipping away at banal circumstances and minute feelings, trying to find jewels in a little space. Until this book he was nearly apolitical and even here he carefully grounds his characters' political opinions in their immediate social and psychological conditions. He is tender, not aggressive. His sexual descriptions are not boastful but reverent. His major characters include women as well as men—which is remarkable in American fiction. He is our finest writer about children. He treats his characters with respect; there are no villains.

In *Rabbit Redux* all is ambiguous, dialectical and yet, finally, novelistically resolved. There are no "Updikean" curlicues of style or yawning gaps between symbol and event. All is dramatized. There are some structural faults, and moments when characters don't ring true. But I can think of no stronger vindication of the claims of essentially realistic fiction than this extraordinary synthesis of the disparate elements of contemporary experience. *Rabbit Redux* is a great achievement, by far the most audacious and successful book Updike has written.

Updike, Malamud, and the Fire This Time

by Robert Alter

Taking certain striking passages out of context from some recent American novels, one might conclude that white writers in this country have been engulfed by a wave of racial paranoia. To begin with, there is the elegantly dressed black pickpocket in Saul Bellow's *Mr. Sammler's Planet* who exhibits his ropy male member to the panicked Mr. Sammler as an ominous lesson in "lordliness." Still more emphatically, Bernard Malamud's Willie Spearmint, the black novelist in *The Tenants,* stirs an acrid literary brew in which black guerrilla squads round up "wailing, hand-wringing Zionists" to finish them off with pistols or, in another version, stab "Goldberg" to death and taste his sour flesh. In the last confrontation of the novel—or is it only the protagonist's final fantasy?—Willie's slicing knife unsexes Lesser, the Jewish writer, at the very moment, to be sure, when Lesser's ax cleaves the skull of the black man. John Updike's *Rabbit Redux,* moreover, demonstrates that these visions of menacing black power unleashed are not restricted to Jewish writers. Updike's working-class white Protestant protagonist, contemplating the eerie, manipulative Negro fugitive he has taken into his home, suddenly sees him as "evil," mentally comparing him to the backyard cesspool he used to poke into as a boy. "Now this black man opens up under him in the same way: a pit of scummed stench impossible to see to the bottom of."

The peculiar nature of the white-black confrontation in Malamud, and the limits of its range of implication, will become clearer through a comparison with the encounter between the two races in the new Updike novel. It is intriguing that two such different writers should have produced simultaneously novels in which the plotting of the racial situation is so similar. By an uncanny coincidence, the white protagonists of both novels even turn out to be exactly the same age, thirty-six, and to have the same first name, Harry. (Updike's Harry Angstrom is German-American, so the name is as probable for him as for the Jewish Harry Lesser.) In each case, a vague, passive, ineffectual character is discovered trying to hang on to a viable sense of self in the eroding terrain of his early middle years, sustaining himself with the fading memory of youthful success (Lesser's first novel, Rabbit's brilliant career as a basketball player that antedates the action of *Rabbit, Run*). Lesser, of course, has his dogged sense of vocation; Rabbit has only his ticky-tacky house in a low-cost suburb, his passionless marriage, his long-haired adolescent son whom he does not understand.

In each of the two novels, a black man insinuates himself into the dwelling place of the white. Each of the Harrys sees his black visitor, spun out of the inferno of the ghetto, as a wild, hostile, threatening figure who also somehow manages—through the white man's guilt?—to exercise a weird attraction. Both Angstrom and Lesser become willing if profoundly ambivalent hosts to their black guests, entering into a relationship of teacher and disciple, though in *Rabbit Redux* it is the white man who is the disciple. In each novel, there is a white woman sexually shared, in rather different ways, by the black and the white man. In each case, the protagonist's persistence in the role of host becomes a crazed acquiescence in his own destruction. "My God, Lesser," cries Levenspiel, the distraught landlord, finding his tenant in bloody battle with Willie, "look what you have done to yourself. You're your own worst enemy, bringing a naked nigger into this house. If you don't take my advice and move out you'll wake up one morning playing a banjo in your grave." Much the same advice is given Angstrom by his two menacing neighbors, Brumbach and Showalter, who come to warn him that he had better get the black man out of his house if he doesn't want serious trouble. Finally, each of the black visitors is involved in an act of fiery destruction toward the conclusion of the action. Willie burns Lesser's novel, the anguished work of ten years, so that the Jewish writer sees himself "buried in ashes," while Updike's Skeeter flees the Angstrom house in a suspect midnight blaze that destroys most of Rabbit's material possessions as well as the pathetic girl Rabbit had not quite managed to love.

Cautiously, one might draw certain general inferences from these similarities of plot. The sustained assertion of black militancy, a decade after James Baldwin's the "Fire Next Time," seems to conjure up for white literary imaginations a recurrent vision of—quite literally—the fire *this* time. Angry blacks force upon white consciousness the bitter knowledge of their collective pain and degradation; in the novels, Willie does this through his writing, Skeeter through his nightly lectures in Rabbit's living room on black history. The white man responds with guilt, a concomitant feeling of obligation, and, above all, with an apocalyptic fear that such suffering must issue in a destructive rage of unimaginable proportion and effect. The female character shuttling between races in each of the novels embodies a renewed insight into the profoundly sexual nature of the guilt, fear, and attraction that exist between the two races. In both books, the principal characters carry out bizarrely altered reenactments of the historical sexual exploitation of blacks by whites. In *The Tenants,* the white man "emasculates" the black, takes his woman from him, though she is in this case white, first attracted to her lover by his blackness. In *Rabbit Redux,* the white girl, Jill, is forced by Skeeter to assume the historical role of the black woman in a sinister psychodrama where he plays the "white" male, sadistically exploiting her, humiliating her before her lover, making her worship his sex.

Finally, a central awareness most clearly shared by both novels is a white failure of nerve, or at least a flagging sense of white identity, in the face of black assertiveness. Rabbit and Jill, a generation apart, are in their different ways both rudderless people, caught in the powerful undertow of the black man's vehement self-affirmation, and the same is true of Irene in *The Tenants.* Even Lesser, with his habit-bound commitment to the writer's vocation, has only a vague sense of identity, unmoored in the world of experience outside his manuscript, and his black visitor's certainty about self, however manic, exerts its magnetism on him. Willie makes this general point succinctly in describing his relationship with Irene: "She had nothing she believed in herself.

I straightened her out in the main ways because I gave her an example, that I believed in my blackness." The white man's fading belief in himself and in his inherited values is brought forth with comic poignancy in one of Lesser's dreams, where, clad in raffia skirt and anklets, he dances before the thatched huts of an African village. Suddenly his decrepit father appears:

> "You should be ashamed to dance like a *shvartzer,* without any clothes on."
> "It's a ceremonial dance, papa."
> "It's my own fault because I didn't give you a Jewish education."
> The old man weeps.

Although these tentative generalizations about the common implications of the two novels may have a degree of validity, a closer examination of the imaginative texture of each book will suggest that the two writers make very different use of the same racial preoccupations. In order to convey this difference in texture, I would like to set end-to-end two descriptions of city scenes that occur at the beginnings of the two novels. In each case, we see an older neighborhood in an Eastern city scarred by the characteristic contemporary blight of demolition and parking lots. Here is Lesser, stepping outside his apartment building:

> In front of the decaying brown-painted tenement, once a decent house, Lesser's pleasure dome, he gave it spirit—stood a single dented ash can containing mostly his crap, thousands of torn-up screaming words and rotting apple cores, coffee grinds, and broken eggshells, a literary rubbish can, the garbage of language become the language of garbage. ... Next building on the left had long ago evaporated into a parking lot, its pop-art remains, the small-roomed skeletal scars and rabid colors testifying former colorless existence, hieroglyphed on Levenspiel's brick wall; and there was a rumor around that the skinny house on the right, ten thin stories from the 1880's (Mark Twain lived there?) with a wrought-iron-banistered stoop and abandoned Italian cellar restaurant, was touched for next. Beyond that an old red-brick public school, three stories high, vintage of 1903, the curled numerals set like a cameo high on the window-smashed façade, also marked for disappearance. In New York who needs an atom bomb? If you walked away from a place they tore it down.

To this one might usefully compare Updike's initial description of downtown Brewer:

Now in summer the granite curbs starred with mica and the row
houses differentiated by speckled bastard sidings and the hopeful
small porches with their jigsaw brackets and gray milk-bottle boxes
and the sooty ginkgo trees and the baking curbside cars wince beneath a brilliance like a frozen explosion. The city, attempting to
revive its dying downtown, has torn away blocks of buildings to
create parking lots, so that a desolate openness, weedy and rub-
bled, spills through the once-packed streets, exposing church
façades never seen from a distance and generating new perspectives
of rear entryways and half-alleys and intensifying the cruel breadth
of the light. The sky is cloudless yet colorless, hovering blanched
humidity, in the way of these Pennsylvania summers, good for
nothing but to make green things grow. Men don't even tan; filmed
by sweat, they turn yellow.

The obvious difference between Updike's omniscient overview
and Malamud's rendering of the scene through his character's
point of view has broad ramifications in the way each novel
handles its larger subject. What engages us in the passage from
The Tenants is the manner in which it catches the special inflec-
tions of Lesser's thought and, at the very end, of his speech as
well. This means, however, that we get nothing of the outside
world that does not somehow mirror the struggling novelist's
peculiar predicament. Indeed, the world outside his writer's
refuge is first seen simply as a dumping-ground for his physical
and literary wastes. The only details he picks up of the cityscape
around him are reminders that his own fifth-floor hermitage
stands under the shadow of the wrecker's ball. The external re-
flections, in fact, of his own plight are even more specific. A
demolished building leaves a hieroglyphic testimony of its colorless existence—which is about what can be expected from Lesser's life, from his career as a writer. A neighboring tenement is
lingered over momentarily partly because Lesser thinks it once
may have given shelter to a novelist, Mark Twain. One even
suspects that the condemned old school with the smashed windows echoes a sense the protagonist has of his own anachronistic
bookishness in a landscape of urban violence, ascetic devotee of
a Flaubertian concept of the writer's craft in a high-decibel age
where activism passes for art.

In the Updike passage, on the other hand, there is a pervading
sense of the city scene, the houses and streets with their human

population, even the weather, as a coherent ensemble expressing a whole mode of life at a particular time and place. The informing authorial intelligence, personifying porches and cars,
sunlight and open space, has an emphatic interpretive view
which gives the scene its sharpness of definition, makes it mean
something as a moment in social history. Thus, the final observation about people turning yellow instead of tanning hovers
somewhere between plausible fact and literary conceit but serves
as a firmly cinching summary of the feel of existence in this life-
forsaken town.

Updike has a keen eye for those minute details which remind us
just how such a milieu looks, which suggest how its parts fit
together—the granite curbs starred with mica, the sooty ginkgo
trees, the speckled sidings on the row houses, the jigsaw brackets
and gray milk-bottle boxes on the porches. The Malamud passage
does have two analogous details—the curled numerals on the
school façade and the wrought-iron banister of the tenement
stoop—but these are not part of a panorama or descriptive catalogue, and in any case they show a degree of specification quite
untypical of the novel as a whole, which is notable for its abstract-
ness. Although urban "renewal" is going on in *The Tenants,* pot
is smoked at parties, and blacks are talking of revolution, Lesser's
tenement dwelling, scantily furnished and sketchily rendered, is
virtually interchangeable with Manischevitz's flat in "Angel
Levine" (1952) or Harry Cohen's in "The Jewbird" (1963): and
Lesser himself, essentially unmarked by history, could serve as a
stand-in for S. Levin, Fidelman, Henry Freeman, Leo Finkle,
any of those hapless, stranded Malamud protagonists vaguely
longing for a new life, for achievement, and above all for love.

By contrast, *Rabbit Redux* is that rare thing, a convincing sequel, largely because the Harry Angstrom of the Eisenhower
years portrayed in *Rabbit, Run* (1960) reappears here thoroughly
a creature of his changed time, caught in its social crises, shaped
by his class and surroundings as they have evolved into the late
1960's. For this reason, the frequent allusions to current news
events are genuinely functional, unlike the lamentable *Couples,*
where an unintegrated use of the same device seems a mere af-
fectation of historical realism. Bringing to bear an old-fashioned

novelist's instinct for the defining details of ambience, Updike places the thirty-six-year-old Rabbit in a precise social context linked to the recent years of relative affluence, deepening national malaise, and mass-produced inauthenticity. For example, the contents of Rabbit's living room, surveyed in the early morning light, have a "Martian" look: "an armchair covered in synthetic fabric enlivened by silver thread, a sofa of air-foam slabs, a low table hacked to imitate an antique cobbler's bench, a piece of driftwood that is a lamp, nothing shaped directly for its purpose, gadgets designed to repel repair, nothing straight from a human hand, furniture Rabbit has lived among but has never known, made of substances he cannot name, that has aged as in a department store, worn out without once conforming to his body." Elsewhere, the novel is punctuated with reminders of a national era vanished, the most remarkable of these being a virtuoso description of a sparsely-attended baseball game, the magic of an American ritual turned into an empty charade because "the poetry of space and inaction is too fine, too slowly spun" for this crowd of the late 60's, and "the old world of heraldic local loyalties" recalled in the team insignias has become alien, almost forgotten.

Updike, it seems to me, is at his best when he is being a rather traditional kind of novelist—which means broadly when, as in both *Rabbit* novels, the clarity of his social perceptions is not unduly vexed or obfuscated by stylistic mannerisms. I do not mean to suggest in making this general contrast between *Rabbit Redux* and *The Tenants* that social realism is intrinsically a superior mode of fiction. The thinnesss and schematism, however, of Malamud's new novel could lead one to infer that his real strength as a writer is in the short story rather than the novel because his vision is too private, too detached from the realities of society, his imagination too inclined to fable and parable, for the needs of novelistic elaboration of character, event, and setting. At any rate, I think none of his five novels equals his best short stories in originality of conception and persuasive force, while *The Tenants* seems to me clearly the weakest volume of fiction he has published. As a fabulist of the frustrated, isolate self, as a wry fantasist of grubby failure, Malamud has invented brilliant things. In *The Tenants,* the insistent presence of the new black militancy impinges upon his imagination, but one senses his limitations here precisely because in the end he can only make of a crisis in national consciousness grist for his private mill.

Willie Spearmint duly recalls for us ghetto squalor and degradation, Southern persecution, black anger and pride, but all this finally dissolves in Malamud's claustrophilia, his fixation on the allures of withdrawal and sordid self-interment, and that preoccupation has no intrinsic connection with the racial situation. Here is Lesser near the end of his sad story: "Nights he lay nauseated in piss-smelling hallways, sick, grieving, the self to whom such things happen a running sore." The nastiness of this has to be explained in terms of the loathing Malamud must feel toward the self-defeating masochistic character he is condemned to invent again and again. It has nothing to do with the conflict between black and white. The running sore of the self—a self unrepresentative in its special neurosis—fills the canvas of the novel, blurring the delineation of racial relations within it. Willie Spearmint, as I intimated earlier, becomes another Lesser, like him withdrawing from the world into a dilapidated trap, cultivating a destiny of self-immolation, wallowing in dirt, and at the end, again like his Jewish mentor, dabbling in excreta (each searches daily through the garbage cans outside to fish out the rejected drafts of the other). The ultimate moment of mutual slaughter is less a novelistic ending than an idea, a means of symmetrically finishing off both self-destructive characters since there is no way out of the claustral morass they have entered. The schematic conception of the ending is reflected in the neatness of the reversal by which the black man, having felt himself threatened with emasculation, castrates the white as the latter smashes the brain of the aspiring black writer. The whole working-out of the plot is so caught up in Malamud's private preoccupations with filth, womb-like enclosure, the inability to love (Lesser hopes to learn that by writing about it), and a writer's fear of losing creative élan, that it is extremely difficult to read it as a resonant prophetic warning about the actual relationship between the races.

With *Rabbit Redux* the case is rather different. Updike exhibits, I think, a certain boldness in placing at the center of a novel about our time an average, unintellectual, politically conservative, working-class figure. By successfully representing the confusions, anxieties, and blind longings of such a character, he manages, in a time-honored tradition of the novel, to bring us the "news" about something going on in our society, enabling us to see a familiar phenomenon more sharply, from within. Indeed, if a German-American laborer (laid off in the end by automation) can be granted title to ethnicity, one might contend that this is the first notable novel about the much-discussed anguish of the neglected ethnic amid the upheavals of the Vietnam years, the revolutions of the young and the black. I find the rendering here of one ordinary American's feelings toward blacks generally persuasive because those feelings are represented without authorial attitudinizing, as a visceral perception of the black's otherness. Harry Angstrom is physically uncomfortable in the presence of blacks yet fascinated by their seemingly impenetrable alienness; hidebound by prejudices of class and race against blacks yet paradoxically open to their suffering because, after all, he cannot entirely muffle his awareness that they are men like himself. "Talking to Negroes makes him feel itchy, up behind the eyeballs, maybe because theirs look so semi-liquid and yellow in the white and sore. Their whole beings seemed lubricated on pain." In the bizarre character of Skeeter, Updike strains the idea of black otherness to the limits, Skeeter at times seeming more a projection of Rabbit's fantasies than an independent personage. For me, however, the strategy finally works through its extremeness: the conventional Angstrom is hypnotized into a trance of passivity by the black man's sheer *outrance*, compelled to a dazed attentiveness quite unlike his ordinary mental habits by the psychological and rhetorical contortions of the utterly alien black.

But this is not, one can be thankful, a homiletic novel about the conversion of a bigot. Rabbit is deeply shaken by his extended encounter with Skeeter, literally and figuratively burned by it, but he plausibly remains more or less what he was. At the end he still supports the war in Vietnam, still has scorn for Americans who defame America, still feels prejudice toward "Spics" (his wife's lover is Greek-American) and others who have dark skins or foreign origins. His loyalty to the idea of America remains, but now, after Skeeter's bitter lectures, it is shot through with doubts about what America has really been. His sense of distance from blacks is almost the same, his fear of them surely enlarged, but he also sees them more clearly as human beings, understands in some way the exigencies of their troubled condition.

What emerges most prominently from Rabbit's confusions is a sense of complicity. He can no longer see the nation altogether as a division between "we" who are all right and "they" who make the trouble, for he has reached some inner knowledge that we all have a hand in the trouble. The result, for better or for worse, is not a resolution but a new kind of confusion, a free-floating guilt that as yet has no proper outlet. Harry Lesser's self-victimization is a matter of individual obsession; Harry Angstrom's self-victimization bespeaks a publicly shared feeling of guilt. Implicated in violent destruction, he thinks of himself as a criminal, wonders why the police don't arrest him, and with his sense of punishment coming to him he has an open ear to Skeeter's new gospel for the defeated: "Chuck, you're learning to be a loser. I love it. The Lord loves it. Losers gonna grab the earth, right?"

His attraction to the fire this time is of a piece with the relief so many frustrated, socially and emotionally trapped Americans must feel in the outlet of violence, in glimpses of an apocalyptic end "You like any disaster that might spring you free," his sister tells him, and the jibe strikes home not only for the predicament of one Harry Angstrom. In Updike's *Rabbit* novel of the late 50's, the prisoner of family, class, and place could still dream of winning freedom by getting into a car and heading for open country. Now the only way out he can readily imagine is through the burning down of the whole house: "Freedom means murder," Rabbit muses moodily during a visit to a Negro bar, "rebirth means death." Mere flirtation with the apocalypse, however, reinforces feelings of impotence and guilt, and it is on this uncertain note that the novel appropriately concludes. Rabbit is back again with his wife, unable yet to make love to her after their pained separation, unsure what their new relationship will be or what he will do with the terrible shocks of new awareness he has absorbed during the *Walpurgisnacht* of his strange ménage with Skeeter and Jill. The dialogue between him and his wife before they drift into an exhausted sleep is curt, impatient, restive. The first voice is Rabbit's:

"I feel so guilty."
"About what?"

"About everything."

"Relax. Not everything is your fault."

"I can't accept that."

As a way of bringing a novel to a close, this may seem indefinite, hesitant, denying us the satisfactions of a resolution—even an apocalpytic resolution like Malamud's—but it says something that sounds right about where we are now. After all that has passed in political and literary history, it is reassuring that some novels still perform that prosaic but necessary task.

MARRIAGE NOVELS

The bourgeois novel is inherently erotic, just as the basic unit of bourgeois order—the family unit built upon the marriage contract—is erotic. Who loves whom? Once this question seems less than urgent, new kinds of novels must be written, or none at all. If domestic stability and personal salvation are at issue, acts of sexual conquest and surrender are important. If the issue is an economic reordering, and social control of the means of production, then sexual attachments are as they are in Mao's China—irrelevant, and the fewer the better.

UPDIKE
Picked-Up Pieces

Updike's American Comedies

by Joyce Carol Oates

> ...I must go to Nature disarmed of perspective and stretch
> myself like a large transparent canvas upon her in the hope
> that, my submission being perfect, the imprint of a beauti-
> ful and useful truth would be taken.

THE CENTAUR

His genius is best excited by the lyric possibilities of tragic
events that, failing to justify themselves as tragedy, turn unac-
countably into comedies. Perhaps it is out of a general sense of
doom, of American expansion and decay, of American sub-
religions that spring up so effortlessly everywhere, that Updike
works, or perhaps it is something more personal, which his extraordinary professional art can disguise: the constant transformation
of what would be "suffering" into works of art that are direct appeals to the *her* of the above quotation, not for salvation as such,
but for the possibly higher experience of being "transparent"—
that is, an artist. There has been from the first, in his fiction, an
omniscience that works against the serious development of tragic
experiences; what might be tragedy can be re-examined, re-
assessed, and dramatized as finally comic, with overtones of
despair. Contending for one's soul with Nature is, of course, the
Calvinist God Whose judgments may be harsh but do not justify
the term *tragic.*

Like Flannery O'Connor, who also studied art before she concentrated upon prose fiction, Updike pays homage to the visual

"Updike's American Comedies," by Joyce Carol Oates. From *Modern Fiction
Studies*, Vol. 21, No. 3 (Fall, 1975), 459-72. Copyright © 1975 by Purdue Research Foundation. Reprinted by permission.

artist's "submission" to the physical stimuli of his world far more than most writers. He transcribes the world for us, and at the same time transcribes the experience of doing so, from the inside. His world, like O'Connor's, is "incarnational"—vividly, lovingly, at times meanly recorded—perhaps because, in Updike, such a synthesis of fidelity and inventiveness allows an escape of sorts from the tyrannical, unimaginative cosmology of Calvinism. O'Connor was affirming her faith through allegorical art; Updike usually affirms it in words, but the act of writing itself, the free lovely spontaneous play of the imagination, *is* salvation of a kind. Does the artist require anything further? Updike's prose style resembles Nabokov's, of course, and yet it seems to me that in Updike the activity of art is never for Nabokovian purposes— never to deceive, to conceal, to mock, to reduce Nature to an egoistic and mechanical arrangement of words. On the contrary, Updike seems at times too generous, too revealing. His energies are American in their prolific and reverential honoring of a multitude of objects, as "Nature" is scaled down, compressed, at times hardly more than a series of forms of The Female.

Museums and Women makes the point explicitly that both "museums" and "women" are mysterious structures which, once entered, once explored, somehow lose their mystery; yet they are, to use Peter Caldwell's phrase, "high religious halls" that attract the artist again and again. Flannery O'Connor's interest was in love of a distinctly spiritual nature, but Updike speaks with Alexander Blok, surely, in saying, "We love the flesh: its taste, its tones/ Its charnel odor, breathed through Death's jaws..." ("The Scythians," epigraph to *Couples*). Because O'Connor's Catholic faith was unshakable, she could invent for her allegorical people ghastly physical-historical fates, assuming that their souls, encompassing but not limited to their egos, were unkillable. Updike's faith is possibly unshakable as well—which, judging from observations scattered throughout his writing, in a way alarms and amuses him—but his sympathies are usually with those who doubt, who have given up hope of salvation as such, wanting instead to be transparent, artists of their own lives. The "beautiful and useful truth" that Peter Caldwell prayed for has little to do with religious convictions, but everything to do with the patient, reverential transcribing of Man comically descended into the flesh: into Nature. Once in the flesh, once individualized, Man can then attempt some form of rebellion against "fate"— enjoying the very absurdity of his position.

The hero of *Couples,* Piet Hanema, is a man of artistic imagination, somehow trapped by his work, his marriage, the unholy and entertaining town of Tarbox, and he is, despite his despair and his promiscuity, a religious man. Foxy tells him that "his callousness, his promiscuity, had this advantage for her; with him she could be as whorish as she wanted, that unlike most men he really didn't judge." Piet answers that it is his Calvinism: "Only God judged." But more than this, Piet believes that God already judged: it is all over, history, melodrama, comic arrangements and re-arrangements of adulterous couples, the Day of Judgment is—as Kafka has said—a perpetual event, the court always in session and the judgments known ahead of time because everything is predestined. Updike understands women well in allowing Foxy to compliment her lover on character traits that, ironically, activate less-than-admirable traits in her, but she speaks more generally for the sly truth that must gradually but inevitably dawn upon the Puritan Calvinist of any intellectual capacity: one can do exactly as one wishes, since salvation or damnation are accomplished facts, impersonal, boring, finally irrelevant. A sense of determinism, whether religious or economic or biological, has personal advantaged never dreamt of by those who believe in free will. When Updike explores the non-Protestant possibilities of the imagination, when he sends out his soul, let us say, in the guise of an atheistic Jew, we have the fantastically funny and despairing Bech who, in being elected to a society of arts and letters to which Updike was himself elected in real life, precociously, muses:

His mother was out there in that audience!

But she had died four years ago, in a nursing home in Riverdale. As the applause washed in, Bech saw that the old lady ... was not his mother but somebody else's. ... The light in his eyes turned to warm water. His applause ebbed away. He sat down. ... Bech tried to clear his vision by contemplating the backs of the heads. They were blank: blank shabby backs of a cardboard tableau lent substance only by the credulous, by old women and children. His

knees trembled, as if after an arduous climb. He had made it, he
was here, in Heaven. Now what?   [*Bech,* pp. 204-5] [1]

Bech is Updike's projection of an Updike unprotected by women,
children, God; though attached to his mother, as Updike's characters are often attached to their mothers, he "ascends" to this mock-
Heaven only after her death, when it is too late. His adventures must
be seen as comic because they are so desperate, so horrible. In
this way Updike explores wittily the very real possibilities of a
shallow imaginative life "free" of Calvinistic gloom, though it
must be said, in my opinion at least, that he does not convince us
of Bech's "Jewishness"—Bech is a man without a soul. In the brief
reverie "Solitaire," in *Museums and Women,* a husband contemplates leaving his wife for his mistress, but contemplates it only
with one part of his mind—the aesthetic; he knows very well that
his identity would be lost outside the confining and nourishing
circle of wife and children: in fact, he married young, had several
children almost at once, in order to assure his being trapped.
Bech escaped the trap, but at great cost to his soul.

By isolating those lines from *The Centaur* in which Peter-as-
Prometheus speaks so eloquently about submitting himself to
Nature, I am deliberately giving more weight to the pagan-
classical-artistic-"immoral" side of Updike's imagination than to
the Calvinistic, though, in fact, the two are balanced. *The Centaur,* being a relatively early and emotionally autobiographical
work, is valuable in its obvious statement of the dichotomy in the
author's imagination between the "pagan" and the "Christian."
Critics may well disagree about the merit of the uses to which
Updike put his childhood interest in "old Greek folk stories told
anew," and surely the example of Joyce's *Ulysses* was always in
his mind; but, unlike Joyce, he did not evoke the classical in order
to give structure to quantity[2] or to comment ironically upon it,

[1]Rpt. New York: Fawcett World Library, 1970. Subsequent quotations from
Updike's works all refer to the Fawcett editions—Ed.

[2]When someone denounced Gothic architecture as a fussy multiplication of
accents that demonstrated only "a belief in the virtue of *quantity,*" James Joyce
stated that he did something similar in words; there was no need to force the
trivial into a symbolic expression of "beauty" since it is already, by simply existing, beautiful. The emotional and artistic consequences of such a belief, however
admirable the belief, are sometimes dangerous: the writer finds himself unable
to stop the multiplication of specific detail. There is a scholastic maxim *(omnis*

but to provide for himself,, for Peter, for George Caldwell, another spiritual dimension in which they might be heroic without fear of being heretical. Significantly, the "pagan" world is really a feminine world; Updike alludes to the whimsical and tyrannical figure of Zeus, but it is Venus Aphrodite who speaks to Chiron at such length in Chapter 1 and even offers to embrace him, though he is part-beast, and Venus Aphrodite in the form of Vera Hummel, the girls' gym teacher, with whom the young impressionable Peter Caldwell imagines himself "sharing a house" in a concluding chapter. Venus, not Zeus, presides over the pagan world. Unlike the woman who awaits Peter and his father back on the farm, in that fertile but uncultivated land that is more a burden than a place of retreat, Vera Hummel is all warmth, simplicity, radiance, nourishment. *She,* of course, is promiscuous; Cassie Caldwell is someone's faithful wife, herself trapped, complaining, and bitter and yet, ultimately, fairly satisfied with her lot. Vera is the promise; Cassie the reality. Vera forever beckons, but is not known; Cassie is known. Though Peter and his father return to the farm, and will always return (as the narrator of *Of The Farm* returns — to betray his wife with his mother!),[3] it is Venus Aphrodite who

---

determinatio est negatio) that, in psychological terms, warns against the generous dissolving of the ego in its submission to all that is outside it. What some critics dislike in Updike is this tendency toward detail for its own sake, as in *Couples* at the start of a dramatic scene one is sometimes given the setting at too great a length, or in *Rabbit Redux* one is dizzily informed of the furnishings of the Angstrom's house while scandalous events are taking place. The "external circumstances" of the visual world can be an exhausting burden. One example from *The Centaur:* "Vera enters the back of the auditorium by one of the broad doors that are propped open on little rubber-footed legs which unhinge at a kick from snug brass fittings" [p. 175]. This naturalism, this fidelity to the concreteness of things, shades into the "absurdistic" techniques of Céline, Beckett, Robbe-Grillet, Ionesco, and many others, as faith in the divinity of things as things is lost.

[3]*The Centaur* (1963) and *Of the Farm* (1966) illuminate one another, just as, scattered in his fiction but always recognizable as *the* nuclear fable of Updike's life, a certain set of tensions appears and re-appears. At the center is the Mother who waits out in Nature, patient, diabolically clever, more than a match for any female rival who would tempt her son away from her, and more than a match for the son himself. Hence the rudeness, the bluntness, the devastating accuracy of Mr. Robinson of *Of the Farm,* who, when her thirty-five-year-old son challenges her by saying, "You can't reduce everything to money," replies at once: "What would you reduce it to? Sex?" [p. 31]. She knows him completely, from

has the power of altering lives without exactly touching them.
Here is the adolescent Peter:

> The next two hours were unlike any previous in my life. I share a
> house with a woman, a woman tall in time, so tall I could not esti-
> mate her height in years, which at the least was twice mine. A
> woman of overarching fame; legends concerning her lovelife cir-
> culated like dirty coins in the student underworld. A woman fully
> grown and extended in terms of property and authority; her pres-
> ence branched into every corner of the house. ... Intimations of
> Vera Hummel moved toward me from every corner of her house,
> every shadow. ...   [*Centaur,* p. 206]

Always outside the masculine consciousness, this archetypal
creature when embodied, however briefly, in flesh, has the power
to awaken, however briefly, the "religious" experience common to
the entering of both museums and women; she is life itself, the
very force of life, playful, promiscuous as Nature, ultimately uncaring as the ancient Magna Mater was so viciously uncaring of
the beautiful adolescent youths she loved and devoured. Contemplating the naked green lady of the Alton Museum, a foun-
tain-statue, the child Peter is at first troubled by the mechanical
logistics of the statue that forbid its ever quenching its thirst; but,
artist as he is, manipulator of reality as he will be, he tells himself that at night the statue manages to drink from its own foun-
tain. "The coming of night" released the necessary magic [p. 200.].
Because the Venus-figure is experienced as archetypal rather
than personal, she is never connected with any specific woman,
but may be projected into nearly anyone. She is simple, vital,
enchanting, and yet—curiously—she is no threat. Men remain
married or, at the most, remarry women with children (like Peggy
of *Of the Farm;* like Foxy of *Couples,* one baby alive, one baby
aborted, but a mother nevertheless); and as everyone knows
Venus is sterile. She has never entered history. Piet Hanema
perhaps speaks for Updike in diagnosing his eventual dissatisfaction with one of his mistresses, Georgene, because she made

---

the inside, and the means by which Joey is able to transcend his situation—his
mortality—is belittled simply by being named. Here is Venus in her older, wiser,
and more terrifying form: the "Great Mother" who, according to legend, was so
intolerable a religious experience that what we call today the "patriarchal" consciousness (descended in the West from Judaism) was a desperately necessary
evolutionary development.

adultery too easy, too delightful, for his "warped nature." And so in *The Centaur,* Venus Vera attracts her opposite, the Reverend March, he whose faith is so unshakable, intact and infrangible as metal, and "like metal dead." Economically and concisely developed, the Reverend March is a type that appears occasionally in Updike ("The Deacon" is an older, wearier version) and whose function in *The Centaur* is not only angrily to resist the desperate George Caldwell's desire to speak of theological matters at a basketball game, but, more importantly, to be the man whose faith is dead and metallic and yet rather wonderful ("Though he can go and pick it up and test its weight whenever he wishes, it has no arms with which to reach and restrain him. He mocks it" [*Centaur,* p. 178]) and whose faith allows him a psychological insight that, in Updike-as-Peter, would be annihilating when he muses upon the fact that a woman's beauty depends only upon the man who perceives her: Her value is not present to herself, but given to her. "Having been forced to perceive this," the Reverend March is therefore "slow to buy" [*Centaur,* p. 177] .

Because the Feminine Archetype is always projected outward, and the knowledge of this projection ("valuing" or "pricing," in the Reverend March's crude terminology) cannot be accepted except at the risk of emotional impotence, it slips back beneath the level of consciousness and is not accepted at all. It is not seen to be a natural psychological fact in which the perceiver-artist values, creates, and honors everything he sees—not only women —and in which he himself re-creates himself *as* an artist; it is, instead, despairing if and when it is admitted, so grotesque that it had better not be admitted. So, Updike puts into the mouth of Janice Angstrom of *Rabbit Redux* words no woman would say, being in one sense obvious and in another sense completely incorrect: "I'm just a cunt. There are millions of us now." And Bech's horrific vision in "Bech Panics" is the stuff of which religious conversions are made, so intense and incredulous is his experience of the falsity of an old faith:

> He looked around the ring of munching females and saw their bodies as a Martian or a mollusc might see them, as pulpy stalks of bundled nerves oddly pinched to a bud of concentration in the head, a hairy bone knob holding some pounds of jelly in which a trillion circuits, mostly dead, kept old records, coned motor opera-

tions, and generated an excess of electricity that pressed into the
hairless side of the head and leaked through the orifices, in the
form of pained, hopeful noises and a simian dance of wrinkles.
Impossible mirage! A blot on nothingness. And to think that all
the efforts of his life—his preening, his lovemaking, his typing[!] —
boiled down to the attempt to displace a few sparks...within some
random other scoops of jelly. ...   [*Bech,* p. 131] [4]

Bech gives voice to suspicions Updike may play with, but cannot
take seriously; he knows we are not free, and so Bech's lazy "freedom" is mere fiction, the maniacal cleverness of an intellectual consciousness unhampered by restraint, by the necessary admission
of its subordinate position in the universe. And yet—if Bech *were*
correct—one would be free of the tyrannical father as well, and
free of the need to perform, ceaselessly, the erotic activity that
defies him: writing. For Bech, of course, is a writer who cannot
write. Updike may write about him, but Bech requires a week to
compose a three-page introduction to the book. Free, yes, un-
damned and unhaunted—but whoever wanted such freedom?

[4]To realize the depths of Bech's discovery and to sympathize with his near-
psychotic experience, one must know precisely what it is Bech fears losing. One
could select any number of representative passages—all of them beautifully-
written, true "erotic" manipulations of the language itself that strike us as an
attempt to render into prose an essentially mystical experience; here, from *Of
the Farm:*

> My wife is wide, wide-hipped and long-waisted, and, surveyed from above,
> gives an impression of terrain, of a wealth whose ownership imposes upon
> my own body a sweet strain of extension; entered, she yields a variety of
> landscapes, seeming now a snowy rolling perspective of bursting cotton
> bolls seen through the Negro arabesques of a fancywork wrought-iron
> balcony; now a taut vista of mesas dreaming in the midst of sere and
> painterly ochre; now a gray French castle complexly fitted to a steep green
> hill whose terraces imitate turrets; now something like Antarctica; and
> then a receding valleyland of blacks and purples where an unrippled river
> flows unseen between shadowy banks of grapes that are never eaten. ...
> [p. 39].

It is possible to make the statement that such ecstatic experiences absolutely pre-
clude any personalities, in which case "Peggy" is only the fleshly means by which
the lover's imagination, his physical imagination, is activated; he divorced his
first wife, Joan, because she was too like himself, "an adventurer helpless in dark
realms." What is experienced is basically the loss of individuality, the dissolving
of personality itself; at such times the son is united with the archetypal "Great
Mother," ironically enough. Such a loss would be equivalent to the loss of life
itself.

Most of the time, however, the projection is not recognized as such; it is experienced in a religious manner, the woman is "adored," she is associated with Nature, as either the Mother herself or a form of the mother, and is in any case the promise of timelessness within the oppressive context of time. Foxy Whitman is loved when she is pregnant and because she is pregnant; once delivered of her child, her "flat" being somehow disappoints and bewilders her lover. Burdened with the difficult responsibility of making men immortal, the woman-as-adored either tires of the whole thing (as Joan Maple has grown tired in *Museums and Women,* itself a curiously tired book) or shares with her adorer a baffled metaphysical rage: *Why* isn't love permanent?

In asking of love that it be permanent, Updike's characters assert their profoundly Christian and historically-oriented religious temperament, for not many religions have really promised an "immortality" of the ego let alone the Theistic mechanism to assure this permanence. In Updike, Eros is equated with Life itself, but it is usually concentrated, and very intensely indeed, in terms of specific women's bodies; when they go—everything goes![5] Hence Bech's terror, his breakdown, hence the fact, "monstrous and lovely," Peter discovers in kissing his girl, Penny, that at the center of the world is an absence: "Where her legs meet there is nothing" [*Centaur,* p 184]. Because he is an adolescent and will be an artist, Peter still values this "nothing" and equates it with "innocence." *He* experiences his own artistry, through this equation, as Chiron/George Caldwell experiences his own divinity by simply accepting, as an ordinary human being, the fact of mortality. *The Centaur* is the most psychologically satisfying of Updike's numerous books—it may or may not be his "best" book—because it has expressed its author's considerable idealism in the guise of adolescent love, for Woman

[5]The woman who fails to recognize how part, or perhaps most, of her power over men is transpersonal and not personal, is doomed to a steady loss of her faith in her own "identity," because she will experience the natural biological process of aging as a personal egoistic failure—a kind of sin. Updike's meticulous analysis of the love-experience from the point of view of the male turns almost constantly upon the excitation in the male of what is transpersonal, rather than uniquely individual and is, therefore, highly instructive for women: if only Venus Aphrodite is really sought, the individual woman may see how she embodies—temporarily—an ideal of romantic love, but cannot and, indeed, should not care to, maintain it indefinitely. Art must not be mistaken for life.

and for Father, an idealism Updike may not trust in adult terms.
Or perhaps the world has changed, has become more "adult"
and secular and unworthy of redemption—the dismal Tarbox of
Museums and Women is far less attractive than the same Tarbox
of *Couples,* though that was degenerate enough. An earlier novel,
Rabbit, Run, explored quite remorselessly the consequences of a
reduced, secularized, "unimagined" world, Updike's conception
of Updike-without-talent, Updike trapped in quantity. But the
consciousness of a Rabbit Angstrom is so foreign to Updike's
own that it seems at times more a point of view, a voicing of that
part of the mind unfertilized by the imagination, than a coherent
personality. Rabbit is both a poet and a very stupid young man. A
decade later, as Rabbit led back, penned, now finally trapped, he
has become an uneasy constellation of opinions, insights, descriptive passages and various lusts, a character at the center of *Rabbit
Redux* called "Harry"; he ends his adventure in a motel room
with his own wife, Janice, Venus-led-back, he is exhausted, impotent, but agreeable: *O.K.* The *Yes* of *Ulysses* is the weary *O.K.*
of a man imagined as typically "American."

The world itself has not changed, though history—both personal and collective—has certainly changed. *Couples* dramatizes
in infinite, comically attentive detail the melodramatic adventures of "typical" Americans in a "typical" though sophisticated
town in New England; love vies with the stock market in reducing everyone to ruins. Much has been said, some of it by the
author himself, of the novel's religious and allegorical structure,
which is so beautifully folded in with the flow of life, the work-
ings-out of numerous fates, as to be invisible except in concluding
scenes: the Congregational Church is struck by "God's own
lightning," its weathercock is removed, Piet discovers in the ruins
a pamphlet containing an 18th-century sermon that speaks of the
"indispensable duty" of all nations to know that "the LORD he
is God." Piet is not much of a hero, and he does not choose to be
heroic. He has, after all, helped arrange for the abortion of a baby
both he and his mistress really wanted; but he is one of the few
characters in Updike's recent fiction who can somehow synthesize
the knowledge of human "valuing" with a religious faith that
sustains it while reducing it to scale.

Piet does not require that love be permanent—or even "love."
If he is an artist it is at compromises he is best; failing to be an

architect, he winds up as a construction inspector for military barracks, failing to keep his wife from divorcing him, he moves on to the next stage, the next compromise. He has not much choice except to compromise his ideal love (Foxy pregnant) with his real love (Foxy the individual). After the desperate violence of his love ebbs he is able to see the woman clearly, not perfect, not even very charming, at times embarrassingly "tough," "whorish" as if performing for him, her waist thickened by childbirth, her luminous being somehow coarsened into the flesh of historical experience. Yet Piet says, without lying, that she is beautiful anyway; he adores her anyway; he marries her and they move to another town where "gradually, among people like themselves, they have been accepted as another couple." The practical wisdom of the novel's concluding sentence may be interpreted as cynicism, or as a necessary and therefore rather comic working-out of events that made their claim for tragic grandeur, but fell short.

In this way Piet accepts his own mortality, a movement into adulthood, middle-age, in which the adolescent yearnings for an inexpressible transcendence in fleshly terms is put aside. In a powerful paragraph at the end of Chapter 3 ("Thin Ice"), Piet has already come to terms with his own death by recognizing that "the future is in the sky. ... Everything already exists" [*Couples*, p. 287] and this knowledge has the effect of undoing some of the magic of Foxy: "Henceforth he would love her less." The "love" he had experienced for Foxy was a form of delirium in which his terror of death was temporarily obliterated in the body of Venus —but only temporarily, for his real allegiance is to doom, to a future already in existence, a God Who manipulates men according to His inscrutable design.[6]

At the same time Piet articulates what is sometimes kept beneath the level of consciousness in Updike: that the infatuation

---

[6]One of Updike's several undeveloped shadow-selves is that of a distinctly American and therefore "secular" theologian—like Thoreau, though enamoured of the flesh, as Thoreau evidently was not. His essays on Barth, Tillich, and de Rougemont (in *Assorted Prose*, 1965), "The Astronomer" (of *Pigeon Feathers*), and *A Month of Sundays* make this clear, though we should sense it anyway. He accepts de Rougemont's convincing thesis about "love in the Western world," but declares himself still on the side of this perverse and narcissistic love: "The heart *prefers* to move against the grain of circumstance; perversity is the soul's very life" [*Assorted Prose*, p. 233].

with surfaces, the artist's-eye aspect of his imagination, is somehow less basic to him than a deeper and more impersonal tendency toward unity, toward the general. After Angela has asked
Piet to move out of their home he finds himself with a great deal
of time, little to do, very much alone; and out of his loneliness the
discovery that

> The world was more Platonic than he suspected. He found he
> missed, friends less than friendship; what he felt, remembering
> Foxy, was a nostalgia for adultery itself—its adventure, the acro-
> batics its deceptions demand, the tension of its hidden strings, the
> new landscapes it makes us master.   [*Couples*, p. 450]

By a subtle—but not too subtle—shifting from the relatively
restricted third person of "he" to the communal "us" Updike invites his readers to admit, in league with his doomed character,
that the particular objects of any kind of infatuation, however
idealized, are mere stimuli that activate the inborn responses of
"love"; Venus Aphrodite is a figure that somehow unites and in
that way attempts to explain a bewildering multiplicity of love-
urges, but cannot exist "in herself" and cannot be more permanent
than the brain-structure in which these love-urges exist. And yet—
does it really matter? Lying with Foxy in his squalid rented
room, Piet makes comic moaning noises, at first disgusting Foxy
and then drawing her into imitating him; and Updike comments,
again with an ironically confident 19th-century omniscience: *We
are all exiles who need to bathe in the irrational.*

   In a poem, "South of the Alps," the speaker is being driven to
Lake Como by a beautiful Italian woman, is seated in the back of
the car, terrified at the woman's careless speed, while "Her chatting lover occupied the death seat." The elements of an essential
Updikian romance are present: the woman is seen as an "ikon,"
her beauty is "deep in hock to time" and reckless with itself, and
the men around it, slavish, adoring, hopeless. The poet sees himself as a "cowardly word-hoarder":

> Of course I adored her, though my fate / was a midge on her wrist
> she could twitch away; / the old Testament said truly: fear / is love
> and love is rigid-making fear.   [*Tossing and Turning*, 1977]

Unknown in any personal, fleshly sense, unentered, unexplored,
Signorina Angeli, an "angel" as finally remote and rejecting as

Piet's wife Angela, alarms the poet and has the final line of the poem: "Tell me, why doesn't anything last?" And here it is Venus speaking from the disappointed idealism of the male, promised permanence and yet continually denied it.

"South of the Alps" shows us, in beautifully compressed language, the bewildering locked-in fates of the adorer and the adored: the masculine consciousness that, having failed to integrate the "Feminine" with its own masculinity, seeing it as essentially pagan and heretical, must continually project it outward; the feminine consciousness that, having taken on the masculine, Faustian quest for permanence, must be forever loved, a beloved, an ikon with nostrils "nice as a skull's." Male and female here unite only through a declaration of their common predicament. A writer who shares Updike's extreme interest in the visual world as well as his obsession with language is Joseph Conrad who, significantly, could imagine the ideal and the real only as hopelessly separate: when the "ideal" is given historical freedom to experience itself in flesh, in action, we have the tragi-comedy of *Nostromo,* we have the Feminine Archetype (I use this expression, clumsy as it is, because Conrad nearly uses it himself), Mrs. Gould, at the very center of a storm of mirages, each an "ideal," each a masculine fantasy. But Conrad—ironic and witty as he may be—has not finally Updike's sanity, Updike's redeeming sense of humor. Art itself is not redemptive; art may very often make things much worse, for the artist at least; but the sudden shifting of point of view that allows for a restoration of sanity is often redemptive. There is an Updike who is forever being driven along dangerous narrow roads by a beautiful woman with an intriguing, because mysterious past, himself a hoarder of words, hoping only to experience transparency in the face of such wonder; there is another Updike in the guise of Reverend March, knowing his bitter metallic Calvinistic faith so unkillable that he may mock it, betray it, take every possible risk of damnation—because he is already saved, or already damned anyway. And out of this curious duality comes the paradoxical freedom of the true artist: having conquered both his temptation by vice and his temptation by virtue, he may live as ordinarily as anyone else.

The present-action of *The Centaur* is a long "dreaming-back" as Peter Caldwell, now a young adult, a painter who lives with his black mistress in a loft in New York City, tortures himself with doubts—*Was it for this that my father gave up his life?* In *Of the Farm* it is mentioned that George Robinson's death may have been hastened—but it is more his wife's fault, probably, than his son's; and in "Flight" it is the mother, eerily powerful, who insists upon the brilliant young boy's flight, his escape from that part of Pennsylvania in which she knows herself trapped, partly by the burden of her own aged but undying father. Yet though Peter worries about the role he may have played in exhausting his father, the novel as a whole works to liberate him from guilt and would be, for this reason alone, an unusual work for an American writer; O'Neill's *A Long Day's Journey into Night* is its exact reverse. The point is made explicitly that the father, in giving his life for others, enters a total freedom. He is the "noblest of all the Centaurs" and certainly the noblest of all the characters in Updike's now vast canvas: it is not Peter's right to doubt.

From George Caldwell's experience, then, comes a conviction that permeates Updike's work even when it appears in secularized and diminished settings—that one cannot assume any ultimate truths about other people, that they forever elude the word-nets we devise. Fearing he had cancer of the bowels, Caldwell had been more or less ready to die and (like Piet Hanema after the missile crisis) feels somewhat cheated after learning that his X-rays are clear, having been "spoiled" by the expectation of an end to his troubled life. Yet he accepts it all again. Life consists and will always consist of some version of Caldwell's lot:

> The prospect of having again to maneuver among Zimmerman and Mrs. Herzog and all that overbearing unfathomable Olinger gang made him giddy, sick; how could his father's seed, exploding into an infinitude of possibilities, have been funnelled into this, this paralyzed patch of thankless alien land, these few cryptic faces, those certain four walls of Room 204?   [*Centaur*, p. 221]

Yet he accepts it. By doing so he is blessed with the release of death—he is freed of his ego, his concern for himself, and is liberated from the tyranny of the Calvinistic vision of life which his son cannot avoid inheriting. Peter, Prometheus and artist, a Dedalus as well who *must* rebel against so holy a fate in order to honor it, through his art, can encompass this wisdom only in the speculative recesses of his dreaming mind—he imagines his father as "saved," but he dares not accept such salvation for himself, because in giving his life to others (particularly to the mother who so blackmails him with her "love"), he cannot be an artist.

In assembling the short stories and sketches called, simply, *Olinger Stories,* Updike spoke of having said the "final word" in 1964; by having written *The Centaur* and transforming Olinger into Olympus, he closed the book of his own adolescence — the past is now a fable, receding, completed. But the past is never completed; it is not even *past.* It is a continual present. And so, having in a way immortalized and killed the "George Caldwell" of *The Centaur,* the author takes on, perhaps unconsciously, those traits he found so exasperating in the man as an adolescent: "Daddy, why are you so — superstitious? You make everything mean something it isn't. Why? Why can't you *relax?* It's so exhausting!" [*Centaur,* p. 192]. And he has taken on as well that remarkably detached, rather elegantly ego-less ability to glance without judgment on all sides of a melodramatic event, a basic clownishness, that seems to go largely unnoticed in his writing, but which gives it its energy, its high worth. Caldwell is funny, very funny, not with Bech's overwrought and neurotic wit, but with a fundamentally amiable acceptance of mystery. He reduces theological arguments to their basic emotional core and, correctly, presents it all as a cosmic joke: "What I could never ram through my thick skull was why the ones that don't have it [i.e., the non-Elect] were created in the first place. The only reason I could figure out was that God had to have somebody to fry down in Hell" [*Centaur,* p. 189].

When the comic vision is weak in Updike's writing, a terrifying nihilism beckons: there is the skull behind the flesh, the skull's "nice" nostrils in Signorina Angeli's beautiful face, and the middle-aged weariness of *Rabbit Redux.* The truly religious imagination is never tragic, of course, and may be capable, as Flannery O'Connor is capable, of an ostensible cruelty that can alarm the liberal imagination because this cruelty is suggested as part of a cosmic joke. The pattern is always for compromise, for a scaling-down of passions, not even for tragic grandeur when it might be justified in a way by "the plot" — for everything is seen from an omniscient point of view, and that point of view is finally not human. When faith recedes or is lost, at once a half-consciously-willed surrogate will appear, another form of desperation (as at the conclusion of *Couples* the socially-conscious and "radical" younger generation of citizens is taking possession of Tarbox): if it is time-bound, historical rather than eternal, it carries with it the germ of its own disintegration. The process in time is always toward disintegration: the physical conquest of any embodiment of the life-giving Venus is a self-destructing act. And yet—"We love the flesh, its taste, its tones"—what to make of this torment except an art that, being totally transparent, submissive, finally achieves a kind of immortality?

Out of contradictory forces that, taken very seriously, have annihilated other writers or reduced them to fruitless angry quarrels in the guise of literary works, Updike has fashioned a body of writing that is as rich, mysterious, and infinitely rewarding as life itself—which, in fact, it *is,* finally claiming no intellectual or moral excuse for its own being. It is uniquely Updike's, and uniquely American. Updike exiled from America is unthinkable, and America without Updike to record it—unthinkable as well. His special value for us is his willingness to be disarmed of perspective, to allow his intensely-realized worlds to flower with something of the mysterious effortlessness of nature itself, and to attempt to spiritualize the flesh since, for many in our time, the "flesh" may be all that remains of religious experience. The charge that Updike is too fascinated with the near-infinitesimal at the cost of having failed to create massive, angry works of art that more accurately record a violent time is unfair, because it is far more difficult to do what Updike does. Like Chiron/Caldwell, he accepts the comic ironies and inadequacies of ordinary life.

Play in *Couples*

by Howard Eiland

Couples is full of games. There are sports like basketball, tennis, skiing, golf, swimming, bowling, hockey. There are parlor games like Ghosts, Botticelli, Impressions, bridge, and "Wonderful." And there are various less conventional games and contests, some of which overlap or shade into one another. Games have had an important place in Updike's fiction at least since *Rabbit, Run,* with its basketball and golf. But not until *Couples* do they appear so extensively as heightened or concentrated models of the way people act. The dualism of *Rabbit, Run* — which separated an ideal sphere of spontaneous and sanctifying play from a muddled, troubled actual world — gives way in *Couples* to a more complex intermingling of reality and play, a sense that the strategies and controls of games pervade daily life. This is not to say that life is viewed as a *mere* game (as Freddy Thorne claims to view it), that it lacks seriousness or authenticity. Indeed, Updike's use of metaphor here can be contrasted to that of a writer like Nabokov, for whom, especially in his later work, life is a lyric, comic play of illusions, mockeries, artifices — something like Kierkegaard's rich and desperate aesthetic realm, disclosing nothing beyond itself. Updike is fully as self-conscious (though not self-reflexive) a writer as Nabokov, only Updike doesn't flaunt his self-consciousness. His main focus is not on art as such but on the interaction of characters, though he may show that men in society constantly have recourse to illusion, mockery, or artifice. He conceives metaphors of play, in other words, for old-fashioned mimetic, rather than solipsistic or narrowly aesthetic, ends; *Couples* in particular may be said to imply a psychology

"Play in *Couples*" by Howard Eiland. This article appears for the first time in this volume.

and sociology of play. It is not so much Nabokov as Henry James, especially the subtly metaphorical and sexual James of *The Golden Bowl,* the James who finds a stage and arena and jungle in the drawing room, it is James whom Updike resembles.

Although Updike has been more exclusively autobiographical than James, he is no less preoccupied with the exploration of bourgeois manners. They both are distinctly gentlemanly writers: refined (though not without a kinky side), oblique, mindful of moral precept and transgression, interested in the masks or "guises" of civilized life.[1] The mode of their fiction is not so directly "thematic," in the way that Melville's or John Barth's is, as it is densely and equivocally "dramatic," taking its rise in empirical experience rather than in apperceived "problems" or subjective fantasy. If there is a figure in the carpet, it is less in the nature of abstract concept than of large- and small-scale gestures like approach, withdrawal, or surrender. Their dramas are conventionally woven of distinct, fully turned scenes, which together bring into view a manifold subtext of motives. A character's speech betokens more or less ambiguously a set of intentions which may not square with what is overtly stated.[2] Looking thus into the deeper pile or yarn of the carpet, into the strategic moves and constructions informing various human exchanges, such fiction constitutes a kind of psychopathology of everyday life. Which is to say (in the face of the current negatively epistemological criticism) that for writers like James and Updike the things of the lived world necessarily carry meanings, necessarily manifest and deploy themselves like elements in a drama. To the pluralistic and ultimately comic metaphor of play, illuminating both the spontaneity and the stagedness of things, these writers bring a moral epistemology which is largely the heritage of the nineteenth-century novel. Exploring the self not in the light of an absolute ideal (as is still the case in *Rabbit, Run*) but in the context

[1] Updike has said in an interview: "The mythology [in my novels] answers to my sensation that the people we meet are *guises,* do conceal something mythic, perhaps prototypes or longings in our minds." *Picked-Up Pieces* (New York: Alfred A. Knopf, 1975), p. 500.

[2] In "Bech Panics," the skeptical hero observes to himself that "even in an age of science and unbelief our ideas are dreams, styles, superstitions, mere animal noises intended to repel or attract." Updike, I think, would agree, leaving out the "mere." His creative juices pretty much stopped up, Bech seems ("Jewishly") more at odds with animality and the organic than Updike himself.

of interpersonal relations, qualifying but not negating the omniscient narrative voice, they "democratize" the idea of play. One becomes *con*scious of oneself, they suggest, as one comes to *take the part of* the people surrounding one.

The idea of play indeed seems implicit in the idea of democracy, and it is commonplace to point out how preoccupied with playing contemporary American society is—how we hunger for more leisure time and for "stars" and "great games" and the yet more amazing "record," how we so pervasively and often unconsciously color our language with metaphors drawn from sports. The recent best-selling guides to psycho-dramas, body language, group rituals are an outgrowth or popularization of proliferating scholarly work in game theory, "language games," "dramatistic analysis." No doubt *Couples* reflects this general interest in the subject of performance, but, as I have indicated, Updike's presentation is at once less systematic than the sociological studies and more subtly attentive to the ethical dimensions of our playing, to experiences of freedom and suffering.

Alan T. McKenzie has already suggested how in *Couples* the participation of characters in some of the parlor games reflects aspects of their personalities.[3] In fact all of the games in the novel function partly to reveal character. Thus, during the basketball game at the Hanemas in Chapter One (Rpt. New York: Fawcett World Library, pp. 66-77), Foxy on the sidelines shrewdly surmises from Eddie Constantine's low, protective dribbling that he has been raised in a city, while she notices "a certain nice economy" in her husband Ken's movements which comports with his efficient and fastidious nature, though he significantly misses his shot, as he will in his research and his marriage. Harold little-Smith—refined, affected, an expert on savoir-faire off court—on the court has "none of the instinctive moves," and we recall that his wife, Marcia, has found in Frank Appleby the "real man" that she misses in her otherwise sophisticated husband. Ben Saltz, serious-minded and rather skittish at parties, characteristically moves "on the fringes cautiously, stooped and smiling as if to admit he was in a boys' game." When Freddy Thorne arrives, he shows himself to be all talk and no action—"Foxy saw he was nothing of an athlete"—just as he will later in bed with

---

[3]Alan T. McKenzie, " 'A Craftsman's Intimate Satisfactions': The Parlor Games in *Couples,"Modern Fiction Studies,* Vol. 20, No. 1 (Spring, 1974), 53-58.

Angela. Before Freddy's arrival, Piet has exhibited an abrupt fierceness in stealing the ball from Constantine (he later "steals" his wife for an evening and throughout the novel steals his way into several marriages); Piet makes his shot and then, acrobat and clown that he sometimes is, rides on Gallagher's back around the court (in their business Gallagher often finds Piet a burden). The others complain that Piet has fouled, though such judgment is as usual left up in the air. When Freddy enters the game, he keeps bumping Piet until Piet retaliates by tripping and hurting him. Their close antagonism on court reflects their general adversary (love/hate) relations in Tarbox society, and their exchange of fouls foreshadows their later exchange of injuries (when *Freddy* becomes the avenger).

The basketball game thus reflects not only the personalities of the players but various relations of allegiance or hostility between them, relations which continue outside the court. The court is only one area of a larger social arena. Indeed, after stealing the ball from Constantine, Piet comes over to the sidelines and engages in a little "face-off" with Angela, who appears frightened by his sweating, manly body. He is conscious of Foxy's watching him and, irked by his wife, he tells Foxy with a peculiarly courtly emphasis how "endearing of you to come and be audience." His speech is a kind of rebounding or perhaps riposting play for Foxy against Angela, foreshadowing his eventual triangular relationship with the two women. Foxy feels, no doubt accurately but with characteristic vanity, that his play on court has been done for her to see: it has been a play in more senses than one. After Freddy's injury, Piet again comes up to Foxy, again teases, but this time Georgene Thorne, Piet's present mistress, thrusts herself between them as a sort of "screen." Later, after he has begun to see Foxy, Piet falls victim to Georgene's jealous energies in a tennis match between the Hanemas and the Thornes which becomes a dynamic emblem of their relationship: "a fluid treacherous game. Advantages so swiftly shifted. Love became hate" (p. 201). Georgene returns the ball straight toward Piet at the net (the dangerous middle, the crossroads, the edge), but "anger had hurried her stroke slightly and the ball whacked the net at the height of his groin and fell dead on her side." When, a moment later, she prepares to serve, Piet "[bites] down on a shout for mercy." Neither she nor Freddy will show any mercy toward the

Hanemas when they oppose them in the game of adultery. Angela, "whose game was graceful and well-schooled and even, except at the net, where she had no sense of kill," will be as vulnerable in adultery as she is in tennis: "her serves, though accurate, lacked pace and sat up pleasantly fat to hit" ("I'd love to clobber you," Piet later tells her—p. 426).

These games of basketball and tennis exemplify the typical play situation in the novel. That situation is characterized perhaps most generally by a drawing of lines or boundaries of one sort or another. There is an out of bounds for the parlor as for the basketball court. When Freddy, in the parlor of the ski lodge, misquotes the Bard—"To fuck is human; to be blown divine"—the Smiths and Applebys feel that, "as usual, [he] had gone beyond all bounds of order" (p. 158). His penalty, the usual penalty, is to be excluded. To control foul play there are various "unspoken rules" among the couples, one of which Carol Constantine breaks by criticizing Piet's professional work in retaliation for his silent censure of her paintings, which she considers *her* professional work (p. 246). And when, in one of the most comically startling scenes in the novel, Piet escapes out of the Thorne's bathroom window and comes upon Ben Saltz and Bea Guerin necking in the grass, Bea tells him: "you may tell one person...those are the rules"; and in exchange they may tell Roger and Irene about Piet's jumping (p. 331).

Such boundaries and rules seem to evolve for a variety of reasons. Partly they serve the obvious function of maintaining order within social relations, of keeping discreet distances between friends. They bespeak a tacit recognition of the necessary gap between people, the range of possible stances, the ambiguity and relative unpredictability of the other (Piet continually finds Angela "strange," is often frightened that she may reveal unsuspected riches, and late in the novel trails her on the street without recognizing her). They operate further to control and channel impulses of affection or curiosity or aggression, and the more intimate the social climate the more elaborate these controls and channels become. In the keenly sexual "ecology" (p. 116) of Updike's couples, such regulations allow one to "score" without necessarily subverting the communal construct. We have seen an example of such scoring in the scene between Piet, Bea, and Ben mentioned above. The game of Impressions at the end of Chapter

Two allows the participants through a controlled violence to score in a different way on Piet and Foxy by exposing their budding love affair: all except Angela and Ben are quick to see the meaning in Georgene's snide, caustic attacks on Foxy, in Piet's defenses of her, and in Foxy's tears at the end when they tell her she is Christine Keeler (Updike, by the way, continues to suggest Foxy's "whorishness" throughout the novel).

In addition to maintaining a discreet distance and an order, these structures simultaneously *enable* intimacy. Piet and Georgene, "lacking marriage or any contract,...had evolved between them a code of mutual consideration" (p. 57), just as later in the action, between Georgene and Foxy, "a polity existed: rules, a complex set of assumed concessions, a generous bargain posited upon the presumption of defeat" (p. 401). A particularly complicated instance of this double function, a virtual parody, in fact, of the idea of "being civilized," occurs at a late stage in the "Applesmiths'" collective adultery, when the bond of deception is gone and the fact of mutual acknowledgement has changed the rules of the game without cancelling the need for propriety and "obligingness": "they had reached, the Applesmiths, the boundary of a condition wherein their needs were merged, and a general courtesy replaced individual desire. The women would sleep with the men out of pity, and each would permit the other her man out of an attenuated and hopeless graciousness" (p. 179). A similar tact, at once restraining and betraying underlying tensions, emerges in the relationship between Piet and Gallagher: "Piet had developed with Gallagher a kidding pose, a blarneyish tone, useful in both acknowledging and somewhat bridging the widening gap between them. Gradually they were finding each other impossible. Without an act, a routine, Piet would hardly have been able to talk to Gallagher at all" (p. 231). Under more complex circumstances, Freddy Thorne plays the butt, consciously elicits an often exaggerated contempt from the couples, in order to maintain the affection which they also feel for him and for each other. Foxy sees that he "savors" rejection, and that "his being despised served as a unifying purpose for the others, gave them a common identity, as the couples that tolerated Freddy Thorne" (p. 37).

The above examples make it clear that play as game tends to merge in the novel with play as dramatization. Like the classic "psychologists" among novelists and playwrights, Updike is interested in the elaborate role-playing—sometimes unconscious (Ken's "costumes"), sometimes calculated (Harold's French)— by which people orient themselves in social relations, particularly under the broad, vague impetus of sexual desire. A character's thoughts about people, including himself, are seen to be approximations or interpretations. Piet sometimes characterizes himself, for instance, by taking a cue from another's idea of him (the squire, the passive man). Identity, as the passages quoted in the last paragraph suggest, is a conception, a performance, a "routine" (in *A Month of Sundays*, Marshfield's extended self-portrait or self-dramatization becomes a mode of self-discovery). "What did you make of the new couple?" begins the novel; and throughout, characters are "making of" themselves and others. At the Guerins' dinner party in Chapter One (pp. 40-41), for example, we hear various conceptions of absent Piet and Angela by their friends. Bea thinks Angela is lovely and serene, Frank thinks she is a robot "with Jack Kennedy inside her, trying to get out," Georgene thinks she doesn't give Piet very much, while Harold thinks she gives him social aplomb, and Freddy thinks she gives him a bang now and then; though later he tells her in person that he can never picture her in bed with Piet, and she responds that he must be idealizing her. Piet thinks of her as fair and fine and gracious, in contrast to his own "coarseness" (p. 8), and at one point he calls her stoical, to which Freddy objects: "Angela's not stoical, that's your theory. My theory is, she suffers" (p. 373). About Piet the couples have likewise formed divergent but telling conceptions: Marcia calls him sweet and Freddy adds indiscreet, "the biggest neurotic in town"; Roger thinks he does very solid, loving work, and Bea calls him "a dear little old-fashioned kind of man"; Georgene thinks of him as a knight-errant, Foxy as a squire and "the world's husband," Angela as a bully, but a bully who has "tried to batter [his] way into me" (p. 424). There are similar constellations of opinions surrounding most of the major characters (Piet thinks Ken is a computer and Angela thinks he has shown more courage than anyone; Mrs. Roth finds Freddy fascinating and simpatico, while Foxy finds him insidious and odious, etc.). Of course not all these conceptions are equally accurate and some seem self-deluding; they are inevitably influenced by the conceiver's sensibilities and intelligence and by his relation to the person conceived. But they generally reveal actual aspects of that person's multiform behavior or performance in society, and they reinforce the idea that a character's knowledge of other characters—like a reader's knowledge—involves an interpretive assigning of roles.

The characters' role-playing in the novel is often more explicit. The couples' improvised participation in Freddy's pornographic play—"Let's all take parts," cries orange-haired Carol, only to go on pornographically to expose a breast while wrestling with Freddy for the manuscript—their acting here reflects comically on their general "acting" with one another (p. 239). The numerous extra-marital affairs in the novel are, not surprisingly, rich occasions for the playing of roles. Adultery, once again, combines sport and theatre: lovers enact strategies of approach, possession, deception, revenge. While, clubwoman that she is, Georgene conceives her affair with Piet as a "bargain," she also thinks of herself as a "queen" to be served by her knight (p. 403). When challenged, she affects "a playful immigrant accent, part shopgirl, part vamp" (p. 57). She holds him, bodily, "as if captive" (p. 57). A month after their savage tennis game, she tentatively calls him at work—"Allo, dollink"—and with Gallagher's presence as an excuse, Piet uses "his flat contractor's voice" rather drolly to put her off: "'The estimate looks discouraging'...'We're speaking of upright supports'...'In the meantime,' Piet said, 'watch out for seepage,' and hung up" (pp. 228-31). The Applesmiths also find that "intimacy had forced upon each a role" (pp. 172-73). Frank and Marcia, when they first start meeting in the secluded cottage, think of themselves as "conspirators" (p. 127). When Janet finds out, she first tries for a confession from Frank—who, knowing her to be oversensitive about her lack of education, uses his Shakespeare simultaneously to evade, mock, and attack her (p. 125)— and thus failing she then makes a wittily brusque play for Harold, partly to assuage her despair, partly to seek vengeance, and partly no doubt to test her attractiveness. Harold, for his part, feels "that communication between the sexes should be a courtly and dangerous game, with understood rules, mostly financial, and strict time limits" (p. 130). Though he plays as usual the dandy and connoisseur and teacher with Janet, he senses a favorable opening and allows himself to be seduced. His secret liaison with her gives them both an advantage over Frank and Marcia, whose "strategems" now appear "transparent" (p. 147). At the ski lodge Frank shows his hand, and Harold, finding the moment economically opportune, plays along: "He saw that the deceit he had worked with [Janet] would now lose all value. But there is always a time to sell; the trick of the market is to know when. Janet waited like a stack of certain profit" (p. 160). Later that night, when he leaves to rejoin his wife, his face wears "a mask of tenderness" (p. 163). Before the flop of Janet's half-hearted tactic of flirting with Freddy Thorne ("I don't like messy games," she had claimed —p. 174), and before the development of the strained tact that marks the final act of their collective affair, the Applesmiths perform a comically melodramatic climax one evening in the Applebys' living room (pp. 165-67): Janet, despite herself, "speaking as the injured wife," with Marcia returning her fire while "gauging the dismay in the faces [of the others]," and a moment later, "feeling her scene slide away from her," making a stormy exit: "I can't stand any of you and I hate this dreary house."

The idea of strategy, as these scenes suggest, links sport and theatre with hunting and battle. In the tense, late-sixties atmosphere of *Rabbit Redux*, the metaphor of war—of agitation, invasion, siege, and escalating violence—is more pronounced; the shifting rivalries and alliances between the main characters have tumultuous consequences. The violence of *Couples* runs more beneath a surface of routine events, and the dominant predator in this domain (I shall come to her in a moment) is a fox, operating more by wile than main force. The metaphor of the hunt is raised to a literal level fairly early in the novel in the extraordinary scene involving the dead hamster (pp. 82-87)— extraordinary in the physical description, at once tender and slightly gruesome, of the hamster's body, in the evocation of its brief, dim-witted "adventure" before encountering the cat (Piet, "desolated" by the mishap, imagines himself into the dead little male's final hours, its "hopeful sexual vanity," whereas Foxy earlier on wishes she were a cat), and extraordinary finally in the suggestion of an extensive family struggle surrounding this small ambush. It becomes evident under Piet's questioning that the younger daughter Nancy knew the hamster was downstairs when she let the cat in:

He asked Nancy roughly, "Did you see it happen?"
Angela said, "Don't Piet. She doesn't want to think about it."
But she did; Nancy said…"Kitty and Hamster played and Hamster wanted to quit and Kitty wouldn't let him."

"Did you know the hamster was downstairs when you let Kitty in?"

Nancy's thumb went back into her mouth.

"I'm sure she didn't," Angela said.

Later on, thinking she will die because she is not pretty enough, Nancy again defensively resorts to thumb sucking. That conversation ends with her emphatic rejection of Piet in favor of her mommy. Here, under Piet's "roughness," Angela intercedes for Nancy. Piet is rough mainly because Nancy has just seemed to doubt his picture of a hamster heaven drawn to solace and amuse her sister Ruth, who had "owned" the pet. Indeed, loving Ruth's incipient womanhood, Piet is often impatient with Nancy, finds her, with her vanities and anxieties, vaguely threatening; while Angela is oversolicitous with her younger child. "These were the lines drawn," Updike writes on p. 87, "Angela's heart sought to enshrine the younger child's innocence; Piet loved more the brave corruption of the older, who sang in the choir and who had brusquely pushed across the sill of fear where Nancy stood wide-eyed." These divisions of affection are evident in most of the scenes involving the children: on p. 227, Nancy flees Piet for Angela and Piet thinks, "Loves her more than me. Each to each. Symbiosis"; on p. 371, Piet sees that Nancy "had come to trust only her mother"; on p. 445, after Piet has separated from Angela, Nancy tells him "Go now," whereupon Ruth slaps at her sister for her rudeness while Angela defends and reinforces her, "She's telling Daddy it's all right to go now"—Ruth then denounces Nancy's behavior at the planetarium, "*Hurt*ing Daddy's *fee*lings, making him *take* us out *ear*ly," and Nancy, again denying responsibility, attacks her sister with "Liar! Liar!" and with fists. In light of such behavior, one suspects that Nancy allows the cat to kill the hamster at least partly out of jealousy for her sister, and it is not surprising that she later hysterically admits to being at fault (p. 101). It is also possible that her action is a veiled attack on her father, who had liked the hamster's lulling noise, and who comes to see that, "in his towering rank maleness," he represents death to this child (p. 365).

Nancy's attitude toward Piet seems a kind of embryonic reflection of Angela's attitude toward him. She too—maidenly, diffident, afraid of knowing, with "a girl's tentative questing way of moving" (p. 7), most comfortable when she is instructing children—Angela too is intimidated by Piet's "towering rank maleness." The first scene in the novel, introducing the Hanemas, involves a pursuit and attack that prefigures the general course of their relationship as well as all the various hunting games to follow. Piet's question—"What did you make of the new couple?"—functions not just to raise the themes of identity and interpretation, which I commented on earlier. It is also a tactic designed to engage his wife so that he can *make* her. Angela senses his move and answers shortly, evasively, sarcastically. Grudging and accusatory, Piet presses until his aggression becomes more overt: "He took a step forward, his eyes narrowed and pink, partychafed. She resisted the urge to step backwards, knowing that this threatening mood of his was supposed to end in sex, was a plea. Instead she reached under her slip to unfasten her garters. The gesture, so vulnerable, disarmed him" (p. 11). Piet has tried to keep the conversation light, playful, but now Angela is "determined to answer him seriously, until her patience dulled his pricking mood." Before his desperate pounce on her at the scene's end, his unsuccessful ambush, Piet resorts once more to playfulness. He stands on his head as a demonstration of his religiously inspired virility. Angela is not impressed.

Piet's playfulness is an ambiguous phenomenon. In this scene with Angela, it works partly as an attack, partly as a release of frustrated energies, partly as an egotistical exhibition, partly as a plea—love me, I'm physical and fun. And as with all playfulness, there is doubtless present here a spontaneous exuberance, a kind of animal frolicking. Piet often plays the fool or the clown in order to evade someone. Georgene, with her private grievances, tells him that he's never entirely honest, and he tells Angela that solitude is not so bad because "I don't have to play politics" (pp. 316, 443). He seeks to evade Freddy's "menacing mass" by mincing and playing the Irishman—"Never ask an Irishman that question at a wake" (he is also obliquely chiding Freddy for having a party on the day of Kennedy's murder)—and he evades Harold's overbearing attempts at condolence by teasing him about Janet and mimicking his French (pp. 318, 438). In this latter case, Piet's evasion and self-defense turn into mockery and attack, just as, when faced with Ken's charges of adultery, he will clown in order both to seek "invisibility" and to fight against Ken's academic and insulating proprieties. Similarly, at the end of the hamster episode, when Angela questions his appeal to religious consolation, he assumes the manner of an old yeoman: "'Ah,' he said, 'thet's all verra well for a fine leddy like yerself, ma'am, but us peasants like need a touch o' holy water to keep off the rheumatism, and th' evil eye'" (p. 86). This is not only a complex evasion, defense, and attack against Angela's "evil eye," but also a self-mockery — "us peasants" — expressing perhaps an ironically guarded appeal for forebearance on this his vulnerable point, his "superstitious nature" ("Every marriage tends to consist of an aristocrat and a peasant," Updike observes — p. 66). At such moments Piet is reminiscent of Caldwell in *The Centaur*, whose self-demeaning speeches (effectively taking in his son, but not his wife) usually conceal a tactful shrewdness and a shyness, a bid for sympathy sometimes, a desire to ingratiate himself to his interlocutor but also a desire to keep him at a distance. Caldwell's self-dramatization is no doubt part of what makes him a good teacher.

With Foxy, Piet is likewise warily playful. On p. 285, for example, he "comically" bows to her in farewell: "'Charrming,' he said 'to be seeing ye sae fair on so fair a morrning, Mrs. Whitman.'" The burlesquerie serves as a gentlemanly way of rounding off an awkward and inconclusive moment, but also as a gentlemanly way of avoiding a conclusion that may confirm "his sense of certain loss." Their relationship is initiated by Piet's acrobatically looking up her dress at the Applebys' party and her staring him back down — an event that stays in the back of both their minds during their parallel introductions in Chapter One (the scene at the church, pp. 21-28, bridges their initial appearances on successive Saturday nights; each couple talks about the other, flirts with the idea of adultery, reveals frustrations and a sense that they entered marriage blindly and too hastily; Angela and Ken are shown to be similarly abstract and fastidious, etc.). When Piet comes to inspect the Whitmans' house, he is courtly and embarrassed, "ready to put himself back into the hired-man role" (p. 112). He is "shy and circumspect with Foxy and had not wanted to desire her" (p. 206). But Foxy is coyly aggressive with

Piet from the beginning ("I can manage him," she tells Ken before they've even hired him, and in a letter to Piet she blithely lets fall: "Having decided, long before we slept together, to have you..."—pp. 109, 279). Appearing before him in her loosely tied bathrobe, serving him sour lemonade, she draws him out ("Forgive me, I'm not usually so talkative"), burdens him with her "secrets," and offers to kiss him (pp. 206-12). Piet kisses a face "clean of feeling," touches a body "almost wooden yet alive."

This dryness and hardness of Foxy's is emphasized throughout the novel: "her mind in the midst of love's throes could be as dry and straight seeking as a man's" (p. 215); "...a dry mind that sized him up through veils of rapture" (p. 272). Her calculating mind, as this last passage in particular suggests, is continually devising roles: the child and orphan, the slave and whore, the awkward proper girl from Maryland. On p. 349, when it appears that Piet is leaving her for good, she seizes "the high, the haughty, role" of the dismissed mistress. On p. 398, trying to get him back, she frets "with a stagy lassitude learned from the movies," and then hangs up on him because "the script" calls for it. And, on p. 459, having made an effort to recapture him, she parts from him on a "gravel arena...like a stage set in daylight" with "the sad word *'Ciaou,'* learned from the movies." Beneath this posturing would seem to be an increasingly desperate greed ("Her slowness to come," Piet thinks, "had always been a kind of greed" —p. 351). Foxy will not suffer, will not bleed, and Piet is her way out of a dreary marriage, a drafty house, an oppressive social climate. What begins as a "contentious teasing" of her lover becomes a strategic onslaught to make him hers: "I want to own you" (p. 285). After she calls with the news that she is pregnant by him, Piet feels that he has been taken "hostage," been "gulled" (p. 358). Even after the abortion, Foxy continues to use her "sly cunt" to trap him. In town to check on her house, she foresees sleeping with him and brings along her diaphragm; in bed she fights his entrance of her and "then afterwards slyly asked if it had made it more exciting for him, her pretending to resist" (p. 454—"I just lie and lie, Piet," she smiles, p. 356). In spilling the story to Ken after he is tipped off by jealous Georgene, she has likewise foreseen that he will divorce her and that Piet will marry her. And again her tactic succeeds.

Piet's half-willing capitulation to Foxy, as most critics and reviewers have noticed, is presented as a "fall." His life with rare, safe Angela, whom he "adores" rather than loves—his job, his conservative house that keeps out the dark—all this is an imperfect paradise or garden, a vestige perhaps of what he once found in the greenhouse of his childhood which now lives only in his idealizing memory. From this garden, which sometimes seems to him a "cage," he makes adulterous excursions into the world for "knowledge"—but always with the intention of returning to the relative order and security of home. There is still indeed much of the child in Piet, the child who needs to be held after a nightmare and the child who playfully charms those around him, particularly the women. In his great sexual tenderness there may well be, as with Rabbit Angstrom, a narcissism, seeking in the womb oblivion and a refuge from death. He likes the romantic, sinful excitement, and perhaps (with Rabbit) the irresponsibility, of adultery—"its adventure, the acrobatics its deceptions demand, the tension of its hidden strings, the new landscapes it makes us master" (p. 450). His affair (his first) with Georgene "had been a going from indoors to outdoors" (p. 237). And now with Foxy, who is consistently associated with nature and who "had demanded that he know" (p. 394), he finds himself "outdoors" to stay. "Don't make me leave you," he had begged Angela. "You're what guards my soul. I'll be damned eternally" (p. 425); his actual leaving her, in a beautiful scene toward the end, is for him the dousing of a "golden light" (p. 435). His "church" is gone. When he later returns for an afternoon, weeds have invaded the garden.

Exiled into the world, Piet makes his peace with death: he learns from visiting John Ong "how death, far from invading earth like a meteor, occurs on the same plane as birth and marriage and the arrival of the daily mail" (p. 448). Nothing is too ordinary for him to notice, and like Leopold Bloom he accepts with somewhat sad equanimity Foxy's soiled underpants and scratchy armpits. He falls into the messy real world, Updike implies, he lets go of the greenhouse. His protracted fall is an initiation, a "Growing up," as Mom says to Rabbit at the end of *Rabbit Redux*. Like so many of the modern masters, only more modestly, Updike works through the quotidian to a glimpse of the typical and the cyclical—thus the seasonal frame for the action of *Couples* and thus the ending, where it is suggested that the Hanemas will begin a new cycle in Lexington as "another couple."

To view life mythically in this way is finally to return to the ambiguous ideas of play and ritual. For from a mythic perspective, life appears as a subtly orchestrated music on elemental themes of sex, power, and death ("Organic music scores our ancient nerves," he writes in "Midpoint"), an emergent drama in which individuals more or less unwittingly enact variations of archetypal roles—like the serpent and the mostly innocent maiden, the huntress (who is Diana *and* Venus), the father and scapegoat. In myth Updike gives shape to his feeling for life's "ordinary ceremonies" (the term is David Thorburn's), his sense that art's play is really a form of doing reverence.

Post-Pill Paradise Lost: *Couples*

by David Lodge

Discussing some books about Utopia recently, I ventured the suggestion that "Eros is traditionally an anti-utopian force, though he is catered for in the specialized utopias of pornography — what Steven Marcus has called 'Pornotopia.'" I used the word "traditionally" because we have seen in modern times the emergence of a school of thought that may properly be termed "utopian," in that it is concerned to construct ideal models of the good life, but which inverts the values we normally associate with Utopia, recommending not the enhanced exercise of rationality but the liberation of instinct, not the perfecting of the mind, but "the resurrection of the body." The latter phrase is adopted by Norman O. Brown as a concluding slogan in *Life Against Death* (1959), a representative text of the new utopianism. It is not, of course, wholly new, and may be readily traced back to earlier sources — to Nietzsche, to Lawrence and, pre-eminently to Freud, on whom *Life Against Death* is a commentary.

Brown begins with the paradox propounded by Freud, that civilization or "culture" (which is prized by traditional utopists, and which they wish to perfect) is based on the repression and sublimation of erotic energy. Freud himself was shifty about the proportionate loss and gain of this process, but Brown is quite certain and uncompromising: civilization is self-evidently neurotic, and the only solution is to end the tyranny of the reality-principle, to substitute "conscious play" for alienated labour as the mainspring of society, and to restore to adult sexuality, narrowly fixated on genital and procreative functions, the "polymorphous perverse" of infantile eroticism. This utopian adaptation of Freud both feeds and is fed by the sexual revolution in contemporary society, and the third interacting contribution comes from the arts. Thus, in this perspective, pornography is the product of a sexually repressed society and would disappear in the erotic utopia by a process of assimilation. Not surprisingly, therefore, we are witnessing today a determined effort by the arts to render pornography redundant by incorporating its characteristic materials into "legitimate" art.

John Updike's *Couples* seems to me likely to be best understood and appreciated against this kind of background. It is concerned with the efforts of a number of couples in contemporary New England to create a clandestine, erotic utopia; and it is, notoriously, a serious novel which exploits extensively the matter and diction traditionally reserved for pornography. As this latter feature would suggest, the utopian enterprise is treated with a good deal of sympathy; and the novel is notable for its lyrical celebration of the sensual life, including the "perverse" forms of love-making. But whereas Brown, at the outset of his book, asks the reader to make a "willing suspension of common sense," Updike is, as a novelist, basically committed to realism (however much heightened by mythopoeic allusion) from which common sense—and the reality principle—cannot be excluded. Thus in *Couples* the note of celebration is checked by irony, the utopian enterprise fails on a communal level, and the struggle of life against death is ambiguously resolved.

Erotic utopianism is, of course, at odds with conventional Christian morality and with the Christian counsels of perfection through asceticism; yet at the same time it claims to be basically religious in its values, and to have in common with "true" Christianity a virtuous indifference to worldly and materialistic standards of achievement and success. It thus draws on the Christian tradition of a pre-lapsarian paradise, which in turn has literary associations with the ideal world of pastoral. This matrix of ideas is kept constantly before us in *Couples,* sometimes lightly—as when the hero's first mistress stills his fears about conception with the gay greeting, "Welcome to the post-pill paradise"— and sometimes gravely, as in the epigraph from Tillich:

> There is a tendency in the average citizen, even if he has a high
> standing in his profession, to consider the decisions relating to the
> life of the society to which he belongs as a matter of fate on which
> he has no influence—like the Roman subjects all over the world in
> the period of the Roman empire, a mood favorable for the resur-
> gence of religion but unfavourable for the preservation of a living
> democracy.

The couples of Tarbox, a "pastoral milltown," a "bucolic paradise" as it is variously called, within commuting distance of Boston, re-enact or parody the situation of the early Christians.
"We're a subversive cell...," their "high-priest" and "games-
master," Freddy Thorne, the dentist, tells them. "Like in the catacombs. Only they were trying to break out of hedonism. We're
trying to break back into it. It's not easy." It's not easy partly because the Christian religion still retains a vestigial hold over
them. Of the Applebys and the Smiths, who first develop the
protocol of wife-swapping, and earn the corporate title of the
"Applesmiths," Janet Appleby develops an "inconvenient sense
of evil" which the other three try patiently but unsuccessfully to
assuage. The main characters, and most adventurous explorers
of the erotic, Piet Hanema and Foxy Whitman, are also the most
regular churchgoers of the group. Piet, indeed, is burdened with
an inherited Calvinist conscience, much obsessed with death and
damnation. This makes him the fitting culture-hero—and as it
turns out, scapegoat—of the new cult; for in him the struggle of
id against ego and super-ego is most intense and dramatic.

The sex-and-religion equation—sex as religion, sex versus
religion, sex replacing religion—is insisted upon even in the
topography of Tarbox, with its streets called Charity and Divinity
leading to the landmark of the Congregational Church with its
"pricking steeple and flashing cock." At the end of the story this
church is destroyed by lightning in a furious thunderstorm that
has overtones of Old Testament visitations upon sinners; but the
damage reveals that the church has long been structurally un-
sound—in other words, the religious spirit has already passed
into the intimate circle of the couples. "He thinks we're a circle,"
Piet's wife Angela says of Freddy Thorne, "A magic circle of
heads to keep the night out.... He thinks we've made a church
of each other." The American couples, however, though they
copy the early Christians' withdrawal from the public world in

which secular history is made, lack their innocence and con-
fidence. They are apt to feel that they are rejected rather than
rejecting. "God doesn't love us any more," Piet asserts. Their
magic circle is, in this light, not the seed of a brave new world but
a temporary resource "in one of those dark ages that visit mankind between millennia, between the death and rebirth of the
gods, when there is nothing to steer by but sex and stoicism and
the stars."

This ambivalence is maintained by the two alternative notes
that sound throughout the narrative: romantic-lyrical celebration,
and realistic irony. The honorific description of the couples'
attempt to "improvise...a free way of life" in which "duty and
work yielded as ideals to truth and fun. Virtue was no longer
sought in temple or market place but in the home—one's own
home and the home of one's friends," is balanced by the more
reductive comment, "The men had stopped having careers and
the women had stopped having children. Liquor and love were
left." Adultery opens the way to erotic delight which is far from
being selfish or brutalizing, for in changing partners the ageing
couples achieve an enhanced awareness of their own and others'
beauty:

> Harold believed that beauty was what happened between people,
> was in a sense the trace of what had happened, so he in truth found
> her, though minutely creased and puckered and sagging, more
> beautiful than the unused girl whose ruins she thought of herself
> as inhabiting. Such generosity of perception returned upon him-
> self; as he lay with Janet, lost in praise, Harold felt as if a glowing
> tumor of eternal life were consuming the cells of his mortality.
> [Rpt. New York: Fawcett World Library, p. 147]

But adultery also imposes its own demeaning code of intrigue and
stylized deception:

> "Are you sleeping with Janet?"
> "Why? Are you sleeping with Frank?"
> "Of course not."
> "In that case, I'm not sleeping with Janet." [p. 150]

The paradoxes and tensions of the theme are most dramatically
enacted by Piet Hanema (partner in a Tarbox building firm) and
Foxy Whitman (wife of a frigid biochemist who is still competing
in the "real" world, and hence hostile to the world of the couples).

They dare, erotically, more than any of the other couples. Their affair is both the most romantically intense and the most sensual (their oral-genital lovemaking given an extra quality of polymorphous perversity by the circumstance that Foxy is heavily pregnant by her husband); but they also suffer most, both comically and tragically. Mastered by an overwhelming desire to suck the milk-filled breasts of his mistress at a party,[1] Piet locks himself in the bathroom with her, and escapes discovery by his wife only by leaping from the window, straight into the arms of another, sardonically teasing couple—hurting his leg into the bargain. Later in the story a stiffer and more traditional price is paid for sexual indulgence: Foxy, untypically in the post-pill paradise, fails to take contraceptive precautions in her first postnatal encounter with Piet, and becomes pregnant by him. An abortion, with all its attendant anxiety, misery and guilt, is arranged, but fails to conceal the affair. Piet and Foxy are banished by their respective spouses, and cold-shouldered by the other couples, whose disregard for convention does not extend thus far, and who cannot forgive them for making the clandestine cult scandalously public. They go through a bad time; but when the wrath of God that Piet has always feared finally strikes, it does so harmlessly, merely symbolically, on the empty church. After their temporary purgatory of exile and separation, Piet and Foxy are allowed to marry, and settle happily enough in another town where, "gradually, among people like themselves, they have been accepted, as another couple."

Updike is, of course, neither the first not the last American writer to take as his subject an attempt (usually unsuccessful) to found a new kind of human community, one based on values that run counter to those prevailing in society at large. The place of *Couples* in this tradition is not immediately apparent only because the utopian experiment it describes is interpersonal rather than social or economic, and thus, on the outside, scarcely distinguishable from the way of life it is rejecting. Utopian com-

---

[1]Brown quotes from Freud as follows: "The state of being in love results from the fulfilment of infantile conditions of love...whatever fulfils this condition of love becomes idealized." "The desire to suck includes within it the desire for the mother's breast, which is therefore the first object of sexual desire; I cannot convey to you any adequate idea of the importance of this first object in determining every later object adopted."

munities usually signal their intentions more openly: thus, the middle-aged radicals in Mary McCarthy's *A Source of Embarrassment* set off in covered station wagons to found an agricultural co-operative, and the hippies in the movie *Alice's Restaurant* set up their commune in a deconsecrated church. The tradition can be traced right back to *The Blithedale Romance* (1852), and it is interesting to place *Couples* beside that earlier account of "an exploded scheme for beginning the life of Paradise anew" in New England.

Like Updike's couples, Hawthorne's characters have opted out of the competitive, acquisitive rat-race. The narrator, Coverdale, explains: "We had left the rusty iron framework of society behind us; we had broken through many hindrances that are powerful enough to keep most people on the weary treadmill of the established system...." In both novels the utopian experiment founders, eventually, on the reef of sex and sexual intrigue. In *The Blithedale Romance* Coverdale is in love with Priscilla who is in love with Hollingsworth who is in love with Zenobia who is secretly and unhappily married (?) to Westervelt who has a mesmeric hold on Priscilla. Coverdale might almost be describing Tarbox when he says:

> the footing on which we all associated at Blithedale was widely different from that of conventional society. While inclining us to the soft affections of the golden age, it seemed to authorize any individual, of either sex, to fall in love with any other, regardless of what would elsewhere be judged suitable and prudent.
>
> (Chap. IX).

There are differences, obviously enough. Blithedale is, officially, dedicated to work rather than play, and its play never becomes overtly erotic. Nevertheless, *The Blithedale Romance* contains some of Hawthorne's sexiest writing. Coverdale, for instance, is naughtily given to imagining Zenobia in the nude:

> Assuredly, Zenobia could not have intended it—the fault must have been entirely in my imagination. But these last words, together with something in her manner, irresistibly brought up a picture of that fine, perfectly developed figure, in Eve's earliest garment. Her free, careless, generous modes of expression often had this effect of creating images which though pure, are hardly felt to be quite decorous when born of a thought that passes between man and woman.... One felt an influence breathing out of

her such as we might suppose to come from Eve, when she was just
made, and her creator brought her to Adam, saying, "Behold!
here is a woman!" Not that I would convey ,the idea of especial
gentleness, grace, modesty and shyness, but of a certain warmth
and rich characteristic, which seems, for the most part, to have been
refined away out of the feminine system.   (Chap. III).

Coverdale thinks Zenobia should pose for sculptors, "because
the cold decorum of the marble would consist with the utmost
scantiness of drapery, so that the eye might chastely be gladdened
with her material perfection in its entireness." Looking at "the
flesh-warmth over her round arms, and what was visible of her
full bust" he sometimes has to close his eyes, "as if it were not
quite the privilege of modesty to gaze at her." And he is sure that
she is sexually experienced: "Zenobia is a wife; Zenobia has lived
and loved! There is no folded petal, no latent dew-drop, in this
perfectly developed rose!"   (Chap. VI).

There is no such carnal element in Coverdale's "love" for Priscilla—who is, indeed, precisely the kind of de-sexualized Victorian maiden with whom Zenobia is contrasted in the first of
these quotations. He apologizes for his suspicions about Zenobia:
"I acknowledged it as a masculine grossness—a sin of wicked
interpretation, of which man is often guilty towards the other
sex—thus to mistake the sweet, liberal, but womanly frankness of
a noble and generous disposition." But his suspicions prove well-
founded, and Hawthorne evidently shared his narrator's mixture
of guilty excitement and genteel *pudeur* when contemplating a
fully sexual woman, since he is at pains to present Zenobia as a
kind of witch, and sends her eventually to a sudden and sadistically relished death by drowning.

Updike, in contrast, is much more "emancipated," much more
tolerant and sympathetic towards the erotic, and lets his lawless
lovers off lightly in the end. But there is something of the witch
about Foxy, something sinister and depraved, Lamia-like, about
the magnetism she holds for Piet, who is himself quite as much
haunted by the God of Calvin as any Hawthorne hero. Indeed,
the more one dwells on the comparison, the more plausible it
becomes to see Hawthorne as Updike's literary ancestor among
the classic American novelists. Both writers like to temper romance with realism, lyricism with irony; both tend to rely on

ambivalent symbolism at crucial points in their narratives; both are highly literary, highly self-conscious stylists, fussing over every word to a degree that can be self-defeating; and both seem at their best in the short story, over-extended in the long narrative.

Updike's literary gifts, especially his remarkably precise, sensuous notation of the physical texture of ordinary experience, are well suited to the evocation of a suburban pastoral paradise with a snake in the grass. The descriptions of Tarbox, its couples and their way of life—the neglected beauty of the landscape, the comfortable elegance of the expensively remodelled homes, the casual entertaining, the ball games and parlour games, the plentiful food and drink, the intimate uninhibited conversations, as the children watch the blue flickerings of the TV bring meaningless messages of remote disasters and upheavals in the outer, public world (only the assassination of J. F. Kennedy, whose combination of personal stylishness and political weakness makes devious claims on their allegiance, disturbs the couples' calm assumption that "news happened to other people")—all this is exquisitely rendered, so that we feel the charm, the allure of this way of life, and also its weakness, its fragility. The most eloquent passages in the novel are elegiac—for example:

> Foxy said, "We must get back," truly sad. She was to experience this sadness many times, this chronic sadness of late Sunday afternoon, when the couples had exhausted their game, basketball or beachgoing or tennis or touch football, and saw an evening weighing upon them, an evening without a game, an evening spent among flickering lamps and cranky children and leftover food and the nagging half-read newspaper with its weary portents and atrocities, an evening when marriages closed in upon themselves like flowers from which the sun is withdrawn, an evening giving like a smeared window on Monday and the long week when they must perform again their impersonations of working men, of stockbrokers and dentists and engineers, of mothers and housekeepers, of adults who are not the world's guests but its hosts.
>
> [pp. 80-81]

This passage illustrates very well how Updike has taken a large abstract theme about contemporary culture and embodied it in a densely-textured novel about a particular social milieu. On this level, and as long as he keeps our interest distributed fairly evenly over a considerable number of characters, *Couples* seemed to me remarkably successful. But in the latter half of the book the whole weight of the theme and structure is shifted on to the shoulders of Piet and Foxy, and they are not sufficiently realized to sustain it. Foxy is acceptable as a beautiful witch, but as an Eloise to Piet's Abelard, analysing her feelings in long, fey epistles, she becomes something of a bore. Piet is more solidly drawn, but his passiveness in the crisis of his marriage induces tedium; and Updike's incorrigible greed for stylistic effect makes nonsense of his attempt to portray his hero as a kind of primitive, a rough diamond who doesn't really belong among the college educated couples. Walking on the shore, for instance, Piet notices

> wood flecks smoothed like creek pebbles, iron spikes mummified in the orange froth of oxidization, powerfully sunk horseshoe prints, the four-lined traces of racing dog paws, the shallow impress of human couples that had vanished (the female foot bare, with toe and a tender isthmus linking heel and forepad; the male mechanically shod in the waffle intaglio of sneaker soles and apparently dragging a stick), the wandering mollusk trails dim as the contours of a photograph over-developed in the pan of the tide [etc., etc.] .   [p. 449]

This is a poet's, not a builder's sensibility. The rather Shakespearian intrigue whereby Freddy Thorne arranges Foxy's abortion in return for a night with Piet's wife, Angela, who obliges without enquiring into the basis of the bargain, seems to violate the probabilities of the rest of the action. This is reminiscent of Hawthorne, and so is the device by which Updike displaces the catastrophe of his story from the human characters to the inanimate church—an effective set-piece, but too obviously stage-managed, a purely aesthetic climax where we have been led to expect a moral one.

For all that, *Couples* impressed me as an intelligent and skillfully composed novel on a significant theme, and most of the comment I have heard or read upon it seems to me to have done Updike less than justice.

A Month of Sundays: Scarlet Letters

by George Steiner

John Updike has been an enviable problem. Gifted at once
with a supremely alert ear and eye for the pulse and sinew of contemporary American speech and with a passion for the rare word,
for the jewelled and baroque precisions still vital beneath and
around the current of common idiom, he has been able to write
about literally *anything.* Whether it be the stubble in a Pennsylvania field, the swerve of a basketball under gymnasium lights,
the rasp of a tire on gravel, the tightening at a man's temples under pressure of sexual fantasy, Mr. Updike has made these planes
of experience brilliantly his own yet true to the evidence, pene-
trative into the fabric of American discourse and gesture to a
degree that future historians and sociologists will exult in. He has
written of rich and poor, of urban and rural, of science and political intrigue, of gregariousness and cold solitude with an un-
forgiving yet strangely solicitous, almost tender intelligence. The
critic and the poet in him (a minor but sparkling poet of occasion
and humor of a kind infrequent now) are at no odds with the
novelist; the same sharpness of apprehension bears on the object
in each of Updike's modes. But it is precisely this ubiquity, the
sheer range of whatever elicits his luminous dispassions, that has
made it difficult for him to find a mastering theme.

Not only in *The Centaur* but, indeed, in all of his novels
Updike has tested elements of fable and allegory, ancient formal
devices with which to knit into comely and probing shape the
dazzling singularity, the vital ordinariness of his perceptions.
The Poorhouse Fair, still one of his finest achievements, aims

at control, at a sharp and exemplary meaning, through compression. *Couples* is a panoramic mapping. rescued from indiscrimination by recourse to deliberately symbolic, terminal devices (the raging fire at the close). *Bech* is a book held in place, mirrored within a book—again a fine solution to the problem of focus, of finding a structure both firm and supple enough to contain such wealth and scruple of style. Sexuality has over and over provided the key. Because it is simultaneously the most ordinary and the most individual of human rites, because sexual concourse in and out of marriage is not only general to all societies but highly distinctive of each, the erotic has provided Updike with an essential coherence. Our sexual lives are deep-rooted in the locale of our economic, regional, ethnic identity. They call on the masked as well as on the most public, brutal layers of contemporary language. They involve illusions of infinite particularity and recognitions, maturing no less than corrosive, of routine. And, inevitably, the erotic, even at its most vulgar and irresponsible—perhaps there more than elsewhere—touches on myth, on shadow-places and echoes, idyllic, cruel, scatological, as ancient as the human imagination itself. Through detailed accounts of sex, ranging from the physiological to the allegorical, Updike has found a center, a discipline for the prodigality of his art. At its best, the result is poignant and ironic: what is in lesser writers a dispensation is in Updike a severity. The more urgent, the more acrobatic the sexual moment, the tauter, the more contemptuous of facility is the writing. Eroticism is, in a serious artist, an ascetic pursuit.

To invoke the pathos, the enigmatic humanity of lust is, of course, to borrow the language of St. Augustine and of Kierkegaard. Where eros and sadness meet, theology begins. This realization has long been a part of Mr. Updike's work. Looking back, one comes to realize how deeply his sense of American experience is religious, and religious in a vein related particularly to the history of New England Calvinism on the one hand and to the thought of Barth and Tillich on the other. It is a commonplace that recent American fiction and criticism have to a drastic extent been the product of a Jewish tone and explosion of talent. Updike is the counterpoise: his sensibility is, among practicing American novelists, the most distinctly Christian and Protestant. The eroticism of his fiction has been a long prelude to a radically theological view of American existence. In *A Month of Sundays,* the sexual and the clerical, the scatological and the eschatological are intimately, almost violently meshed.

As a result of sensual indiscretions above and beyond the bounds of charity, the Reverend Tom Marshfield has been banished from his Midwestern parish. Under the veil of a nervous breakdown, scandal is avoided. Instead, the holy gentleman is to spend a month in a desert motel specifically intended for clergy in various modes of dishevelment (yielding to Updike's own obsession with puns, acrostics, and word games, one might describe his plot as nightshades of Tennessee Williams' *The Night of the Iguana).* The therapy of the Reverend Marshfield is a balanced diet of golf, masturbation, and written confession. He is to set down the chronicle of his fall from grace, together with his present thoughts, feelings, visitations of the spirit holy or profane. What we have before us is this penitential journal—Marxist jailers call it self-criticism—together with a set of imaginary sermons. In the first place, however, these lucubrations (Mr. Updike's coruscated idiom becomes infectious) are meant not for the reader but for the guardian presence of the sanatorium. Her name is Ms. Prynne. The maiden name of Tom's wife, the name of her theologian father, is Chillingworth.

This, obviously, is the point. *A Month of Sundays* is a meditation on, a contradictory echo of that first classic of the American Protestant erotic imagination, Hawthorne's *The Scarlet Letter.* Adultery was to Hawthorne the crucial, emblematic motif of the American condition, posing the full paradox of the inherited weakness of the flesh and of social institutions in a new Eden, in a world predestined to innocence and the renovation of man. Updike turns the tables on Hawthorne and on the legacy of Calvinist prohibition: "But who that has eyes to see cannot so lust? Was not the First Divine Commandment received by human ears, 'Be fruitful, and multiply'? Adultery is not a choice to be avoided; it is a circumstance to be embraced. Thus I construe these texts." The Reverend Marshfield's exegeses go further. Pondering the meaning of American experience, the location of this experience in God's scheme of things, he arrives at a new definition of American emancipation. It is marriage itself that has proved to be only a tentative sacrament in the crises and dispensations of what is, literally, the new world: "Separation arrives by

whim (the last dessert dish broken, the final intolerable cigar-
burn on the armchair) or marriages are extended by surrender.
The race between freedom and exhaustion is decided. And then,
in a religious sense, there is no more adultery, as there is none
among schoolchildren, or slaves, or the beyond-all-reckoning
rich." (It is in the placing of that word "reckoning" that Updike's
parallel art, his conjunction of the colloquial with the liturgical,
can be seen at its most exact.)

Given this doctrine and Marshfield's deepening doubts about
the patriarchal deity of the Protestant tradition, his debauches
seem at once inevitable and incidental. Alicia is something of a
sexual athlete, Frankie's scapulae glint in the afternoon light of
the motel—but these are the mere trappings of a subtler, sadder
heresy. Ned, the curate, has taken to copulating with the beloved Alicia. Half-naked, the Reverend Tom has been peeping at
their windows. Reviewing the desolate pain of the discovery, our
confessor—observe the antique duplicity of the term—resorts to
"Plotinian language." What is being violated is no less than "the
body of my soul." Marshfield no longer accepts the bargain of
transcendence. American spirituality is of the flesh, flesh-rooted
and bound. Grace is of this world or it is of none. When John
Updike launches on one of his inventories of the material scene:

> also visible through the window: houses with conical roofs, dor-
> mers, protrusions, scallop shingling, jigsawed brackets, ovals of
> stained glass tucked up under eave-peaks like single eyes under a
> massive gingerbread eyebrow; and hedges and shrubs, and a mail-
> box painted in patriotic tricolor, a birdfeeder hopping with feathered
> mendicants, a covetously onlooking squirrel, streetsigns, street-
> lamps, etc., etc. ...
> [Rpt. New York: Fawcett World Library, pp. 110-11]

he is not primarily displaying his masterly eye and lexical virtuosity (that superbly apt "mendicants"). He is making an insistent point about the ephemeral substance of reality, about the
possibility, profoundly heretical and grievous, that there is beyond the skin of things no firmer realm, no compensating deep.
Poor Tom's gratifications have long been immanent: "Even the
purgative sweep of windshield wipers gratifies me" (note "purgative"). Now, having by desultory license disrobed himself and

been driven to the desert whence Christianity came in its dawn of promise, he finds himself "stripped." If there is a grace note at the close, it is, in the true sense, terminal. He who is down need fear no fall.

Working so near the innermost of his concerns, that congruence—at once farcical and tragic—of sexuality and religious feeling in post-Puritan America, Updike trusts himself almost blindly to his verbal skills. His use of puns, Freudian malapropisms, and portmanteau words—themselves symptomatic of Marshfield's nervous extremity—runs riot. Too often the level is that of a Hasty Pudding script in an off year: "navish" for "knavery" in church; "Nixema, the noxious salve for liberal sores;" "Andman Willsin" for one of Mr. Updike's illustrious colleagues in American letters; "Near-Mrs.," no explanation needed. The prose is febrile in a manner expressive less of the Reverend Marshfield's troubles than of the writer's ungoverned cartwheels. An upper lip becomes "an arch of expectation, a gem of moisture;" passing car lights set Alicia's hair "on false fire;" a Dart is sea-changed into "a hydrofoil skimming above the asphalt waves of the highway of life;" golf-course sprinklers do "a dervish dance to keep the heartbeat of green alive." During a poker game, beer and tension induce dizziness. The result is "betting losers and folding winners in boustrophedonic alternation." Is there anything sadder than fireworks that last into the day?

However, as in Joyce, so in this latest Updike it is in the puns and acrostics, even at their most brutal, that the heart of meaning lies. When a wife's sexual organs (Updike's word is much shorter and simpler) are defined as "indentured," the triple connotation (pictorial, "pornographic," legal-economic) brilliantly, nauseatingly concentrates the intent of the book— its critique of those values and hypocrisies implicit in the Puritan ethic. When the Reverend Marshfield descants on "prick, pic, truthpic," he is not only mocking the mendacities of photographic realism or echoing back to "indenture" via "toothpick." He is proclaiming what he, and very probably John Updike, takes to be the locale and function of honesty, of authentic recognition. These are ugly devices toward an urgent vision.

Whether *A Month of Sundays* is substantial, controlled enough to make this vision emotionally plausible is less certain. It is an impatient text enforced by rather than enforcing its pyrotechnics. One would guess that it is a transitional novel in Updike's work, a rapid staking-out of territory that the next fictions will map at leisure. In the present instance the letter bullies the spirit. And is this not precisely the cause of Tom Marshfield's insurgence, of his peregrinations—randy, autistic, but fundamentally desperate —to the deserts of the heart?

Updike as Matchmaker: *Marry Me*

by Josephine Hendin

John Updike's novels show a man's marriage as his fate. No one has done more to explode male freedom as a myth than Updike in novels of American men whose lives, from cradle to grave, are structured by women. His characters are the philanderers who seem freewheeling until the press of Updike's intelligence reveals them as captives in that velvet glove, the female presence. Often accused of being narrow in his concerns, Updike may in fact have anticipated that, of all the revolutionary currents of the past decade, the one that would last is sexual. No other male writer has probed so single-mindedly a man's need of women or the anger dependency inflames. *Marry Me* is about a man who, bewitched between his mistress and his wife, finds his destiny is sexual calamity. This superb, irresistible novel is a subtle exposure of what you might call tender malice.

Jerry adores his beautiful blonde mistress, Sally, who drops her children elsewhere to come to him on an idyllic beach. Breathing her pleasure in her lover's ear, she hears him softly inquire: "Do you mind...the pain we're going to cause?" About to make love to Ruth, his as yet unknowing wife, Jerry purrs, "Tell me about Sally." Each woman furiously believes the other is his favorite subject. Jerry uses even his death anxiety as a jealousy hook. To Sally: "I look at your face, and imagine myself lying in bed dying, and ask myself, 'Is this the face I want at my death-bed?' I don't know. I honestly don't *know*, Sally." To Ruth: "Whenever I'm with Sally I know I'm never going to die." "And with me?" "You?" "You're death. I'm married to my death." But packing his medi-

"Updike as Matchmaker," by Josephine Hendin. From *The Nation*, Vol. 223, No. 14 (October 30, 1976), 437-39. Copyright © 1976 by *The Nation*. Reprinted by permission.

cated inhaler to leave Ruth, he interrupts his complaints with the sweet inquiry: "Shall I wait until you fall asleep?"

Updike's groaning humor captures the disparity between the dreamlike pleasures expected between the "lover" and his "mistress" and the hesitancy of the suburban swinger. His wit blooms in the gap between the euphoric outburst "Marry me," and the failure of those magic words to change one's soul. In the most sophisticated situation comedy imaginable, Updike achieves an absolutely hypnotic novel of sexual suspense in which a man and woman find their perfect love moves leave them checkmated. Why can't *amor vincit omnia?*

Updike uses an ordinary suburban love affair for the exposure of that failed warrior, the American prisoner of sex. Jerry's chains are forged by psychological and social trends that split the dream of love from a man's capacity for loving. Updike is the D.H. Lawrence of our time, opening up the male heart not in terms of myth but in realistic fiction that unsentimentally shows those relations between the sexes that head toward antagonistic love. The sexual revolution emerges in Updike's fiction as those psychological and social trends that both define maleness as sexual responsibility for women and at the same time produce men who cannot help but needle, belittle and wound the sweetest blonde beloved. Jerry and Sally are not just superbly realized characters but Updike's prototypes of those new "revolutionary" products: the man engulfed by self-hatred and anger, the woman who is all unambivalent sex.

What Updike bares in his beleaguered male chauvinists are the forces that keep men riveted on women as the solitary source of meaning in life. His novels open up a feminized world. The Updikean Connecticut suburb where Jerry lives is remarkably without the usual male obsession with work or sports. Jerry's appetite for advancement as a commercial artist has been sated by an even money-flow. He competes only in mixed volleyball. Feminization is to love as mulch to roses, for the traditional triangle (two men fighting for one woman) is replaced by one (two women competing for one man) produced by the sexual availability of women and the scarcity, that Jerry loves to note, of men as interesting as he is.

Beneath Jerry's boyish arrogance beats the heart of Updike's Rabbit Angstrom, the working-class hero of the brilliant novel

Rabbit, Run (1960), which *Marry Me* resembles, and *Rabbit Redux* (1973). To find out how Jerry became a lady-killer, consider his brother Rabbit. Momism flourishes in the American housewife of *Rabbit, Run* who is controlling, ironic and relentlessly involved with her son, whose narcissism she alternately wounds and strokes. At 26, aged by his humiliating job, his heavily pregnant wife, his toddler son, Rabbit knows he has lost the sense of exaltation he felt in high school as a basketball star. He has no star status in his wife's eyes. He runs away. At 36, returned, he becomes a hard-working linotyper, husband and father. He seems to have become his passive, joyless father. But he cannot take his father's path because the world has changed all the road signs. He is automated out of work by a photo-offset machine. He is displaced from his wife's bed by a man who is a better lover. Janice, his wife, works and has an income of her own. Technology has changed his mother's life too. Old and ill, she is propped up and pepped up by a pill that brings her sexual fantasies she presumably never had as a healthy young woman.

Is sex the medicine of the 1960s? Only for women. For Rabbit there is no tonic for frustration but revenge. He takes in a black nihilist who expresses his own darker impulses, and a pretty young girl who has become a drug abuser. He lets the man insult him and takes out his rage at women passively by letting him kill the girl. His destructiveness and self-destructiveness get his house burned down. Rabbit is the dark side of any man who realizes his ideals and his power are gone. Updike connects the decline of masculinity with the social trends that undermine Rabbit. He compresses into the fall of Rabbit's house and marriage the war between the sexes, the dissidence between classes and races, the efficiency economy that undermines a man's sense of himself. Houseless, jobless, wifeless, Rabbit crumbles. Giving up on being a father to his son he goes back to his ever-loving Mom.

St. George has his dragon, Sir Galahad his grail; Updike's men have only their women to justify their aggression and define them as men. Rabbit and Janice, Jerry and Ruth are matched pairs whose collusive entanglement with each other, however unhappy, is crucial. When Rabbit runs out on his wife, Janice drunkenly drowns their infant daughter. When Janice runs out on Rabbit, he lets his young girl friend die. Neither Janice nor Rabbit is happy with the other yet the presence of her husband helps

Janice function, and the presence of his wife helps Rabbit behave like a man. Janice is the control on his anger and self-hatred. When Jerry seems to be about to leave Ruth, she has an accident that demolishes her car. When Jerry must confront Sally's husband, he feels like groveling to the man and giggling in bed with Ruth.

Updike puts life together as a sophisticated Oedipal knot in which a man is tied at both ends. His men fear being in control, in charge, but are equally afraid of being suffocated and controlled. Their inhibitions bring them the worst as sons and lovers. Lawrence's famous son thought he would be a lover when his mother died. Updike's heroes know how to keep their mothers alive forever by remaining in the box of coolness and contempt that is their mothers' personality. Jerry virtually marries his mother or rather maneuvers his wife into an asexual, maternal protectiveness toward him. Resenting the flatness of their life together, he is drawn toward a woman who is wonderfully greedy for pleasure. Yet he does his best to ruin her need for him, uses sex as an instrument of revenge and his shows of tenderness to tie his women in knots.

At their worst Updike's men are victims of forces which he understands but they do not. When they find the woman of their dreams, they invariably begin to hate her. When Rabbit runs out on Janice he meets a good-natured, sexy woman who makes him feel as alive and competitive as he did on the basketball court. He wants to oust all her other lovers from her mind. He succeeds. But afterward he dreams he is back in his mother's kitchen with his call-girl sister, Mim. Mim opens the icebox door and they see a block of ice in which something that looks like a heart is frozen. His mother begins scolding Mim for opening the door. Mim turns into Janice, her face melts. But it's Rabbit who is furious at women for trying to melt him. That Janice melts into oblivion reflects his angry fear that to lose your cool is to die. He wants to keep his heart on ice not only to stay in his mother's box but to ice his explosiveness. Sister, wife, mistress are interchangeable as women who are in danger if his feelings are unleashed. This is the dark side of sex where romanticizing a woman is better than having her, because intimacy arouses destructiveness. What makes Rabbit feel alive is ironically the total conquest that makes him want to destroy.

Jerry conquers Sally, overpowers her concern for her children, her marriage, her financial security. But he is unwilling to thaw or to change and unable to remain the same. He thinks he wants a warm woman, but seems able to live only with a cold one who keeps his contempt alive and his anger in check. He looks to his mistress to be a stronger force, capable of freeing him. But getting into her means getting back to the frustration and anger he would have toward any woman who threatened to melt the iced anger that binds him to motherly Ruth.

Jerry's mastery of the instant turnoff is the sign of his enthrallment. Updike developed how much more deeply a man can be spellbound in his fine short novel *Of the Farm*. There a man virtually fuses with his mother by seeing his wife through her disparaging eyes. Contempt is a bond between them. When Joey Robinson and his new wife arrive at his mother's farm, he watches his sexual wife, whose body he loves, walk towards his mother. Knowing his mother will see her only as a large, gross, painted woman, he develops a kind of double vision, sees her that way too. He begins to belittle her, complain about her promiscuity with men before she knew him; he hates himself for being fool enough to marry her. As his mother, who had belittled his first wife during his marriage to her insists, wife two seems not so bright, charming or attractive as wife one. Joey's self-hatred turns to hatred for the wife who is the living sign of his bad taste. Yet his fate is to need the contempt and self-contempt that keep him bound to his mother.

Women are the only masculine pursuit in Updike's novels that offer the promise of relief and rebirth. Rabbit's grace comes from his wish to be made new; his decline from losing his power to believe he can be. Jerry's appeal comes from his boyish hope for heaven in a woman; his rigidity from his blindness to the massive evidence Updike provides that he would wreck an angel. The persistent tragic irony in Updike's novels is the contradiction between what a man wants and what his heart will allow.

What would happen if everything were allowed? Updike has written novels which are comic resolutions of ambivalence. In these the Oedipal situation turns around: youth replaces authority as a value and Mom herself is available. Irony isn't psychological bile but frothy social confusion. Updike is hilarious on the ill manners of marriage in a town where the basic social unit is the man and wife who are sexually disenchanted with each other. In *Couples* when Angela, oft-condemned by her husband for her repressions, begins confessing her interest in sex and asking for help, her husband becomes enraged. He is happy to be unhappy with her because he has learned to make his contempt work for him. He regards her as that perfect ally, the wife who is a defense against life: she holds his hand while the irate husband of his mistress tells him off. Ruth becomes Jerry's sisterly confidante as they face Sally and her husband, making Jerry feel as though he has found a family by loving Sally. Like the long-suffering Mrs. Marshfield in *A Month of Sundays* who knows how to humiliate her husband's mistress almost as well as he does, wives and husbands are "the matched jaws of a heartbreaker." The payoff is for the husband who learns how useful it is to have a wife who loves him just like a mother.

Why can't Updike's men live happily, if incestuously, with both in the post-pill paradise? Sex, Updike implies, frees men for other things, but binds women deeply to the men who please them. After the most ecstatic experience the couple is often left upset: the man wants to please (Updike's men think like gentlemen), but knows he cannot give the woman what he thinks she wants (quaintly, it's always marriage). Sally, who watches her lover rise, dress and run, feels left behind. Jerry finds himself engulfed by death anxiety so profound it must reflect his fear of immanent punishment for betraying both his wife and mistress.

Jerry is helpless before his need to wound. It is not Sally who brings up marriage but he who offers it to withdraw his offer, to tighten the knot of impotence and helplessness in which he holds her. His very passivity, his indecisiveness drips with his coercive attempt to involve her and Ruth into fighting it out between them, absolving him of responsibility, competing to see who can please him more, and mothering him all the while. Cornered between exasperated mistresses and wives, some of Updike's heroes rhapsodize the disparities between what each sex wants, declaring woman is earthbound, man is stargazer. Sally is the "golden staircase" Jerry "can never climb." But the stargazing, the religiosity of Updike's good Christian men invariably involves a wish to look past female pain and their own sexual anger. They want to think well of themselves while blaming the mistresses who draw them with their clear, open sexuality for being too "pushy," and their battered wives for being "frigid and pathetic." While Ruth and Sally practice charity (toward Jerry, not each other), Jerry plays God the father and Christ crucified.

Updike's defense against despair is style, the spectacular management of perspective to overlook disaster. In conversation, he once spoke of a dream he had at fourteen of a knight in armor who pursued a Polynesian girl across Europe. On her island he finds her, looks at her through a palm frond and dies. "I never wrote that novel, the historical one," he remarked. But Updike imprinted its message in novels where to look too closely is to diminish the ideal woman with her own reality and to die a little oneself. Updike's Jerrys regenerate themselves by not seeing the women they make love to. In sex Sally's face is "a mirror held inches below his own face, a mirror of love more than another person. He asked himself who this was and then remembered it was Sally." Then Jerry, the Jerrys! foil, belittle, betray, disappoint, but somehow never cease to involve the women who so imperfectly stand in for the force to which they have given their lives, the Lady of Rebirth.

Updike is not a sexual materialist. He is an idealist, perhaps by necessity. In *Aaron's Rod* Lawrence worshipped the penis. Updike arrives at male narcissism by the modern route of irony, mocking Jerry's vision of his erection as the Bodily Ascension. Updike's Lawrentian religion makes sex the great reconciler. Sex as the origin and the goal, the moment of eternity, the mortality that feels like omnipotence, reconciles the conflicts of characters whose greatest fear is that the dead part of themselves may defeat the living. In *A Month of Sundays* Reverend Marshfield jokes that there is no more beautiful phrase than "sexual object." Updike's characters are so in love with their objective that they cannot help, within the limits of the bed, loving the women with whom they achieve it. How should women feel? Like Yeats's Crazy Jane? She confides: "Though like a road/ That men pass over/ My body makes no moan/ But sings on; All things remain in God." Updike's happiest characters are those who do not lose the power to believe there are Janes who make it all possible.

Updike sees women as a prophecy of something better. The greatest love in *Marry Me* is Updike's. It is evident in his lavish unsparing skill in creating Ruth. Her acid accuracy about her husband's flaws is unaccompanied by any desire for revenge, any critical bent, any interest in throwing him out. Updike's women are mirrors of his appreciativeness of the qualities of patient forgiveness and excitement his Ruths and Sallys divide between them. Ruth has more insight into her man than into herself. And while Updike is more grateful than any other male writer for the nobility of women, while he grants them every palm of virtue, he never seems to try to know how they might judge themselves for staying with a man who offers his arm, his hand in marriage, to help them fall.

The sign of Updike's grace as a writer is the superb clarity with which he renders the man bewitched by his ambivalences. Not since *Rabbit, Run,* one of the finest novels of the past twenty years, has Updike written with such hard beauty of a man endlessly wandering the labyrinth of his own needs, irresistibly childlike in his faith in the magic of a woman, and abusively fearful of broken spells. *Marry Me* is a compassionate judgment of one kind of married man that brings to mind St. Augustine's remark, "I kept my heart from assenting to anything, fearing to fall headlong, but by hanging in suspense I was the worse killed."

OLINGER NOVELS

Is the syntactical sentence plastic enough to render the flux, the blurring, the endless innuendo of experience as we feel it? No aesthetic theory will cover the case; what is needed is a habit of honesty on the part of the writer. He must, rather athletically, instill his wrists with the refusal to write whatever is lazily assumed, or hastily perceived, or piously hoped. Fiction is a tissue of literal lies that refreshes and informs our sense of actuality. Reality is—chemically, atomically, biologically—a fabric of microscopic accuracies. Language approximates phenomena through a series of hesitations and qualifications; I miss, in much contemporary writing, this sense of self-qualification, the kind of timid reverence toward what exists that Cézanne shows when he grapples for the shape and shade of a fruit through a mist of delicate stabs.

UPDIKE
Picked-Up Pieces

The Poorhouse Fair:
A Fragile Vision of Specialness

by Joyce Markle

In *The Poorhouse Fair,* an old people's home becomes a sociological cosmos in which the principal fact is death. But though the poorhouse is, by definition, a place to die, it is important to notice that physical death is not a cause of dread for the inmates. They recall the former prefect Mendelssohn's death, for instance, with tender nostalgia. "In his coffin, I remember saying to Mrs. Haines, he looks like he's come to the end of a prayer, his nostrils still full of its breath. My heart told me to stoop and kiss his hand, but the line was pushing" (Rpt. New York: Fawcett World Library, p. 22). They also exchange enthusiastic accounts of their visions of heaven. "I've always thought I'd be a beauty and my mother not." "I expect we'll all be about the same age." Heaven will be...a mist of all the joy sensations have given us" (pp. 69-74). Hook uses his approaching death as a cause for increased moral vigilance: "We fellas so close to the Line—have our accounts watched very close" (p. 6). And death creates an urgency to communicate a message to Conner as a "testament to endure his dying in the world" (p. 127). Amy Mortis, whose name suggests she is a friend of death, invokes her own death to fortify her rhetoric whenever she feels attacked. To the antique dealer she threatens, "I doubt if next year I'll be able to find any [patterned cloth] but I'll be dead by then anyway, with luck" (p. 101).

Original Title: *"The Poorhouse Fair:* Essential Thematic Principles." Abridged from *Fighters and Lovers: Theme in the Novels of John Updike,* by Joyce B. Markle (New York: New York University Press, 1973), pp. 13-36. Copyright © 1973 by New York University Press. Reprinted by permission of New York University Press.

Mendelssohn understood this essentially sympathetic relationship to death. Unlike Conner who attempts to forestall death with updated health care (his professional success is rated partly by the longevity of the inmates), Mendelssohn encouraged their awareness of death.

> "Can't you picture Mendelssohn now?" Amy Mortis asked at another table. "How he'd have us all singing and shouting prayers and telling us how we all must die?"...
>
> They were seeing him now. ... As the songs grew more religious, the rims of Mendelssohn's eyes grew redder and he was dabbing at his cheeks with the huge handkerchief he always carried and was saying...how here they all lived close to death, which cast a shadow over even their gaiety.... Here they lived with death at their sides, the third participant in every conversation, the other guest at every meal. ...   [pp. 56-57]

This death-consciousness is a mark of their intelligence and independence. To remove death—as Conner has done—to the sterile, closed, anaesthetized west wing is to deprive the inmates of the dignity of being death-foreseeing. With his good intentions but narrow vision, Conner has attended to physical death —which they do not fear—while failing to see the deathly effect of depersonalization, which is the real threat.

In structure, *The Poorhouse Fair* can be seen as a series of juxtapositions contrasting characters who have an ennobling vision (Hook, and to a lesser degree the other old people) with characters whose vision fails to individualize or distinguish people as special entities (Conner, Buddy, or the visitors to the fair). In the opening scene Gregg reacts violently against the name tags Conner has put on the chairs, feeling that they reduce the people to animals ("Is he putting tags on us so we can be trucked off to the slaughterhouse?") and are the product of animal-level thinking: "What birdbrain scheme is this now of Conner's?" Conner's unintentionally demeaning act of tagging is contrasted with a long internal view of Hook which shows his thoughtfulness, intelligence, and sensitivity about people.

Updike uses figurative language and other special word choice to reveal the dehumanizing vision of Conner, Buddy, and visitors of their generation. When Buddy enters the crowded cafeteria, "one vast bright beast seemed contained in an acoustic cage"

(p. 57). To Conner the crowds entering for the fair "bumble like brainless insects" and form "one living conglomerate, through whose sprawling body veins of traffic with effort circulated: a beast more monstrous than any he had told Hook of" (p. 109). David, a youth coming to the fair, recalls seeing the old people in town where occasionally one "waggled a claw at the children."

A belief in the significance of life creates a recognition of the importance of death. Death loses its terror, for Conner, if it can come without suffering. He foreshadows Ken, of *Couples,* who regards without emotion a tray of gutted laboratory mice. This is a result of their vision of life as biological only, its cessation of no great matter. Mendelssohn's dramatic sermons about death and Conner's peaceful west wing are the keystones of their diametrically opposed views.

Any death, even the death of an animal, invokes the fact of human death to death-foreseeing humans. The death of the cat which Buddy kills and the death of the flying squirrel which Hook had to kill supply two contrasting vignettes of the value of life.

> With a sensation of prolonged growing sweetness Buddy squeezed the trigger. The report disappointed him, a mere slap it seemed in his ears and very local.
>
> If his target had been a bottle, liquid wouldn't have spilled more quickly from it than life from the cat. The animal dropped without a shudder. ... The gun exhaled a faint acrid perfume.
>
> Breaking up the screaming ring [of children] he [Hook] had found at its center a grey pelt wildly pulsing with the parasitic life that refused to loosen its grip, and had had to dispatch it himself, weeping and trembling, with a hatchet brought up from the basement.... As he had imagined it there had been a storm brooding that day.   [p. 34]

The widely differing senses of *life* in the animals, the terror on one hand and the sweetness on the other, and the sense of cosmic importance (a storm brooding) versus a sense of no importance ("a mere slap" and "very local") counterpoint each other.

Updike casts the difference between Hook's and Conner's worlds into the imagery of the intricately patterned quilts that Amy Mortis makes. The quilts with their carefully ordered and arranged design are symmetrical, meaningful, and beautiful as is a world fashioned by an intelligent Maker. Amy's quilts contain little worlds—temples and furniture, hills and sky, flowers and rivers, and children playing. Hook makes the analogy at once and looking at the quilt, sees himself as a child "wandering among the rectilinear paths of the pattern searching for the deeper dyed thread" (p. 21). When he was a child a quilt symbolized the necessary sleep after a day's play just as now his faith understands the meaning of death after the span of life. Eight pages later, when Hook prays, he becomes "a point within an infinitely thick blanket," prayer revitalizing a sense of the world as patterned quilt.

Conner, by contrast, sees himself as living beneath "blank skies" in the same paragraph in which he admits his boredom (p. 47). This is an echo of the "plain" cloth which the younger people prefer but which Amy cannot use in her quilts. Standing alongside Hook, who frequently makes long, lyrical descriptions of the view from the poorhouse grounds, Conner sees "nothing, or what amounted to nothing" (p. 47). Although Hook has seen and interpreted the thickening cloud patterns, Conner can only see the western sector of the sky which is "unclouded." This leaves him unable to understand the thunder as he is unable to understand the rest of the world which is given meaning by the pattern in which it partakes.

Conner calls Elizabeth's vision of heaven "tremblings" of her mind, "shy hallucinations," "cartoons projected on a waterfall," for which he has no time. After the discussion, however, Conner daydreams a far more romantic heaven while listening to music:

> grown men and women, lightly clad, playing, on the brilliant sand of a seashore, children's games. A man threw a golden ball, his tunic slowly swirling with the exertion; a girl caught it. No fear here, no dread of time. Another man caught the girl by the waist. She had a wide belt. He held her above his head; she bent way back, her throat curved against the sky above the distant domes. The man was Conner. ...   [p. 87]

Later, Walter-Mitty-like, he daydreams again, revealing the need for romantic heroism which is ignored in his scientific dogma: "He was sitting at a table of dignitaries, not in the center but with becoming modesty at one end. He rose, papers in hand. 'My department is pleased to report the possession of evidence which would indicate,' he said, and paused, 'that the cure for cancer has been found'" (pp. 108-109). And although he refuses to believe in Christ—"Can any sane mind believe that a young carpenter in Syria two thousand years ago *made* those monstrous balls of gas" —he adopts the very recognizable role of a Christ figure when he is stoned by the inmates. He feels their attack is "unjust" but when Buddy arrives to help, Conner huskily orders "Go away." "Then the least expected thing—he stopped and collected a double handful of the stones that had fallen around him and brought them forward to the wheelbarrow." Buddy asks:

> "What are you going to do?"
> "Forgive them.".....
> "But at least you could punish their leader."
> "I'm their leader."   [p. 93]

As the people begin to arrive for the fair, Conner meditates upon his unattractive and uninteresting job, hoping for eventual promotion. Yet he feels he prizes a useful life over a pleasant life, and just before conjuring a daydream he unconsciously repeats the Christian refrain that requests God's will: "Wherever I can serve," he tells himself. Finally the speaker ends this section by maintaining that as the Christian assurance of a spiritual identity gives life to believers, Conner's substitute myths are the source of his life: "he had been mocked—but within he stubbornly retained, like the spark of life in the shattered cat, the conviction that he was the hope of the world."

When Conner dismisses Christ as a carpenter, Hook responds that there is no profession "so native to holy and constructive emotions or so appropriate for God-made flesh to assume" (p. 79). This statement fits into a series of remarks by Hook and the speaker praising the old time craftsmen. When the environment is shaped by the work of human hands, work indicating self-conscious care, the world becomes a human place and this permanent evidence of our causality seems to promise permanence to our existence, buys off the finality of death. "There can't be a foot of earth east of the Alleghenies," says Hook, "where a body can stand and not be within hailing distance of a house. We have made the land very tame" (p. 20).

Just as craft humanizes objects or places, people's history has humanized time. A vapor trail's visibility acts as a mark of the pilot's past and cheers Conner; so too a culture's or a person's memory of the past gives time a visible existence and human appearance. Updike's characters can seek evidence of their identity not only in the physical products of craft or the paths of packed earth but also in their memories of the past—"paths" in time—which preserve in a nonphysical way the marks of their existence. In a sense, Updike even runs time and place together insofar as they supply a basis for knowledge of one's existence and identity. In *The Poorhouse Fair* the setting and characters themselves are evocative of the past; having come to maturity in a time past, they are living symbols or products of American history. This is why, the speaker explains, the younger generation—for whom "the conception 'America' had died in their skulls"—need to come to the poorhouse fair: to seek to revitalize their sense of their past, to seek to identify themselves.

For history-teacher Hook, the past century of American politics acts simultaneously as his cultural and personal identity. It replaces the memories of childhood and adolescence in Pennsylvania to which the other protagonists—and Updike himself—turn for identity and comfort. Hook, like the grandfather in "The Dogwood Tree," is solidly intrenched in loyalty to the Democratic party. His memory focuses on the period beginning just previous to his birth and extending like the Olinger stories, through the years of his adolescence; thus his favorite stories begin with Buchanan ("The last of the presidents who truly represented the *en*tire country" [p. 66]), proceed through Cleveland ("Cleveland had the mettle. He was no Tilden to let the carpetbaggers steal the office from him" [p. 105] , and to McKinley ("Now that McKinley was nothing but Mark Hanna's parade uniform" [p. 22]). Deprived of their past (Hook's "farsighted" vision), the modern generation struggle to construct new sagas, instant history.

Among Updike's novels, it would appear that *The Poorhouse Fair* has the least-ambiguous value system, the least-hedged moral framework. It is the initial definition of people: they are death-foreseeing yet cling to a belief in their significance through a fragile vision of their specialness which must be nourished. Their self-consciousness is evidenced by the products of their craft and by the preservation of their past, both of which disappear in the modern world.

However, in *The Poorhouse Fair* there are four symbolic moments which intrude a doubt into the tightly woven ethical fabric of the novel. These are four sounds which each act as a "summons" of some kind to the old people. "As they hastened toward the porch...the *fourth noise* of the half hour *summoned* them, encouraging their flight, the ringing of the lunch signal..." (p. 48, italics mine). These four sounds are: the shot of the gun, the scrape of the truck, the thunder, and the lunch bell. All of these introduce arguments against Hook's faith and trust in his vision.

The gun brings death to the cat, who like the old people is nearly dead (Gregg's sympathy is a mark of the identification between the two) and who has been cruelly smashed in some violent way. Hook himself sees the cat as a flaw in the world's order ("it was hopelessly out of order") and its existence plays an oblique role in Hook's need to explain to Conner the existence of pain and suffering in the world. The fact of the cat's death presents another theological problem—it appears unjust, even to Gregg, that the life and death of creatures is beyond their own control. And so the first summons is to the problem of suffering and death.

The second sound, the scrape of the truck, breaks open the wall which was constructed by the old-time craftsmen that Hook and the speaker see as so significant. But the wall (like the Congregational Church four novels later) is discovered to be rotten and empty inside. Not only is the product of craft partially a fraud, but it is not permanent. Furthermore, there may be the implication that the Christian church is similarly empty inside — just rubble, and only useful for mindless assaults on antagonists. Thus the second summons attacks the basis of man's belief and the products of his intelligence.

The third sound is the thunder, which threatens to destroy the old people's carefully planned and beloved fair. As "God's own lightning" destroys the Congregational Church in *Couples,* so God's thunder can bring the ruination of the work of human hands and prevent the vitalizing products of the human past from reaching others. The third summons is to man's unimportance in the universe.

The fourth sound is the dinner bell which summons the people to a debate in which Conner attacks, intellectually, their belief in God and in the universe of His creation. Although Hook wages an intelligent and emotionally attractive argument against Conner's atheism, he is defeated in the end by Conner's scientific evidence. His response to the case of the girl with the chemically induced vision of God is "shame" and a feeble criticism, "That was a very cruel experiment" (p. 80). After Buddy's story of his brother's slow death from cancer, which acts as a conclusion to Conner's argument, Hook can only invoke the results of destroying Christian beliefs: "There can be no goodness...only busyness." This final summons, then, invokes the Achilles' heel of any religion: its ultimate inability to prove its own proofs.

These four thematic qualifications act upon the closing of the book—a scene colored by ambiguity and frustration. Hook wants to give Conner a message—presumably his vision, his natural faith—but the message seems unable to form. Moreover this desire to communicate a message places Hook parallel with Conner himself who had earlier expressed the desire to give Hook such a message, "And he felt, important within him, something he should get across, a *message*..." (p. 64, italics mine). As one critic has remarked, these enigmatic closing sentences have become an Updike trademark. But more than a stylistic tendency, the endings of the novels, beginning with *The Poorhouse Fair,* point to the ambiguity, the "yes, but" quality, of the conceptual framework in each book. Updike himself claimed that Conner, here an antagonist, reminded him of his father, the lovable protagonist of *The Centaur.* And to what degree does the old people's simple-minded vision of heaven cast doubt on the reliability of their whole system of belief? This seed of doubt continues to gain thematic strength in each novel until, in an apocalyptic burst of flame, the church deserts the protagonist of the fifth novel, leaving him abandoned, if content, on the nearly animal plane that the first novel so persistently resists.

The Centaur:
Epic Paean and Pastoral Lament

by Larry E. Taylor

For John Milton to have transformed the Cambridge scholar Edward King into the simple shepherd Lycidas in order to ennoble and aggrandise him is a curious inversion of the Hebraic-Christian tradition by which great kings of earth and gods of heaven are shepherd boys (King David of the Old Testament) and humble peasants born in mangers (Jesus of the New Testament). In the Hellenistic tradition, kings and gods are also often disguised as shepherds (for example, Apollo and Paris); and the gods themselves are nagging housewives (Hera), promiscuous husbands (Zeus), blacksmiths (Haephestus), and so forth. The process of linking pastoral simplicity and epic grandeur, along with its pervasive inversion, seems to be a preoccupation within the myths of the Western world. The paradox is central to the entire story of Jesus and his teachings. And far from diminishment, the process has, if anything, been reinforced within the American democratic tradition. In terms of the classic pastoral-epic metaphor, for Abraham Lincoln to have been born in a log cabin on the frontier is as essential to the wholeness of "the myth of Lincoln" as Jesus' birth in a manger is to the wholeness of "the myth of Jesus." Indeed, even in our more minor American myths, we still like our presidents to be simple Quakers from Yorba Linda, ex-country-school-teachers from Texas, or the elegant Bostonian sons of once-poor Irish immigrants. The mind delights in linking the humble with the grand. Theocritus of Alexandria worked in two genres only—pastoral and epic; Virgil is known for his *Eclogues* and his *Aeneid,* as Milton is best known for *Lycidas* and *Paradise Lost.*

John Updike's finest work—the novel which would have established him as a "major" writer, had he written nothing else—rests directly in the mainstream of this pastoral-epic pattern; furthermore, *The Centaur* powerfully illuminates the pattern itself. Rather than merely using the metaphor, Updike contributes to it in the way that James Joyce and John Milton, for example, contributed to it—Milton in adding Christianity, and Joyce in adding post-Darwinian and post-Freudian philosophy. Why are the apparently contradictory and dichotomous pastoral and epic metaphors so important to Western culture, and to the race itself? John Updike's epigraph to *The Centaur* provides part of the answer; his novel provides the rest. The epigraph is a quotation from the theologian Karl Barth:

> Heaven is the creation inconceivable to man, earth the creation conceivable to him. He himself is the creature on the boundary between heaven and earth.

Ipso facto, two creations exist, call them what one will—heavenly and earthly, spiritual and material, ideal and real, unconscious and conscious, imaginative and empirical, divine and temporal, epic and pastoral—it does not matter. Man, unable to conceive one of the creations, employs earth, that creation which he can conceive, to explain the other. Ingenious and ironic animal that he is, he creates exaggerated metaphors befitting his exaggerated, rather absurd position of being "on the boundary between heaven and earth." Unable to conceive a ruler of that other creation, he makes god into an exaggerated version of his earthly father, who, as he knows from experience is capable of both extreme mercy and extreme wrath. Conscious that the role of the shepherd is the lowliest earthly social position, he causes his god to be born in a stable and to become "the good shepherd" as well as "the Son of God." And in an inspired burst of irony, he dresses his popes and bishops (symbolic intermediaries who are kinds of walking metaphors assigned to zigzag across the boundary) in splendid robes, and thrusts a shepherd's crook into their hands—a *golden* shepherd's crook. Or he makes the brightest god of Olympus, Phoebus

Apollo, serve Admetus for a year as a slave; his heroes cleanse stables and cook their own suppers. He places a man's torso on a horse's body, and makes him the teacher of the gods. His saviors are ironically thieves and drifters, stealing fire from the gods and telling paradoxical parables on mountainsides. But in their willingness to suffer on rocks and crosses, in their ability to fully penetrate both the conceivable and inconceivable creations, they become the best comfort that man has. The reciprocal sliding scale between epic and pastoral, I take it, is one way of metaphorically reconciling the imponderable paradoxes involved in the human condition of being "a little lower than the angels" and a little higher than the beasts—like a Centaur. Chiron, the centaur, half man and half horse, can be seen as the perfect symbol for the paradoxical union of epic and pastoral patterns in Updike's novel. Epically, Chiron makes the grand sacrificial gesture which propitiates the crime of the hero Prometheus, and sets him free; pastorally, Chiron teaches the children of the gods in Arcadian groves.

The art of *The Centaur* depends on structure as fully as it depends on theme and metaphor. Indeed, the basic metaphor which compares Olinger citizens to Olympian citizens would merely be a kind of tour de force, a brilliant exercise in analogy and allegory comparable to, say, *Pilgrim's Progress,* were it not for the structure of the novel. Without Updike's arrangement of chapters and his knowledgeable employment of juxtaposed modes and traditions, the surrealism of *The Centaur* would be merely arrestingly clever—like a fur-lined teacup, or a Salvador Dali painting; in Wordsworthian terms, it would be "fanciful" rather than creatively "imaginative." The structure depends on the fact that four interspersed short chapters of the book established the total work as a "pastoral elegy," as certainly and as imaginatively as *Lycidas* is a pastoral elegy. Furthermore, Updike becomes a classicist in writing this novel—in the sense that Milton is a classicist, as opposed to the sense in which eighteenth-century English Augustans were classical. The difference, I take it, is that Milton strove for and achieved the *spirit* of the pastoral epic, and tragic modes, rather than copying the form and letter of the originals: it is Alexander Pope's and Edward Young's distinction—the difference between imitating Homer and Theocritus rather than the *Iliad* and the *Idyls.*

In *The Centaur,* chapters 3, 5, 8, and 9 are all variations of basic conventions of the traditional pastoral elegy. They stand out in the novel because of their brevity and their abrupt tonal shifts. The rest of the novel (the longer chapters 1, 2, 4, 6, and 7) tells the story of the three days Peter-Prometheus and his father George Caldwell-Centaur spend in town, snowed in and unable to return to the mother Ceres and the home farm. The four pastoral chapters declare themselves as legitimate elements of the traditional pastoral elegy through (1) correspondence of conventional subject matter, and (2) correspondence of conventional language and imagery. As to subject matter, the pattern works as follows:

(1)   Chapter 3, only five pages long, shows the pastoral hero Chiron involved in his daily tasks of teaching the children of the gods in Arcadian groves. Idyllic in the strictest sense, the passage includes a conventional catalogue of flowers and herbs and celebrates the tranquility and beauty of the hero as he was in life. Roughly, it corresponds to lines 25-36 of *Lycidas.*

(2)   Chapter 5, four pages long, is a newspaper obituary, giving a coldly factual account of Caldwell's life. It suggests the conventional expression of communal grief. It is the elegiac announcement of death, roughly comparable to the flat shock value of the fact, "For Lycidas is dead, dead ere his prime," lines 10 and following of *Lycidas.*

(3)   Chapter 8 (the first four pages) is the expression of Peter's personal grief for the loss of the pastoral hero. Here Peter-Prometheus sings his lament to his Negro mistress. He questions the meaning of his father's death in a version of the elegiac interrogation of the universe, roughly analagous to lines 50-85 of *Lycidas.*

(4)   Chapter 9, four pages long, is a consolation and reconciliation, an account of the Centaur's acceptance of death, and his son's reconciliation to it. The short epilogue is an account of the Centaur's apotheosis as a star. Roughly, it corresponds to lines 165-93 of *Lycidas.*

The structural continuity of these seemingly fragmented chapters provides the touchstone necessary for reading the entire novel, for seeing it as a unified whole. Boldly shifting from Olinger to Olympus would be comic, like mock-epic, if it were not for Updike's employment of the conventions of the pastoral elegy.

The language of these touchstone chapters provides the lyricism and formality required to keep the novel from being ironic, satiric, and comic. Seen as a highly personal expression of both Updike's and Peter's sense of loss (Updike has left Shillington to become a writer for the *New Yorker,* and Peter is painting abstractions in a New York loft), *The Centaur* appeals to the impersonality of stock pastoral conventions as a vehicle for transforming life into art—the personal into the universal. The very stockness of the language in these chapters—from the idyllic song and catalogue in chapter 3, to the journalistic jargon in chapter 5, to the mixture of love lyric and lament in chapter 8, to the elevated statement of apotheosis in the epilogue—provides a stable point of reference for the almost schizophrenic imagery shifts and linguistic jerks in the rest of the novel. When we come to chapter 3, we recognize the purely stock language and subject matter of the Theocritan pastoral, and we can rest; when we arrive at chapter 5, we almost gratefully recognize the stock jargon of obituaries, and so forth. Grief and loss must be pinned down and stabilized if perspective and sanity are to be retained. Formal language—even to the point of *stock* language—is needed to accompany that "formal feeling" which Emily Dickinson says comes "after great pain." This, I take it, is the purpose of the language of rites and ceremonies—the rationale behind the language of eulogies, obituaries, and pastoral elegies.

Explicitly Arcadian in the strictest classical sense, chapter 3 subtly merges pastoral description with a paean to the gods, "slim pale reeds of a single pipe harmoniously hymning the god of existence pure." Thus, even in this passage Updike merges the pastoral with the heroic, the catalogue of flowers and herbs with the epic paean. The conventional language of the passage is, in kind, straight out of Theocritus' *Idyls.* Compare the stock language of Updike's idyl and Theocritus' idyl. From Updike:

> Chiron hurried, a little late, down the corridors of tamarisk, yew, bay, and kermes oak. Beneath the cedars and silver firs, whose hushed heads were shadows permeated with Olympian blue, a vigorous underwood of arbutus, wild pear, cornel, box, and andrachne filled with scents of flower and sap and new twig in the middle air of the forest. Branches of bloom here and there dashed color across the shifting caverns of forest space that enclosed the haste of his canter. He slowed. The ragged and muted attendants of air escort-

ing his high head slowed also. These intervals of free space—
touched by the arching search of fresh shoots and threaded by the
quick dripdrop of birdsong released as if from a laden ceiling rich
in elements (some songs were water, some copper, some silver,
some burnished rods of wood, some cold and corrugated fire)—
were reminiscent for him of caverns and soothed and suited his
nature. His student's eyes—for what is a teacher but a student
grown old?—retrieved, from their seclusion in the undergrowth,
basil, hellebore, feverwort, spurge, polypody, bryony, wolf's-bane,
and squill. Ixine, cinquefoil, sweet marjoram and gilliflower he
lifted, by the shape of their petals, leaves, stems, and thorns, from
their anonymity in indiscriminate green. Recognized, the plants
seemed to lift crisply in salute, hailing the passage of a hero.

[Rpt. New York: Fawcett World Library, p. 74]

From Theocritus:

Then they went forth upon the shore, and each couple busily got
ready supper in the late evening, and many as they were one bed
they strewed lowly on the ground, for they found a meadow lying,
rich in couches of strown grass and leaves. Thence they cut them
pointed flag-leaves, and deep marsh-galingale. And Hylas of the
yellow hair, with a vessel of bronze in his hand, went to draw water
against supper time, for Heracles himself, and the steadfast Tela-
mon, for these comrades twain supped ever at one table. Soon was
he ware of a spring, in a hollow land, and the rushes grew thickly
round it, and dark swallow-wort, and green maiden-hair, and
blooming parsley, and deergrass spreading through the marshy
land. In the midst of the water the nymphs were arraying their
dances, the sleepless nymphs, dread goddesses of the country people, Eunice, and Malis, and Nycheia, with her April eyes.[1]

In chapter 3, the inclusion of the heroic hymn in the Homeric
manner is a convention of one version of the Theocritan *Idyl.*
For example, "Idyl 22" is a paean:

We hymn the children twain of Leda, and of aegis-bearing Zeus,—
Castor, and Pollux, the boxer dread, when he hath harnessed his
knuckles in thongs of oxhide. Twice hymn we, and thrice the stal-
wart sons of the daughter of Thestias, the two brethren of
Lacedaemon.[2]

---

[1]Theocritus, "Idyl 13," *The Idyls of Theocritus, Bion, and Moschus,* trans. A.
Lang (London: Macmillan Co., 1932), p. 69.

[2]*Ibid.,* p. 103.

The echo in Updike is,

> Lord of the sky
> Wielder of weather,
> Brightness of brightness,
> Zeus, hear our song!
>
> Fill us with glory,
> Crest of the thunderhead,
> Shape us with gradualness,
> Source of the rain!

[pp. 76-77]

Thus, Updike includes the highly conventional language of the Homeric chant. The result of this purely pastoral chapter is to establish a basis for the reading of the whole novel. The reader is calmed and soothed and reconciled by the familiar conventional language—he begins to think that there is some order to what is taking place in the novel—some coherence and meaning to it all. To this extent, the language of the four touchstone chapters is highly important. The chapters become the formal structural clues for reading the whole book. Idyl, hymn, obituary, love lyric, lament, epitaph—these recognizable forms within the pastoral elegy form give the novel its coherence, its dignity, its eloquence as a universal statement.

The first pages of chapter 8 are also pastoral. Here we find the combination of love lyric, pastoral reminiscence, lament, and interrogation of the universe. Here Peter speaks to his Negro mistress, and combines his love song for her with his memory of his father and Olinger. The reminiscent description of the Alton Museum employs language straight out of Theocritus:

> Quickly crossing the harsh width of a three-lane highway, we would enter on a narrow path the museum grounds, and an even older world, Arcadian, would envelop us. Ducks and frogs mixed flat throaty exultations in the scummy marsh half-hidden by the planted lines of cherry, linden, locust, and crabapple trees.

[p. 198]

Explicitly "Arcadian" like the world of chapter 3, the museum and its grounds are associated with the "only treasury of culture accessible to us"—i.e., it is associated with *art*. In addition, the museum exists in ideal nature, in Arcady, as opposed to the harsh reality of real nature.

In the basement, indeed, free classes in "nature appreciation" were held in the summer months. At my mother's suggestion I once enrolled. The first lesson was to watch a snake in a glass cage swallow a chattering field mouse whole. I did not go for the second lesson.   [p. 199]

The passage is important because Peter-Prometheus is now an artist in New York. The struggles of his parents, the sacrifices of his Centaur-Father, have been made so that Peter can be freed to be an artist. It is here that Peter questions the validity of such sacrifice. He sees the role of artist as a deterioration from that of priest and teacher: "Priest, teacher, artist: the classic degeneration." And he asks, "Was it for this that my father gave up his life?" It is the type of question found in *Lycidas:* "Where were ye nymphs...?" and "What boots it with uncessant care/ To tend the homely slighted shepherd's trade...?"

But his father The Centaur has given Peter-Prometheus another gift—the ability to love. We see this in Peter's version of the love lyric to his mistress, which is interwoven with the interrogation of the meaning of his father's sacrifice:

Listen: I love you, love your prim bruised mouth whose corners compress morally when you are awake and scolding me, love your burnt skin ceaselessly forgiving mine, love the centuries of being humbled held in the lilac patina of your palms. I love the tulip-stem stance of your throat. When you stand before the stove you make, all unconscious, undulant motions with the upper half of your body like a drinking hen. When you walk naked toward the bed your feet toe in as if your ankles were manacled to those of someone behind you. When we make love sometimes you sigh my name and I feel radically confirmed.   [p. 200]

Like the language of the obituary of chapter 5, the language of this chapter is curiously stock; we can recognize the forms and idiosyncrasies rather in the way we recognize the clichés like, "The couple was blessed with two offspring, of which George was the second." Though seemingly opposites, the language of newspaper obituary and the language of pastoral love lyric are, in kind, parts of the same pattern: in form and function, they relate to the pattern of elegiac pastoral conventions, as outlined above. In the way that the obituary serves as the required expression of communal and social grief, Peter's song to his love is a part of his expression of intense personal grief. Even in the prototypic Theocritan *Idyl,* the shepherd sings his lament to a close friend or lover.

The final chapter of *The Centaur* provides the required consolation, and the one-sentence epilogue provides the conventional apotheosis. The acceptance of death is associated with the return to the rural home, to Ceres and the earth. It is winter, and the landscape contrasts to the warm pastoral scene of chapter 3. On the realistic level, we learn that George Caldwell does not have cancer as he had feared (at least, the x-rays show nothing); on the metaphoric level, we see Chiron's necessary death and his subsequent rebirth as a constellation. The pointed consolation is that "all joy belongs to the Lord," and that "only goodness lives."

The final chapter is no longer a celebration of the beauty of the earth, with scenes from idealized pastoral nature. It is winter, the time of death. In this last chapter the imagery is based on the coupling of Uranus (sky) and Gaia (earth), heaven and earth. The union echoes Karl Barth's two "creations," the inconceivable and the conceivable. The coldness and bleakness of winter, the "brutish landscape," are not so important now, because the Centaur is approaching death, and his apotheosis into the heavens. And in accepting his fate, he becomes the hero, the savior, the sacrificial figure who mediates between heaven and earth. Having provided the conventional consolation, Updike resorts to a Greek sentence to describe the death of Chiron. Translated, the sentence reads,

> And having received an incurable wound, he went off to the cave. And he willingly went there to die; and although he was immortal and thus not able to die, when Prometheus exchanged fates with him, in order that Chiron might die in his stead, then the Centaur died.

The inclusion of the Greek sentence between Chiron's final word, *"Now,"* and the terminal statement, "Chiron accepted death," is a way of finally thrusting the novel back into the classical, primitive archetypes of the race. The story is not merely a myth retold, or a tribute to a good and noble man of our time; rather, it is an *old* story, originally told in Greek. It is the story of all sacrificial heroes who endure suffering and death for other men. It is the story, for example, of all fathers who have worked hard and devoted themselves to duty in order that their sons might have better lives than they have had.

Like Lycidas, who becomes a "genius of the shore," Chiron becomes the constellation Sagittarius. Apotheosis completes the novel as a pastoral elegy.

Thus, *The Centaur* achieves its aesthetic unity and thematic wholeness through the adaptation of elements of the traditional pastoral elegy. It is a brilliant and a bold adaptation; and, in its own way, the novel ranks with John Milton's adaptations of pastoral and epic modes. Updike follows the Horatian injunction that the artist improve on his models. And I take it that the Horatian idea of improvement is partly a matter of historical immediacy—that is, making a tradition valid and significant *for one's own time,* a transmutation rather than a translation. John Milton did this in writing a "Christian pastoral elegy"; John Updike does this in writing what might be called an "existentialist pastoral elegy." Both *Lycidas* and *The Centaur* are eloquent tributes to the validity of the prototypic form. This process of adapting the conventions of the pastoral elegy to a contemporary theme is, itself, an American tradition aligned to Walt Whitman's "When Lilacs Last in the Dooryard Bloom'd" and to James Agee's *A Death in the Family.* For example, Updike's substitution of a newspaper obituary for the traditional expression of communal mourning is not greatly different from Whitman's substituting a funeral train for the traditional flower-decked bier. The substitutions are alike in spirit and in kind.

Although he employs a version of the pastoral elegy for the unifying structure of *The Centaur,* Updike deals with the pastoral and anti-pastoral theme in still another way in the novel. He continues the old pattern of the primary tensions between rural and urban values—the tensions first presented in the earlier *Olinger Stories* and in *Rabbit, Run.* First, the Caldwell Farm is the same one we earlier encountered in "Pigeon Feathers." And it is the one we later encounter in *Of the Farm.* In very real ways, the mother and father in the story "Pigeon Feathers" are the mother and father in *The Centaur,* and the young son is the same. Updike's preoccupation with reconciling opposites (heaven and earth, masculine and feminine, urban and rural, for example) is further developed in *The Centaur* by the facts that the intellec-

tual, heroic Chiron is married to Ceres, the goddess of the harvest
and the earth. Ceres (or Demeter) is mentioned more than any
other diety in the Theocritan *Idyls*. Half man and half horse, the
Centaur is, by his very nature, a conciliatory and unifying creature—embodying the best of two worlds. Primarily a teacher,
scholar, and intellectual, he travels between the worlds of matter
and the worlds of mind and spirit. Symbolically, he daily com-
mutes from the farm to his teaching job in town. His marriage to
Ceres is as essential to his horse's body as the academic world is
to his man's torso. And he loves his wife, the earth, even as he
shudders at her earthiness. In the realistic sections of the novel—
i.e., those where the hero is clearly George Caldwell, rather than
the Centaur Chiron—we find attitudes toward nature which seem
to be contradictions. For example, Caldwell loves his wife, but
hates the farm; he advises, "Don't take an animal out of nature,"
but he also tells his wife, "I hate nature. It reminds me of death."
These attitudes *are* contradictory; but they are contradictions
consistent with the basic contradictions which the Centaur embodies as half horse, half man. In a way, the Centaur, in both the
Greek tradition and in Updike's adaptation, strangely represents
the harmony of human and animal realms, rather than the conflict between them.

Chapter 2 of the novel realistically describes the life on the
farm. Narrating the life to his mistress, Peter refuses to idealize
or pastoralize that rural life. Still, it is one of the most beautiful
portions of the novel; here we see affection and human interaction which cannot be found in the urban environment, at least
in the rarefied ether of Olinger-Olympus. To the extent that
Peter, as narrator, is looking back on the *entirety* of agrarian life
(including both the farm and Olinger) from the standpoint of
the alienated New York artist, the chapter is idyllic—like all the
Olinger stories. It becomes a lament for something lost. But, at
the same time, the farm is a reality *because* it is ugly as well as
beautiful, as the Centaur himself is a beautiful grotesque. Whereas "the land represented purity" to the mother, it represented "rot
and excrement" to Peter. As in "Pigeon Feathers," the mother is
associated with the feminine element, the earth, "Mother Ge."
The son and the father revolt against the farm; mind and thought
are masculine in Updike's fiction.

But the boy is perfectly willing to celebrate nature in the *ideal*

—that is, pastorally. In the way that he had been repelled by the brutal "nature lesson" in the museum basement, he associates the real land and farming with "rot and excrement." In order to be made meaningful and unchaotic, nature for Peter must be transformed into art. On the morning before he and his father leave the farm for the three-day sojourn in the city, Peter contemplates a juvenile painting he had made of his old backyard, the yard belonging to the house in Olinger where the family had lived before moving to the country. The picture and Peter's feelings about it suggest the pastoral attitude: the artist and the pastoralist enjoy the ordered grace of a painted or created backyard more than the "rot and excrement" of "the land." Peter admires the painted landscape because it is a "potential fixing of a few passing seconds." This comment on the purpose of art—the purposefully firm "potential fixing of a few passing seconds"—is as good an explanation of John Updike's Olinger stories and his fundamental lyricism as any reader or critic should desire; likewise, it is an adequate explanation of the aesthetics of Theocritan *Idyls.* At the end of *The Centaur,* the return of Peter and his father to the mother's farm, after staying in town three days, is connected with Peter's insight about art and nature: feverishly, the boy thinks,

> The stone bare wall was a scumble of umber; my father's footsteps thumbs of white in white. I knew what this scene was—a patch of Pennsylvania in 1947—and yet I did not know, was in my softly fevered state mindlessly soaked in a rectangle of colored light. I burned to paint it, just like that, in its puzzle of glory; it came upon me that I must go to Nature disarmed of perspective and stretch myself like a large transparent canvas upon her in the hope that, my submission being perfect, the imprint of a beautiful and useful truth would be taken.   [p. 218]

Prometheus is to be freed from his rock by Chiron's sacrifice; and he must be freed for some heroic task. In the novel, the equation of Peter with the artist suggests that the creation of Art is that heroic task. In several ways, the character of Peter Prometheus is a "Portrait of the Artist as a Young Man," and he is like James Joyce's portrait of Stephen Dedalus—even to the extent of directly associating the artist in our time with the classical hero. Updike's *Olinger Stories* can be seen as forerunners to the epic-idyllic sweep of the surrealistic novel *The Centaur,* rather in the way Joyce's *Portrait of the Artist as a Young Man* can be seen as a forerunner to *Ulysses.* And both authors employ adaptations of classical mythology in their works. But in the way that Joyce's fiction as a whole is peculiarly Irish, Updike's fiction as a whole is peculiarly American—and that means that Updike must handle the "agrarian myth" in some way; he handles it by making it part of the far-reaching pastoral and anti-pastoral pattern in his fiction.

The matter of art is also related to Peter's hatred of "the land" in other passages in the book. This hatred of real farms and "the land" is perhaps more an "anti-agrarian" attitude than an "anti-pastoral" attitude. But, by the same token, Updike's refusal to idealize the farm itself (with its lack of plumbing, its chill and bleakness in winter, its inconveniences) is an element of anti-pastoralism in the book. Peter and his father flee "the land" each morning; on one symbolic level, this is flight from the femininity of matter (Ceres and the earth) to the masculinity of mind and spirit (Mount Olympus, the classroom, heaven). Peter's hatred of "the land" can be seen as a flight from his mother's domination—rather in the way Huck Finn's flight from "the land" is also flight from the domination of Miss Watson and the Widow Douglas. It is Peter's mother who arranges for those brutal "nature lessons" in the basements of museums and churches. And Peter escapes those stifling lessons on "cattle diseases and corn pests" by fleeing to his book of Vermeer reproductions. Nature acted upon by art (the idealizing pastoral norm) is preferable to raw nature (the realistic and anti-pastoral norm).

The daily flight into Olinger-Olympus is associated with the safety of turning from the rutted dirt road onto the "firm macadam" of the highway. Highly symbolic, the action of either leaving the dirt road or turning onto it is always a clue to Updike's theme: for example, the first line of *Of the Farm* reads, "We turned off the Turnpike onto a macadam highway, then off the macadam onto a pink dirt road." In *The Centaur,* the pattern is especially complex. Although the son and father flee in the mornings, they look forward to returning in the evenings. Since Olinger is Mount Olympus, and therefore a version of "heaven," the daily trips back and forth from the farm suggest an integrated shuttling and familiarity with both heaven and earth, mind and matter, the "inconceivable creation" and the "conceivable creation." In addition, returning to the farm is like returning to the past—it is temporal as well as spatial. The mother, Ceres, symbolically wants to break the new red plastic clock her husband has bought for her. She hates time, because the earth is timeless; she, like her farm and all it stands for, is a physical negation of the passage of time. Representing matter, she cannot be destroyed, but merely change in form, through the slow, clockless processes of erosion and decay, and subsequent re-composition and rebirth.

In his foreword to the *Olinger Stories,* Updike comments on his "Olinger Theme"; speaking of the collected stories, he says,

> Not an autobiography, they have made one impossible. In the last of them, Olinger has become "like a town in a Fable"; and in my novel *The Centaur,* by turning Olinger explicitly into Olympus, I intended to say the final word, and farewell. Perhaps I exaggerate; it is an inherited fault.

The "final word and farewell" to the memory of his youth and innocence requires the epic metaphors found in *The Centaur.* Employing a technique fundamental to a comic mode (i.e., mock-epic,), he tempers and molds the simple story of Peter and George Caldwell into the epic-idyllic story of Prometheus and Chiron. Aware that the elevation of rural rustics into heroic sophisticates is a tricky business, he follows Thoreau's technique of smiling first—of making the analogies and metamorphoses so striking and absurd that the reader's own imagination is engaged from the beginning, where the wounded Chiron walks down the hall and defecates in front of the high school trophy case.

Making the high school principal Zeus and the girls' gym teacher Aphrodite is the kind of shocking artistic boldness that we find in Thoreau's *Walden,* where Thoreau makes the weeds of his bean patch into an epic army. In art, camels are often easier to swallow than gnats, and considerably more palatable. Then, after hitting the reader with his farfetched analogies, Updike structures the entire novel around the conventions of the traditional pastoral elegy—complete with the list of formal subjects, and versions of highly stock language. The result is *not* mock-epic and comic. Rather, because of the structural significance of the four interspersed "touchstone chapters," the novel retains the eloquence and dignity of an elegy. If there is any fundamental irony within the novel, it is not that Olinger becomes Olympus, and that George Caldwell is explicitly metamorphosed into the heroic Centaur; rather, it is that human beings so easily overlook genuine heroism when they see it. The difference between genuine heroism and psuedo-heroism can be demonstrated by comparing Rabbit Angstrom with George Caldwell. Rabbit sees himself as a questing hero and is considered such by some of his contemporaries; in reality, he is a sentimental antihero, a kind of parody of the real thing. On the other hand, George Caldwell is a decent, self-effacing, humble, plodding school teacher, capable of love, sacrifice, duty, and compassion. Like Apollo disguised as Admetus' slave, and like provincial rustics born in stables, Caldwell *is* the genuine hero who frees Prometheus. Rabbit Angstrom, on his nearsighted quest for heroship, becomes a destructive moral anarchist associated with death. George Caldwell, in his plodding daily commitment to duty and work, and in his capacity for love and sacrifice, becomes Chiron, who gives life and freedom to Prometheus. Rabbit Angstrom is a miniscule, scared little animal, a pathetic cipher. George Caldwell is *The Centaur,* the brightest constellation in the heavens.

In *The Centaur* John Updike sings an epic paean and a pastoral lament, and the songs mysteriously emerge as one melody with two sets of words.

A Note on Character in *The Centaur*

by Martin Price

In *The Centaur* John Updike superimposes the myth of Chiron on the situation of George Caldwell, a high school teacher in a small Pennsylvania town. Caldwell has no trust in himself, nor does he have even the tenacity of ego that demands reassurance. He goes about his life apologetically, expecting scorn and often receiving it. The strain of facing his classes or his principal demands all his effort, and he clearly wants to slip out from under the effort into death. At fifty he has exceeded his own expectation of life (his father died at forty-nine), and he is convinced that he is dying of cancer.

Caldwell, his doctor tells him, has never come to terms with his body. "You believe in the soul. You believe your body is like a horse you get up on and ride for a while and then get off." Caldwell's wife remarks testily on the kind of man who hates sex, and we see him, as he plunges in hysterical pain toward the close of a classroom lecture, overcome by a horrified vision of fornication all about him: "the whole room smelled like a stable." Olinger High is no country for old men, or for men of fifty who have chosen to die. Caldwell feels pity rather than passion; he can entertain all points of view, suffer all kinds of guilt or remorse. There is nothing left in himself to assert or impose.

Caldwell cannot afford to die, however. His fifteen-year-old son needs his help, and the novel studies their relationship over three days when they are held together by a series of accidents. The son, Peter, has his own quarrel with his body; he is afflicted with a skin disease whose scaling he tries to cover up, until he comes at last to learn that it doesn't matter as much to his girl as to himself. Peter is both impatient with his father and devoted to him, and he is unnerved by the threat of his father's death. He is the Prometheus for whom Chiron, tormented by a wound that will never heal, gives up immortal life in atonement.

The portrait of George Caldwell is quite remarkable. With fine precision Updike shows us pain turning into sweetness, as it might so readily into something else. The cheerful inanity of Caldwell's words somehow conveys the full range of his feelings: the pain, the helplessness, the incredulity, the outward-turned pity and warmth, "the sudden white laughter that like heat lightning bursts in an atmosphere where souls are trying to serve the impossible." Presumably, Caldwell's gift is to bring God's infinite mercy ("I can't see how it's infinite if it never changes anything at all," he exclaims) down to earth in the only form it can take. Having learned that "All joy belongs to the Lord," Caldwell has the power to recognize it wherever it occurs and to sustain it in others.

But, fine as the portrait is, the mythical dimension hardly seems to deepen it. The myths, as Updike uses them, are too fluid to give form to the novel. They keep before us suggestions of a profound life that takes on the improbable incarnation of Olinger High, and they remind us that the actual is always in some sense improbable. Their language, with its ironically fulsome Lang-Leaf-Myers tone, serves to heighten the actual idiom, like Caldwell's, into which it must be translated. The example of Joyce may lie behind Updike's book, but the result is rather more like Thornton Wilder at his most benign, where the effect of ironic juxtaposition is to soften focus and magnify the actual by means of a gentle blur.

Shrine and Sanctuary: *Of the Farm*

by Edward P. Vargo

American novels in which the land itself becomes a character generally flow out of our experience in the open spaces west of the Mississippi. In the midwestern farm novels of Ole Rölvaag or Willa Cather, the land takes on the role of realistic antagonist or fructifier of life. When Alexandra Bergson of *O Pioneers!* looks to the land "with love and yearning," the land brings forth harvests of human passion and aspiration as well as of grain. Recalling his first experience of Nebraska's warm earth, Jim Burden of *My Antonia* equates happiness with dissolution into its completeness and vastness. In *The Professor's House*, Father Duchene reveals a sense of mystery around man's struggle with Nature when he speaks to Tom Oatland about the former hardy residents of the lofty mesa: "Like you, I feel a reverence for this place. Wherever humanity has made that hardest of all starts and lifted itself out of mere brutality, is a sacred spot." Man may be brutalized in his struggle for survival or defeated in his confrontations with the land. But more often than not, he must actively accept the earth to become a complete human person and to transcend the earth's limited yet inspiring force.

The New Mexican novels of Frank Waters and William Eastlake, less ground-tied and more aware of the sky as transcendent being, develop an "out and up" view of salvation. A kind of mysticism grows out of the meeting with the high plains and vistas of the Southwest. William Eastlake, for example, concludes *Portrait of an Artist with 26 Horses* in this manner: "They flew lightly and all together up a gaudy-thrown profusion of raging color and the sharp high scent of Indian Country until they topped out on the end of a day, on a New Mexican sky infinity of burnished and dying gold." Leaving behind the physical world, the low-lying place of trials, they share in the expansiveness which is part of a religious experience.

The eastern land which is the place of action in *Of the Farm* is not the open country of Nebraska or New Mexico. It is the same compact Pennsylvania countryside which is the setting for the Olinger stories. It is not a land from which man must wrest his existence, but a fallow land of no particular use, in danger of being encroached by housing developments for suburban living. Like the Indian country of the Southwest, this Pennsylvania Dutch country is permeated with presences. It emanates a sense of transcendence and wholeness, out of its integration with the Pennsylvania sky, which an older generation could substitute for belief in God, but with which a younger generation can hardly communicate.

Filled with many of the same memories, *Of the Farm* appears to be a sequel to *The Centaur*. Joey Robinson's mother is an aged version of Peter's mother; her tales of how her father lost his money during the depression, of how she had managed the move back to the farm, of how her husband, a school teacher, and her son Joey hated the farm, are reminiscent of elements in *The Centaur*. Likewise the throatclearings, dignified gestures, and love for newspapers of Joey's dead grandfather, and the clowning, restlessness, and frantic activity of his dead father recall Peter's grandfather and father. Like *The Centaur, Of the Farm* presents an action that occurs over a weekend, from Friday through Sunday. Where one of the primary concerns in *The Centaur* was the investigation of the relationship between the adolescent Peter and his father, a central problem in this novel is the relationship between Joey, now in early middle age, and his mother. Where the adult Peter was an artist with a Negro mistress, Joey is recently divorced and now married to the woman with whom he had been running a protracted affair. Where *The Centaur* dealt with man's exercise of freedom in relation to God and the sky, *Of the Farm* deals with man's exercise of freedom more in relation to other human beings and the earth. *Of the Farm* continues the theme of *The Centaur,* presenting a solution to the struggle between desiring freedom and giving love different from the sacrifice of Chiron for Prometheus.

At first reading, what ostensibly happens on this particular weekend seems to warrant the accusations of thinness in plot and evasion of responsibility so often charged against Updike's fiction. Joey Robinson, with his new wife and her eleven-year-old son Richard, visits his widowed mother, now living alone on her Olinger farm. Over the weekend Joey will mow the field which she is no longer strong enough to do; meanwhile, his second wife and his mother will get acquainted. Upon the arrival of Joey's reconstituted family, Mrs. Robinson feeds them, and the adults talk into the night. On Saturday, Joey begins to mow the field, in fulfillment of regulations from the soil bank, but an afternoon rainstorm forces him to stop prematurely. Richard reads, talks to Grammy (as Mrs. Robinson tells him to call her), mediates the minor differences that arise. Peggy prepares breakfast, does the dishes, sweeps the house, sunbathes, and hoes. Sunday morning, Joey and his mother go to church. On the way home, she has one of her mild attacks, probably brought on by the emotions which she has been experiencing this weekend. As Mrs. Robinson settles down to rest after the doctor's visit, Joey and his family, the field partially mowed, acquaintances set up, bargains made, turn to the city. This is the stuff of ordinary life colored by the pastoral lyricism of Joey's first person narration.

Behind this deceptively static situation, however, an extremely subtle inner activity is in motion. Much of the dialogue of the three adults takes on the characteristics of the trout fisherman's technique: the devious and careful approach, the judgment on how much freedom to give, the setting of the hook before exerting full pressure. This applies to Mrs. Robinson in particular; Peggy is more impatient, blunt, and direct; Joey is usually the fish. As Joey's wife and mother catch him and pull him one way or the other, a delicate emotional balance is constantly being threatened, broken, or re-established. On the side of Joey's mother are his associations with the farm and the past; on the side of his wife are the hopes that he has for his freely chosen future life.

What further enriches this struggle over personal freedom and allegiances is its placement into a context of cyclical structures. Through the Friday-to-Sunday time span, with its freedom from the responsibilities of the ordinary work week, the novel has the potential for developing a sense of holiday similar to that which surrounds the annual poorhouse fair. This possibility is aborted, however, by the point in the cycle of the seasons at which Joey makes his return to the farm: early fall, the season of oncoming death, visible on the land and in the growing weakness of his mother. Peggy's menstrual cycle, analogous to those of the moon and earth, in juxtaposition with the notion of womanhood expressed in the Sunday sermon, emphasizes woman's role in the continuous renewal of life and the conquering of death. Finally, the physical mementos, the reminiscences, the associations which present sights and actions arouse, all lead Joey to return to the past, to the values of his former way of life. "Past relationships evoked by the farm influence present ones. Joey's father and first wife, though physically absent, ...become palpable as sights, sounds and smells trigger Joey's memory. ...As in James' *The Turn of the Screw,* those absent roam the house exerting pressure, influencing decisions, determining emotional alignments."[1]

While these recurrent patterns underlie the entire novel, they are muted in comparison to their use in the previous two novels. Here, these basic elements of ritual are representative of a way of life irrevocably lost to Joey. Through the use of ritual, Harry Angstrom tried to rebel against the materialistic world around him, and George Caldwell, as well as Peter, found a *modus vivendi* to meet alienation. Joey Robinson, by accepting the values of the modern world, has effectively divorced himself from the world in which his mother lives and has practically made it impossible for himself to achieve any transcendent communion through ritual.

The moment that Joey sets foot on the farm, he finds himself in a world where past and present constantly interact. His first sight of his mother is a shock to him; her movements are so slow in comparison to the young woman who had outraced his father from the barn. The old pink blouse that she is wearing brings back to his mind "childhood Easters." Upon entering the house, he sees the gifts that he had sent his mother over the years. Rather than give him pleasure, they confront him with his present corruption; his expensive gifts have been cheap substitutes for the

[1]James R. Lindroth, *"Of the Farm,"* review in *America,* November 27, 1965, p. 692.

giving of his love. With each of his visits home, Joey has increasingly resented the pictures of himself, the schoolboy gifts and certificates on display: "I was so abundantly memorialized it seemed I must be dead." He cannot shake the impression that "the invisible mementos and objects around me seemed gathered into the intense expectance of the votive implements in a shrine."

One of the most vivid presences in this "shrine" to the past is that of Joey's first wife, Joan. He immediately notices that a formal portrait of her, which had been taken twelve years ago at his mother's request, had been removed from its usual place on the living room wall. But when he puts Richard to bed that evening, Joey discovers the picture above the bed. Attempting to evade Richard's question about the "attractive girl" on the wall, Joey can only shakily explain, "'This house is too full of me.'" Coming downstairs with the image of Joan still fresh in his mind, he finds himself comparing his mother's inferior position at the sink with Peggy to the dominant position in housework that she insisted upon with Joan. When his gaze returns to the photograph while he is talking with Richard on the second night, it takes on the character of a religious picture: "She seemed engaged in some vigil, her eyes uplifted, her arm glowing; and it seemed unlikely that her hope, whatever it was, would be rewarded here in this old lonely farmhouse." This saint-like after-presence of his first wife is similar to the remote, inward, and cool beauty suggestive of romantic poetry that attracted him to Joan in the first place.

Although there are no photographs of Joey's father, his presence is also very real. Shaving with his father's razor on Saturday morning and nicking the curve of his jawbone just as his father often did, Joey enters into communion with his father in a way that he had never experienced before. He gets into his father's skin, remembers the sheepish smile with which he used to come down the stairs, realizes for the first time that his father's clumsy shaving "was one of the many small self-abuses with which my father placated the specter of poverty." The sharpness of the knives in the kitchen, while surprising Joey, also reminds him that his "father had cared about knives and tools, and might have made a good craftsman had he not been expected, like me, to work with intangibles."

Everything about the house leads Joey back to the past. Even something as insignificant as "a rhomboid of sun mottled with the slightly shivering shadows of grape leaves" on the kitchen floor strikes a resonance in him. "This patch of sun had been here, just this shape, twenty years ago, morning after morning." When he is removing his wet clothes upstairs, he feels that he is in "a glade of ghosts." The spot on the floor where his grandmother had last fallen invokes her death. The window through which his grandfather had watched for the mailman gives substance to the old man. But the most powerful reminder of his past life in this house is the type of conversation that will also be significant on this weekend: "Talk in our house was a continuum sensitive at all points of past and present and tirelessly harking back and readjusting itself, as if seeking some state of equilibrium finally free of irritation."

In such an atmosphere, Joey feels himself being pulled into the mythology which his mother has created for the values that have meaning in her life and for the kind of life that she wants Joey himself to remember and continue. He understands the complexities of her thinking: "As primitive worshippers invest the indifferent universe with pointed intentions, so my mother superstitiously read into the animate world, including infants and dogs, a richness of motive that could hardly be there—though like believers everywhere, she had a way of making her environment supply corroboration." He also realizes that Peggy, who shares nothing of their past life, cannot possibly be in sympathy with this thinking: "My mother within the mythology she had made of her life was like a mathematician who, having decreed certain severely limited assumptions, performs feats of warping and circumvention and paradoxical linkage that an outside observer, unrestricted to the plane of their logic, would find irksomely arbitrary. And, with the death of my father and my divorce of Joan, there was no inside observer left but myself—myself, and the adoring dogs" (Rpt. New York: Fawcett World Library, pp. 22, 28).

Joan and his father have been drawn into his mother's platonic esthetic of Nature and Art. As his mother reminisces about the experiences that he and his first wife shared on this farm, however, Joey is startled to discover that his mother is incorporating him in her myth in such a way that it will separate him from his present wife who is very different in character from Joan. To avoid this distancing, he attempts to qualify her words and later, after a scene in which his mother deliberately smashes some dishes, he also suggests that she smash all the pictures of himself with which she has filled the house. In a sense, his present life with Peggy demands an annihilation of his past.

Central to Mrs. Robinson's mythology is the special attitude which she bears to the farm. The house itself has become a kind of shrine to her dreams for Joey. More significantly, the entire farm is not just a tract of unused land; it is a sanctuary, a sacred place. At his first glimpse of the unused land, young Richard poses the crucial question that has often tempted Joey to have the land sold, "What's the point of a farm nobody farms?" Told to ask Mrs. Robinson that question, Richard receives an unexpectedly pleasant answer. "'Why,' she said rapidly, 'I guess that's the point, that nobody farms it. Land is like people, it needs a rest. Land is just like a person, except that it never dies, it just gets very tired.'" For Mrs. Robinson, as for the mothers in "Pigeon Feathers" and *The Centaur,* the farm has a living quality; man and the soil mutually mirror each other, though man will not live forever. Even more, the farm is her sacrament, her means of communication with God, her handle on human wholeness: "'If I couldn't see and touch Him here on the farm, if I lived in New York City, I don't know if I'd believe or not. You see, that's why it's so important that the farm be kept. People will forget that there could be anything except stones and glass and subways'" (p. 55).

Stimulated by the boy's fascination, Mrs. Robinson even weaves a fantasy in which she and Richard will develop the farm into a *"people* sanctuary" for refugees from the trials of modern existence. Still later on Saturday, when Richard speaks of his boredom in the city, Mrs. Robinson expresses the pleasure, tinged with nostalgic sadness, which she experiences in the rhythms of the year on the farm: "'Well I don't wonder,' my mother said, 'living in that air-conditioned city where the seasons are all the same. Here on my farm every week is different, every day is a surprise.'" In fact and fantasy, the farm is "a kind of resonator of the sacred" for Mrs. Robinson. It is a center in the middle of chaos. It is a fixed point in the "formless fluidity of profane space." It makes possible communication between heaven and earth. It gives wholeness and orientation to those who are open to its beauties. This Nature religion, a fusion of Mrs. Robinson's vague notion of God and her dedication to the land, is an inheritance from which Joey has excluded himself through his life choices. He is no longer able to "touch" God.

As the weekend wears on, two confused motives emerge for the clashes that Mrs. Robinson precipitates: the fear of her approaching death and her distaste for Peggy. In her utopian people sanctuary, Richard was to "mark the diseased people for destruction." When Peggy remarks that it sounds more like a concentration camp, Mrs. Robinson reacts with the tearful remark that "'people must be told when they're no longer fit to live, they mustn't be left to guess at it, because it's something nobody can tell herself.'" Coupled with the fear of her physical death is Mrs. Robinson's frustration over the death of her dreams for Joey. She wanted him to leave Olinger, to become a poet, to stay married to the esthetic Joan. In the parrying between Mrs. Robinson and Peggy, Joey's mother "swept forward with a fabulous counter-system of which I was the center, the only child, the obscurely chosen, the poet, raped, ignorantly, from my ideally immaterial and unresisting wife and hurled into the shidepoke sin of adultery and the eternal damnation of my children's fatherlessness" (p. 100). Mrs. Robinson is convinced that Peggy will bring about her death in the next twelve months as well as the destruction of her son Joey. In his eagerness to mirror and answer his mother's fright at her coming death, Joey finds himself agreeing with her: "*Ruin.* It pleased me to feel myself sinking, smothered, lost, forgotten, obliterated in the depths of the mistake which my mother, as if enrolling my fall in her mythology, enunciated: 'You've taken a vulgar woman to be your wife'" (p. 104).

Just as Mrs. Robinson has created her own mythology, through which she incorporates her son into her own private demesne, so Peggy also has her own mythology. She appropriates Joey through her sexuality. Her opposition to the life-style of Mrs. Robinson becomes clear when Peggy asks Joey's mother what she gave her husband in return for the farm that he self-sacrificingly gave her. Peggy is angered by Mrs. Robinson's answer that she gave her husband his "freedom" because she considers this a failure to possess Joey's father; "it had touched the sore point within her around which revolved her own mythology, of women giving themselves to men, of men in return giving women a reason to live." As Howard Morrall Harper, Jr., has pointed out,

Peggy's mythology is akin to D. H. Lawrence's idea of sexual polarity. Her gift to Joey has been "to let him be a man." Finally, in the climactic contest of words between the two women on Saturday evening, all the points of Peggy's dissatisfaction with Mrs. Robinson as a woman, wife and mother, merge in one massive complaint: "My mother had undervalued and destroyed my father, had been inadequately a 'woman' to him, had brought him to a farm which was in fact her giant lover, and had thus warped the sense of the masculine within me, her son."

Peggy's belief that women are to give themselves to their men and that men are to possess their women finds concrete expression in her marital relationship with Joey. While Joey always felt as if he were smothering in sexual intercourse with Joan, with Peggy he feels a sense of "pelvic amplitude," of sky, space, and freedom. Peggy is truly his possession; her largeness is a sign of his weath. Joey takes pride in his ownership, and Peggy apparently discovers a renewed purpose for life in the way he takes her. During their adulterous affair, she had already explained to him how he succeeded where her husband McCabe failed to make her feel like a woman. *"You act as though you own me. It's wonderful. It's not something a man can do deliberately. You just do it."* So then, both Peggy and Joey interpret sexual possession as a freeing agent. The platonic ideals of Joan and McCabe are smothering in the bedroom.

These clashing mythologies, the sacrality of the land and sexual polarity, underlie the resentments which Mrs. Robinson and Peggy feel toward each other and which occasionally burst into verbal differences. Much of the tension, however, simply grows out of misunderstandings and misinterpretations, innocent enough, even foreseeable to Joey. When Mrs. Robinson speaks of her own father as "a pretty ugly customer," Peggy feels obliged to remark how fond Richard is of his father. Her failure to see Mrs. Robinson's use of the word *ugly* as a term of endearment irritates Joey. The ideological differences come through more clearly in conversations such as the one about Joey's father. Peggy cannot accept "the frame of assumptions and tolerances in which my mother's description of my father's anguished restlessness as 'his freedom' was beautifully congruous." Puzzled, she can only ask a further question, "Can you give a person freedom?"

Under Peggy's frontal attacks, Mrs. Robinson's barbs have to give way to more direct statement. When Joey's mother attempts to get Peggy's permission for Richard to drive the tractor with the gently sardonic question, "'How can Richard manage my people sanctuary if he can't drive a tractor?'" Peggy cuts in with a gratuitously ruthless reflex, "'He's not going to manage anything for you. He's not going to be another Joey.'" With her subtlety crushed, Mrs. Robinson is reduced to the weak reply, "'Dear Peggy, one Joey is enough for me.'" Even when Mrs. Robinson speaks of Joey's three children by his previous marriage, whom she is convinced she will never see again, Peggy accuses her of trying to needle Joey and herself.

Mrs. Robinson does have her moments of ascendancy, however. When she feels that Peggy is jealous of the relationship that is growing between herself and Richard, she boldly states her grievances about Peggy: "She takes my grandchildren from me, she turns my son into a gray-haired namby-pamby, and now she won't let me show this poor disturbed child a little affection, which he badly needs!" Although Peggy strives to maintain the upper hand by a remark about Mrs. Robinson's treatment of her husband, Joey's mother manages to sink Peggy into tears with the counterthrust: "'Poor Joan had ideas as to how I should do my wash, but at least she never offered to revise my marriage for me.'" At this point, Joey, who normally remains a passive observer of the conflict, comes to his wife's aid: "'You ask for advice, for pity. You carry yourself as if you've made a terrible mistake. You pretend you emasculated Daddy and when some innocent soul offers to agree with you you're hurt'" (pp. 84-85).

So the tensions emerge, grow, break forth, and subside. They reach a kind of climax on Saturday evening when Mrs. Robinson deliberately breaks some dishes in the kitchen because she hears Richard whispering in the living room. No longer attempting any subtleties, Mrs. Robinson speaks out of her frustration: "'I'm tired of being hated. I've lost everything but this child's respect and I don't want him whispering.'" Peggy, just as tired of what she terms "so much neuroticism," decides to return to the city that very evening. Within an hour's time, however, Richard convinces his wife to stay and, between eight-thirty and ten, the two women engage in the kind of conversation that was the purpose of the visit, even though its tone restlessly moves from disagreement to peaceful reminiscence. The dialogue, as Joey the non-participant (reading a book) perceives it, is a quest into the past for the identities of himself and his father: "Two exasperatingly clumsy spirits were passing, searching for, and repassing one another; deeper and deeper their voices dived into the darkness that was each to the other, in pursuit of shadows that I supposed were my father and myself." In this clash of personalities and mythologies, each is testing her own freedom, attempting to curtail the freedom of the other, being forced to recognize the other's freedom in the end.

While Joey seems to be the subject rather than an agent of the conflict, it is through his sensibility that we experience the entire weekend. Through his narration we become aware of his own conflicting emotions as well as of the rivalry over him. He is convinced that his mother had ruined his first marriage, and he wants her to be polite to Peggy on this visit. In bed with Peggy on the first night, he blurts out the resentment which he feels against his mother: "'I'm thirty-five and I've been through hell and I don't see why that old lady has to have such a hold over me. It's ridiculous. It's degrading.'" He is still not free of his mother; neither is he totally secure in his wife. One of his fears, renewed after he learns that Peggy had intercourse with McCabe after their divorce, is that he had been tricked into marrying someone that McCabe was glad to discard. He also senses a certain lack of accommodation toward his mother's foibles on Peggy's part. In the "collision of darknesses" of which the Saturday evening conversation is composed, he feels that his "mother's darkness was nurturing whereas Peggy's was cold, dense, and metallic. Surely in becoming my wife she had undertaken, with me, the burden of mothering my mother, of accommodating herself to the warps of that enclosing spirit."

He sees the farm as a trap and a menace to this marriage. But he also comes to appreciate the farm as a symbol of his mother's freedom, of the freedom she thinks that she has given him, and of their common heritage. On this weekend, Joey responds to his participation in nature with the breathlessness of a primitive man, despite his avowed dislike for the farm. At an outside pump, he enters into mysteries beyond Olinger: "I drank from the tin measuring cup that my mother had carelessly left on the bench one day and that under the consecration of time had become a

fixture here. Its calibrated sides became at my lips the walls of
a cave where my breath rustled and cold well water swayed.
Against my shut lids the blue sky pressed as red; I would gladly
have drowned" (p. 52). A sense of enchantment, with sexual overtones, overcomes Joey when the rain begins to fall upon him in
the field. Everything speaks to him a language beyond the material: "Moving in air, I feel even dust, which makes me sneeze,
as the sofa's angel, and pollen as immanent flowers."

The central episode of the novel, in which Joey early combines
the two mythologies, is the mowing of the meadow, a simple
physical act which is also "a complex symbol of filial piety, the
sexual act, the fulfillment of seasonal rhythms and the foreshadowing of the death of the mother."[2] On the night before the
mowing, Joey reflects upon his wife in terms of possession of earth
and sky. Peggy, "surveyed from above, gives an impression of
terrain, of a wealth whose ownership imposes upon my own body
a sweet strain of extension; entered, she yields a variety of landscapes. ... Over all, like a sky, withdrawn and cool, hangs—
hovers, stands, *is*— is the sense of her consciousness, of her com-
posure, of a noncommittal witnessing that preserves me from
claustrophobia through any descent however deep" (p. 39). Joey
then floats into a dream that used to recur while he was considering
divorce from Joan. In the dream Peggy, "so in love with the farm
and so eager to redeem, with the sun of her presence, the years
of dismal hours I had spent here," brings joy to his existence on
the farm. In dream and reflection, redemption and wholeness
are his through Peggy.

These thoughts influence Joey's reaction to the actual mowing.
The manner in which he attacks the job amounts to a rite of war,
of taking possession of the land. His mother imitated the motions
of love when she mowed the field, tracing its borders in an embrace and ending with a small central triangle of grass. Joey slices
up the middle "in one ecstatic straight thrust" and then whittles
away at each side with various maneuvers. He becomes so completely and intimately absorbed in his rhythmic movements that
his communion with nature is transformed into communion with
his wife:

[2]Peter Buitenhuis, "The Mowing of a Meadow," review of *Of the Farm* in
The New York Times Book Review, November 14, 1965, p. 4.

Black-eyed susans, daisy fleabane, toadflax, goldenrod, butter-and-eggs each flower of which was like a tiny dancer leaping, legs together, scudded past the tractor wheels. Stretched scatterings of flowers moved in a piece, like the heavens, constellated by my wheels' revolution, on my right; and lay as drying fodder on my left. Midges existed in stationary clouds that, though agitated by my interruption, did not follow me, but resumed their self-encircling conversation. Crickets sprang crackling away from the wheels; butterflies loped through their tumbling universe and bobbed above the flattened grass as the hands of a mute concubine would examine, flutteringly, the corpse of her giant lover. The sun grew higher. The metal hood acquired a nimbus of heat waves that visually warped each stalk. The tractor body was flecked with foam and I, rocked back and forth on the iron seat shaped like a woman's hips, alone in nature, as hidden under the glaring sky as at midnight, excited by destruction, weightless, discovered in myself a swelling which I idly permitted to stand, thinking of Peggy. My wife is a field.   [pp. 47-48]

Although Joey does not touch God, the sexual transcendence that he feels comes very close to a union with the cosmos. This experience makes it possible for Joey to attempt a harmonization of the farm with his marriage later in the novel.

Joey attends the Sunday service with his mother for much the same reasons that Harry Angstrom or David Kern in "Churchgoing" attends liturgical services: to regather himself and to renew old ceremonies. The youngish minister, reminiscent of Reverend Eccles, preaches a sermon that offers Joey the possibility of touching God through Peggy as his mother touches Him through her farm. With Genesis 2:18 as his text, the minister presents an exegesis of the creation of Eve, in the course of which he makes several points about the nature of women: that Man and Woman were put upon earth, "not, as some sentimental theologies would have it, to love one another, but to *work* together"; that Woman, taken *out* of Man, is less than equal to man; that Woman, made *after* Man, is the finer and more efficient creation; that Woman is the life-principle for death-oriented Man:

A rib is rounded. Man, with Woman's creation, became confused as to where to turn. With one half of his being he turns toward her, his rib, as if into himself, into the visceral and nostalgic warmth

wherein his tensions find *re*solution in *dis*solution. With his other
half he gazes outward, toward God, along the straight line of infinity. He seeks to *solve* the riddle of his death. Eve does not. In a
sense she does not know death. Her very name, *Hava*, means
"living." Her motherhood answers concretely what men would answer abstractly. But as Christians we know there is no abstract
answer, there is no answer whatsoever apart from the concrete
reality of Christ.   [p. 112]

What the minister further suggests is a recognition of differences, of a necessary partnership in the performing of God's
work on earth. Woman in her very existence reminds man of his
responsibility to be kind as well as to be strong and to believe.
Adam, in naming Eve, accepted this responsibility and tied himself ethically to the earth. In identifying Peggy with "a field,"
Joey has staked out his property, he has tied himself to the earth.
Whether he has accepted the concomitant ethical responsibility
is questionable. When his mother interprets the sermon as an excuse for some woman's pain, he changes the subject.

As mowing the field stirred in Joey the desire to own it instead
of selling it, so the possibility of lingering on to care for his sick
mother after her attack excites him. He sees the farm as numinous.
When Peggy disrupts this vision with the practical suggestion
that his mother will probably need a trained nurse, he suddenly
and angrily realizes that in reality he will be unable to harmonize
his newly found love for the farm with his love for Peggy: "I
knew it was by accident that she had come between me and my
momentary vision of the farm, the farm as mine, in the fall, the
warmth of its leaves and the retreat of its fields and the kind of
infinity of its twigs. ... But my failure to be able to see both her
and the farm at once seemed somehow a failure of hers, a rigidity
that I lived with resentfully, in virtual silence, until at two-thirty
promptly the doctor came, smelling of antiseptic soap and sauer-
kraut" (p. 124).

In the end, even at the bedside of his mother, Joey's thoughts
irresistibly turn to New York, the city of his escape. The weekend was marred by quarrels and now, his mother's attack. The
mowing remains unfinished. In his last words, using their old
allusive and teasing language, Joey speaks to his mother of *our*
farm. Non-committal about what he will do with the farm after
her death, Joey pretends the weekend has changed nothing of

the past. An equilibrium is set. But he knows that he cannot contain both Peggy and the farm, so he is simply evading his true feeling and the decision he has already implicitly made.

The loss of things from his past life haunts Joey throughout the novel. When he notices the geraniums on the window sill of his mother's bedroom, he realizes that their existence depends on his mother's care, and he feels "a thousand such details of nurture about to sink into the earth with her." This sense of loss had already permeated his dream on Saturday night. While mowing in the dream, Joey nicks something that he fears is a nest of pheasant eggs. Upon investigation, he discovers it to be his son Charlie from whom he is separated. But he does not become aware of this at once and sees only "a stunted human being, a hunched homunculus, its head sunk on its chest as if shying from a blow." When he finally recognizes his son, he vows never to be parted from him. Yet in real life he is.

In this sense of losses, *Of the Farm* is a sad and tragic story. Kenneth Hamilton has expressed it well:

> It is not merely that Mary Robinson, who is "of the farm" and of the rich, natural life that it represents, is left alone to die, deprived of grandchildren who might inherit the land she loves. The tragedy is Joey's, who has by his own decision lost his past and given away his children. He recognizes that he cannot "see" both Peggy and the farm at once, so he gives up the farm. Change and death are inevitable on a farm; but there is continuity there, and mutual support between the generations. Joey has lost the right to say "our" of anything. He cannot say to Peggy that Richard is "our" child. He cannot share a common past with her—he does not even know the circumstances that led to Peggy's divorce. ... The links that tie us to nature and to one another have all been broken, and the faith that alone supports human values has been made impossible. Joey the frog who seeks a treasure, has, all unknowingly, sold it cheap.[3]

The drive for power, the pride of possession, has replaced the drive for love and sacrificial sharing in Joey Robinson. ... In his progress toward freedom, he discards one thing after the other. For all practical purposes, he has discarded any sacred commitment to God. By divorce, he has discarded his personal commit-

[3]*John Updike: A Critical Essay* (Grand Rapids, Michigan: William B. Eerdmans, 1967), p. 45.

ments to his first wife and children, though he still has bad dreams about them. He discards the shackles of the past with which his mother tries to bind him. He discards an ideal, transcendental view of life for an earthy sexual view.

In theory, then, this is a novel about freedom. Peggy is the way of escape for Joey from his past, from the world of the farm and from his first wife. But one captivity is simply exchanged for another. Peggy does not offer any real alternative to his mother, as this weekend makes clear. Both women are struggling to gain dominance over Joey, the one through the myth of the sacred past, of Art and Nature, the other through the myth of male owner-ship. Peggy, through the denigration of her own personhood in this myth of male sexual dominance, controls by submission. The openness and freedom which she gives Joey is a temporary illusion.

Joey and Peggy are members of the self-indulgent new gen-eration. They are affluent, selfish, sensuous people who easily confuse sexual attractions with a need for freedom, who dis-regard the needs of others to do what they please. They *exist,* and Updike presents them for what they are. They are not seekers after truth like Harry Angstrom, with whom they otherwise close-ly identify. They are not too concerned with the meaning of life like George and Peter Caldwell. They cannot truly love, because they do not give unselfishly. ... Joey does not understand that *freedom from* is an illusion unless it includes *freedom for.* He is a new kind of leading character for Updike's novels.

Rachael Burchard has considered the characterization of Joey a flawed production in which two distinct voices emerge: the voice of John Updike the narrator in Joey's poetic insights and sensitivity to nature, and the voice of Joey the actor in his banal dialogue and insensitivity to human emotions and need. As a con-sequence, she finds the characterization incredible but suggests that the problem could have been solved if Updike had employed an omniscient point of view instead of first person narration. For me, the disparity between Joey's thoughts and actions is quite ac-ceptable for the simple reason that a sensitivity to beauty in Nature by no means leads automatically to a sensitivity for human beings. A sensitivity to others demands a willingness to care, to sacrifice, to give. Joey responds to beauty only so long as it makes no demands on him. He is not as emancipated from his mother's platonic idealism as he thinks he is. Neither is he as loving as the wife with whom he is sexually infatuated leads him to believe.

Finally, then, the significance of ritual is less obtrusive and more subtle in *Of the Farm* than in any of the previous novels. In the cyclical rhythms of nature with which Mrs. Robinson is in harmony, the total pattern of the universe is presented to us. Her mythology as well as Peggy's, with their opposing views of giving and receiving, is clear enough. What is missing, however, is the sense of celebration that Harry Angstrom craves and through which George Caldwell is able to face life with joy and strength. Although Joey's ritual taking possession of the farm approaches this sense of celebration, there is never any question of his communion with any ultimate reality. He has freely chosen a way of life in harmony with the contemporary world. As a consequence, he refuses to accept any responsibility for his past or for his family, and the refusal kills any ceremonial connection between himself and tradition. The question remains—and it will be given full attention in *Couples*—can belief in heaven persist at all once man has rejected the right order in creation?

Family Quarrels in *Of the Farm*

by Charles Thomas Samuels

Of the Farm offers a complex consideration of nostalgia and of man's relationship to his family. Short, plotted simply enough to be classified a novella, *Of the Farm* is actually Updike's subtlest piece of autobiographical fiction. Though smaller in scope than his masterpiece, *Rabbit, Run,* it is artistically more polished, without taint of obviousness. For Updike's belief that ordinary relationships contain manifold complications, this book provides impressive evidence. In general, Updike's mimetic emphasis makes his fiction peculiarly resistant to summary; *Of the Farm* is the most irreducible of his works.

Its surface seems irreducible by being so meager. When the book first appeared, most reviewers pronounced it uneventful, and its plot is certainly bare:

Since his mother is getting too old to care properly for her farm, Joey Robinson promises to leave Manhattan for a weekend of chores that include mowing the meadow. Returning home with his new, second wife and her adolescent son, he experiences a rivalry between Mrs. Robinson and Peggy so intense as to threaten his marriage. As the weekend wears on, quarrels break out, only to subside without warning. Melodramatically, the mother rages; suddenly "hysteria [falls] from her like a pose." The wife seems daunted, but soon she fights back. On Sunday, Joey takes the old woman to church. His mother had wanted him to retain the farm after she died; now she agrees that it be sold. Soon the city-dwellers will depart.

"Family Quarrels in *Of the Farm*" (editor's title). From *John Updike* by Charles Thomas Samuels (Minneapolis: University of Minnesota Pamphlets on American Writers, no. 79), pp. 22-27. Copyright © 1969 by the University of Minnesota. Reprinted by permission.

What does it all mean? The Sartrean epigraph offers a clue: "Consequently, when, in all honesty, I've recognized that man is a being in whom existence precedes essence, that he is a free being who, in various circumstances, can want only his freedom, I have at the same time recognized that I can want only the freedom of others." To Sartre, freedom means doing; to Updike seeing. To Sartre, we redefine our lives by changing our acts; to Updike, we change our attitudes. But for both writers, the past brings the threat of imprisonment in its potential for rigid definition.

"All misconceptions," Joey Robinson asserts, "are themselves data which have the minimal truth of existing in at least one mind. Truth, my work had taught me, is not something static, a mountain-top that statements approximate like successive assaults of frostbitten climbers. Rather, truth is constantly being formed from the solidification of illusions." The truth of his mother's life had solidified into her shared illusion of their special fate. As the novel progresses, that illusion melts; at its conclusion, Joey is able to remount the stream of life.

Like Allen Dow in "Flight," Joey had been only partly liberated from his mother's influence. "'I've always felt young for my age,'" he tells us by way of introduction; soon we learn why. Entering his house, he habitually "resent[s] how much of myself [is] already here. . . . I [am] so abundantly memorialized it seem[s] I must be dead." Since, like all Updike's sensitive heroes, Joey longs for a kind of ongoing immortality, in which no moment is ever wholly lost, for him, maturation means decay more than growth. Looking at Richard, standing next to Peggy, the boy's mother, Joey becomes jealous, even though Peggy is his wife, for he wishes to possess in her both wife and mother, going to her in Richard's "size."

Drawn to his mother's vision of his promise, Joey has made only frail gestures of self-assertion. He married, but his first marriage failed. He denied his mother's wish that he become a poet, but he lives in the grip of poetic nostalgia. Marrying Peggy was another bid for freedom, but this too is incomplete. That his mother can so challenge his choice shows how little he has made peace with it. That he so fears Peggy's past (both in her child and the husband he suspects she may still love) shows how fervently he seeks the support of total acceptance. Therefore, desiring a perfect corroboration of his own identity, he comes home. But, as Peggy says, it is cowardly to expect either his mother or his wife to give him self-direction.

Rather Joey can only stand on his own if he frees himself from the figure he cuts in both their myths. Mrs. Robinson neglected her husband to devote herself to Joey, for Joey was, so to speak, the objectification of her own self-image. When Peggy charges her with this neglect, and Mrs. Robinson counters by calling it liberation, Joey witnesses the clash of alien perspectives. "I saw," he thinks, "that my mother's describing as a gift her failure to possess my father...had touched the sore point within [Peggy] around which revolved her own mythology, of women giving themselves to men, of men in return giving women a reason to live."

For a time, Joey tries to simulate freedom through the most basic fact of manhood. Conceiving Peggy as a field, he sows the seed of his possession; but in so doing, he takes his wife on his mother's terms. Making of Peggy an ersatz farm, he turns to her for sex, not love, and thus confirms his mother's denigration.

As in "Flight," Updike's hero cannot be free until he accepts the truth about both of his women; for only then will he acknowledge the change that has taken place in himself. His mother is no longer "the swift young" woman of whom he has felt himself deprived. She has "entered, unconsciously, a far territory, the arctic of the old," where her vision of his life will also die. Peggy may be inferior to Mrs. Robinson, but she is Joey's choice and now deserves his loyalty. Time has indeed passed; Joey is a man. Now he must accept a man's responsibilities.

This he does in two scenes, both of which involve the process of revision. First, Joey tells Richard a fairy tale that recalls the similar device in "Should Wizard Hit Mommy?" But in that story the teller is drawn back to his mother's self-referring vision of his character, whereas in this novel Joey uses the fairy tale to express his freedom, his ability to break out of the past. The fairy tale concerns a frog-prince with a watertight skin. One day the prince's self-delight turns to boredom until he learns of a treasure in his guts. "'So he went down a circular staircase out of his head ...and the lower he went, the smaller he got, until finally, just when he was sure he had reached the dungeon where the treasure was, he disappeared!'" But with the return of spring, the frog runs upstairs, throws open his lids, and looks out. After Joey finishes, he goes downstairs expecting to perceive "some nostalgic treasure unlocked by the humidity within the stones, plaster, wood, and history of the house," but instead he smells the dampness of Peggy's hair.

This affirmation of present joy is approved by his mother after both she and Joey hear a Sunday sermon on Adam's obligation to the living Eve. "'In reaching out to her,'" the preacher says, "'Adam commits an act of faith.'" Woman, as Karl Barth says, is an invitation to man's kindness, and "'kindness needs no belief.'" Joey's love for Peggy will not bring him the self-confirmation of filial love, but it is nonetheless "'implicit in the nature of Creation, in the very curves and amplitude of God's fashioning.'"

A deeply religious woman, Mrs. Robinson apparently now sees that it would be a sin to try to maintain her hold on Joey. Therefore, she admits that Peggy suits him better than his first wife, Joan (later symbolizing the admission by asking Peggy to have a picture taken, which will probably replace Joan's). Then, after admitting Peggy's right to her son, she has a seizure, foretelling her death. But when, in her weakness, she pledges Joey to get a good price for her farm, he repays her respect for his freedom by affirming the reality of their bond: "'*Your* farm?'" he retorts. "'I've always thought of it as our farm.'"

The book's action is a record of those shifts, feints, self-dramatized assaults and stage-managed climaxes which are the universal components of family quarrels. Its power is an expression of thematic counterforce. Filled with the loveliness of primal pleasures — the farm, early mornings, one's youth — it also depicts the danger of fixation upon them. Definition requires that we keep faith with our past; freedom demands that we move beyond it. Grand though she is, Mrs. Robinson must yield to Peggy, just as Joey the boy must give way to Joey the man. But the three principal characters can only make their mutual adjustments after they have seen their situation from the individual perspectives that make it up. Subtly, naturally, *Of the Farm* performs this feat.

THE COUP

The 20th-century novelist finds himself in competition with a mode of storytelling—motion pictures—that is astonishing in the directness with which it presents and manipulates imagery and virtually tyrannical in its possession of the viewer's attention and in its power to compel emotion. The novel, rooted in the historical past tense of the histories, legends, journals, and epistles from which it is descended, cannot but envy this constant present that does not tell but simply *is*, dancing and slicing through space, juxtaposing in montage landscapes and faces, swords and roses, violence and stasis—a new poetry, a wordless vocabulary that engulfs us like an environment. ...[Yet] a man sitting with a book in his lap is a creature quite different from a man sitting hypnotized in a dark theatre. The mind translates verbal imagery into familiar images innocent of a photograph's staring actuality; it seizes on a single detail and enshrouds it in vague memories from real life. An image, to have more than this hazy recollective vitality, must be weighted with a momentum beyond itself, by that movement of merged relevance that Aristotle called an "action."

UPDIKE
Picked-Up Pieces

Updike in Africa

by Robert Towers

Like Evelyn Waugh and Paul Theroux and others before him, John Updike has betaken himself—imaginatively, at least—to Africa. The trip has done him good, for he has returned with one of his strongest novels—a book much superior to the (relatively) disappointing *A Month of Sundays* and *Marry Me;* a book that stands with the two *Rabbit* novels and *The Centaur* as an example of what this extraordinarily prolific novelist can do when his imagination, as well as his language, is strenuously engaged.

Like *Black Mischief* and *Jungle Lovers, The Coup* is a comedy of racial and cultural incongruities; but whereas Waugh and Theroux use a white protagonist (an upper-class British rascal, an American ingenue) to clear a path for us into the Dark Continent, Updike has the fictional audacity to project a black among blacks, a militant and culturally, though not sexually, puritanical Marxist Muslim, the redoubtable Col. Hakim Félix Ellelloû, as the commanding figure and voice of his novel.

Ellelloû is the president and dictator of a sub-Saharan nation with the biblical name of Kush, "a land of delicate, delectable emptiness"; once governed by France, Kush is now "a constitutional monarchy with the constitution suspended and the monarch deposed." Ellelloû's story, written in exile, slips easily back and forth between the first and third persons—between "the one who acts and the 'I' who experiences."

It begins in 1973, at a time when the chronically impoverished country has been devastated by a five-year drought. Camels and cattle are dying; people are starving. Colonel Ellelloû, accompanied by bodyguards, drives north in his Mercedes-Benz on a tour of inspection, stopping to visit a Soviet missile base along the way. When he reaches the border with Sahel—"our geographical twin but ideological antithesis, a model of neo-capitalist harlotry..."—he finds a mountainous pyramid of crates, sacks and boxes containing American breakfast cereals, potato chips, Carnation dried milk, cream of celery soup and the like—all sent as aid to Kush by the United States Government.

The vast pile is presided over by an earnest young American in a seersucker suit who cannot understand the Colonel's rejection of what he scornfully refers to as "capitalist intervention" in the form of "table scraps of a society both godless and oppressive." Climbing onto the pile, the American tries a hard sell: "...Here you go...Carnation...add three parts water...." "But we have no water!" calls Ellelloû. "In Kush, water is more precious than blood!" Enraged by the young man's foolishness, the colonel orders torches set to the pile, which becomes a pyre, incinerating not only the foodstuffs, but the American as well: He "did not cry out for mercy, or attempt to scramble and leap to a safety that was not there, but, rather, climbed to the pinnacle and, luridly illumined, awaited the martyrdom for which there must have been, in the training for foreign service provided by his insidious empire, some marginal expectation and religious preparation" (New York: Knopf, 1978, pp. 42, 43).

This killing, naturally enough, has repercussions. So does another act of blood—the public beheading, by Ellelloû himself, of the blind old King who has been kept a prisoner since his deposition following "l'Emergence" (i.e., revolution) of 1968. The repercussions—more farcical than grim—involve, among other episodes too intricate to trace, the "caputnapping" (by Russians disguised as Tuareg nomads) of the old King's head, which is then used as a mouthpiece for anti-Ellelloû propaganda; the arrival in Kush of the martyred American's wife, accompanied by a State Department official named Klipspringer, and the surprising discovery by Ellelloû that the American consumerism he so detests has already established a thriving outpost, complete with a luncheonette, a drugstore and an oil refinery, in a remote valley of Kush itself. The serpentine plot also accommodates scenes with each of Ellelloû's four wives, one of them a perpetually veiled American, and extensive flashbacks to the four years he spent at a college in Wisconsin during the Eisenhower era.

Elleloû himself is an extraordinary tour-de-force of a character, an ideologue who reminds one of Nabokov's mad narrators, a Humbert Humbert or a Charles Kinbote; like them he is obsessed, self-destructive, nimble and often endearing. Single-minded in his devotion to Allah, given to quoting the Koran on all possible occasions, Elleloû is heroic, if quixotic, in his determination to keep his starving land a model of Islamic Marxism, a beacon for the third world, a bulwark against spreading Americanism. But Elleloû is also a witty man, capable of delicate perceptions, of tender as well as sensual or cruel impulse. He is, I suppose, a fictional cousin of Updike's wayward Protestant minister, Tom Marshfield, in *A Month of Sundays*—but much more powerfully and complexly conceived. The African wives, too, are distinctively fleshed-out and memorable, as are the old King and Elleloû's elegant and treacherous associate, Michaelis Ezana. Oddly, the American characters are the least successful; in their case, Updike has contented himself with satirically outlined pinups.

Updike loves to show off his special areas of knowledge, whether Protestant theology or, in this case, the geography, geology and history of sub-Saharan Africa. As the acknowledgments at the front of *The Coup* indicate, considerable homework has gone into the construction of the land and people of Kush. Part savanna, part desert, part forest, Kush seems to be a composite of Mali, Niger and Chad, all of them carved out of what was once French West Africa. The drought is based, in its grisly details, on the real drought that recently brought such suffering and death to the entire area. Whatever the effort involved, Updike's imagination has thoroughly assimilated his erudition, enabling him to render, with sublime authority, the look and feel of this gritty, sun-struck region.

His stylistic virtuosity is more problematic. It is an aspect of his writing that annoys some readers and probably attracts many more. [In a recent review] of John O'Hara's letters, Updike, always the most tenderhearted of critics, asks himself what, if anything, is lacking in the art of his fellow Pennsylvanian, and he comes up with a possible answer. What is lacking in O'Hara's fiction is a love of language—"language as a semi-opaque medium whose colors and connotations can be worked into a supernatural, supermimetic bliss." O'Hara, he continues, "is resolutely unmetaphorical, and language seldom led him with its own music deeper into the matter at hand."[1] Exactly the opposite applies to Updike's own practice. Never was a writer so resolutely, so irrepressibly, metaphorical as he:

> Why did the king love me? I ask myself this in anguish, remembering his infinitely creased face surrounded by wiry white hair and in color the sunken black of a dried fig, his way of nodding and nodding as if his head were mounted on a tremendously balanced pivot, his cackle of mirth and greed like a fine box crushed underfoot, his preposterously bejewelled little hands, so little thickened by labor as to seem two-dimensional, so lightly gesturing, lifting in a wind of hopeless gaiety and sadness such as lifts puffs of dust in the street.   [p. 10]

Many of Updike's images are arresting, a delight to contemplate both for their ingenuity and accuracy; but too often he is tempted into glibness or excess, to a kind of overwriting that leaves the reader surfeited and slightly ill ("Directly overhead, an advance scout of the starry armies trembled like a pearl suspended in a gigantic goblet of heavenly nectar"). Updike's verbal exuberance is indeed "supermimetic." No one, I hope, will complain that Ellellou's language cannot possibly be grounded in the background, education or psychology attributed to that character. But the narcissistic, self-intoxicating element in Updike's style can also serve as a cover for certain defects of structure or narrative in his novel. Many aspects of Ellelloû's career remain improbable or unexplained in ways for which "creative license" is not an adequate excuse. We never learn with any precision how he managed his rise to power—or what transformed the crude Black Muslim allegiance he acquired in America into the pure and erudite devotion to Islam he later displays. The premises of the novel are just realistic enough to make these questions nag. Self-indulgence also accounts for the tedium that occurs in those passages where the characters make speeches at each other—brilliant speeches, to be sure, but speeches where the Updikean music leads *away* from the matter at hand.

[1] *The New Yorker*, Nov. 6, 1978, p. 213.

Still, what a rich, surprising and often funny novel *The Coup* is. I had never thought of Updike as a particularly witty writer before, but *The Coup* displays an epigrammatic talent that again reminds me of Nabokov. "Freedom," says one of the characters, "is like a blanket which, pulled up to the chin, uncovers the feet." And another complains that "life is like an overlong drama through which we sit being nagged by vague memories of having read the reviews." Updike is masterly, too, in the way he can set up a scene of mounting comic intensity. On one occasion, when the colonel is surrounded by a hostile mob and vainly keeps repeating, *"Je suis Ellelloû"* as he is struck and spat upon, his bodyguards at last step in, "gleaming in the nakedness of power, Opuku's machine gun a beautiful *mitrailleuse* after a design by Berthier, oiled like a Nubian whore, and Mtesa's Magnum .44 scarcely less enchanting." They unfurl a patriotic poster next to Ellelloû's face to establish his identity. But confusion persists: "Due to the poor photogravure of the poster, my identity was unsettled until one of the Soviets came forward and shook my hand; I recognized, amid the cocoa-paste of his absurd disguise as a nomad, the shallow, tilted, alert, hunted yellowish eyes of his race. 'Colonel Ellelloû,' he said, *'je présume' "*[p. 217].

This comedy of absurd cultural juxtaposition (which, like Waugh's, can sometimes bare a wonderfully menacing set of teeth) is sustained beautifully through much of Updike's fine novel.

Boy's Life

by Deborah McGill

The dismays and conceits of suburban family arrangements have consistently possessed John Updike's talents and imagination. Up from the row houses of blue-collar Pennsylvania in *Rabbit, Run,* his protagonists have moved north to split-levels, jobs in the city, and Sunday afternoon tennis, taking anxiety and ambivalence with them. Rabbit Angstrom segues effortlessly into Piet Hanema of *Couples* and (more recently) Jerry Conant of *Marry Me,* many short stories securing the links between.

These characters share an uneasy witness to the American dream vision: acknowledging the possible, ideal beauty of carpools, PTA, and seasoned marriages, of community and the fidelity on which it battens, they chafe at middle-class confinements nonetheless, as teen-age boys chafe at curfew, and yearn for rebellion, being temperamentally incapable of sustained revolt. Updike's qualified heroes remain persistently adolescent as they progress through middle age; in this latest novel, it is observed "that a man, in America, is a failed boy."

An odd remark, considering the remote terrain—a fictive sub-Saharan country—that inspires it. With *The Coup,* Updike surveys the impoverished kingdom of Kush—"landlocked between the mongrelized neo-capitalist puppet states of Zanj and Sahel," "a land of delicate, delectable emptiness"—and discovers Darien. The book is not so much a new direction as a last, extraordinary resort: the novelist at the end of his rope and stretching it out for all the tension it will bear.

In fact, this is not the first appearance of Kush in Updike's fiction. "God Speaks," a...story written more than a decade ago [and reprinted in *Museums and Women* (1972)], introduces the word to identify a mountain range in the remote fastnesses of Afghanistan governed by Gish Imra, Harvard alumnus of indeterminate vintage, master of a powerful tennis forehand, possessor of a red MG, and—until his ascension to tribal divinity and absolute rule—a Marxist materialist. The undergraduate Gish considers religion "a hoax. It's a method whereby the powerful keep the ignorant from rebelling." But at home in Kush, he apparently reconciles Marxist austerity with the brutalities of cult worship "in the name of cultural autonomy," disdaining the vain luxuries of Harvard Square for the hard purity of native tradition and political isolation.

And so from the sketch of Gish Imra to the amplified narrative of Colonel Hakim Félix Ellelloû, Commander-in-Chief of the Armed Forces, Minister of National Defense, and President of a Kush "as many miles as years removed from the [Asian] original" whose name it bears. Gish Imra is an alien, an enigma, a curiosity; Ellelloû, in contrast, is Jerry Conant in sunglasses and military khaki.

In *Marry Me,* Jerry wished to abjure the banalities of domestic routine for a transcendent chivalry; the result was comic daydream: the Romance of the Rose as annotated...by the Wife of Bath. Similar divisions and deflations are at work in *The Coup: Bananas* scripted by Frantz Fanon. Ellelloû has returned to Kush from years of service with a colonial regiment of the French Army (in Indochina and, later, Algeria, where he deserted) and an undergraduate tenure at (surely Joseph) McCarthy College in Wisconsin with an aversion to Western glut and a vision of a pristine, truly indigenous African state. He allies himself with the country's puppet-king Edumu to cast out the French, places Edumu under house arrest (and later beheads him, for lack of anything better to do), installs himself as military dictator, and repudiates native magic and superstition—*juju*—for the teachings of Allah (first learned at Muslin Temple Two in Chicago). The symbols of French dominion—a guillotine, bottles of cognac, monocles, and missals—are housed in the People's Museum of Imperialist Atrocities, and the importation of such Western corruptions as Coca-Cola and elastic underwear—"spicy brands called Lollipop and Spanky"—is banned.

To his infinite distress, Ellelloû's rigorous policies are wantonly rebuked by the stubborn receptivity of the natives to Western infiltrations—a counterrevolutionary sensibility that makes the penultimate coup of the novel's title, deposing the dictator, a bloodless and casual inevitability. Kush, chaste daughter of Ellelloû's fantasy, is not raped, but slips gleefully into modernity's embrace, the clues to her treachery a bewildering and comic tax on the dictator's patience. Thus, sipping cocoa (a permissible Muslim indulgence) and lost in the Koranic epigrams that modulate his speech, Ellelloû is startled by a familiar taste: "Ovaltine!" Traveling across the desert, he is troubled by the mirage of two golden parabolas, later to find they are the golden arches of a degenerate McDonald's. At morning prayer, he finds the incantatory rhythms of the Koran syncopated by the faint descant of infidel rock 'n' roll—"Momma don't mind what Daddy say/ we're gonna rock the night away"—and a furious search for the contraband radio ensues. The novel takes its own rhythm from the steady downbeat of such revelations.

Ellelloû, like Jerry Conant, is a man beset by the evidence of his inability to remake the world with a thought. Ellelloû is himself a failed boy, smarting from the abandonment of his father. His hyperbole has the tone of an eager child, determined to please at last. He would have his four wives—one of them American, the prize of his extended Wisconsin sabbatical—faithful and satisfied. Yet they bear him no children and remain steadfastly unmoved in bed, leaving him to fret over his bewildering and chronic impotence as any Northeast commuter might do, worrying his midlife crisis on the train ride home. He would devote all his energies to the creation of a Muslim earthly paradise but is distracted for most of the book's pages by unreconstructed memories of life in the U.S.A.: drugstores, cold beer, snow, and car trips. He lacks the canny, manipulative sense of expedience apparently necessary to administer the post-colonial state. Instead, his is the after-school clubhouse politics of gesture: a head rolls, bullets fly, and in the telling the suffering is as insubstantial as the butterfly's when its wings are plucked. Ellelloû's acts are perhaps even less real to him than the words with which he exhorts the people to greater rigor and sacrifice. Failing to inspire them, he wanders the desert searching for the source of the country's disease.

At last, too infirm of purpose to summon the people from their opulent dreams, Ellelloû withdraws, defeated, to an exile in southern France, in apposite parallel to Jerry Conant's wistful retreat to St. Croix at the conclusion of *Marry Me*. *The Coup* stands as his memoir, narrated by turns in first and third person: "There are two selves: the one who acts, and the 'I' who experiences. This latter is passive even in a whirlwind of the former's making, passive and guiltless and astonished." The alternation of perspective is resonant: this African cannot put the pieces of experience—rich tribal custom, enlightened European cynicism, amiable American pragmatism—together in a coherent image of himself. As he says, he exists "between two worlds," robbed even of a language with which to give himself a name: Americans call him "Happy," his tribal kin "Bini," and "Ellelloû" is lifted from the Berber, for "freedom," and not his native Salu. Colonial French, imperial English, the babel of tribal dialects: no single idiom is sufficient even to the routine demands of daily intercourse. Ellelloû's failure to reform his country becomes in his own estimation, a simple failure of language, of names sufficient to the "idea of Kush" that might reconcile that idea with postcolonial realities. The disjunction between Ellelloû's idealizing language and the demotic events the words describe does not yield the intended transubstantiation, but instead an antic, ingenuous satire, shadowed by the pathos of Ellelloû's incomprehension and bafflement.

Accounting for the origin of his country, Ellelloû exults: "Africa held up a black mirror to Pharaonic Egypt, and the image was Kush." One might say of *The Coup:* it holds up a white mirror to postcolonial Africa, and the image is Connecticut. Passing through Kush, Ellelloû has adopted disguises to lose himself among the people and take their measure: orange vendor, troubador, magician. It is appropriate, then, that in his penultimate avatar, he should appear as an insurance claims adjuster, in his last as a beggar. Updike here seems to be saying that as "the fertile and level moral prairie of America" extends to flatten the world, only such diminished adjustments are possible. Certainly in Updike's fiction none more elevated ever seems to be possible.

There is no anger in *The Coup,* nor in any of Updike's novels. As high priest of middle-class morality, Updike offers his readers a peace that passeth understanding. In his fictive universe, moral values are suspended: we are not allowed to judge the dic-

tator who acts because he is known to us only through the minis-
trations of the detached and personal voice who watches "guiltless
and astonished." We cannot condemn American rapaciousness
because it is manifest only as the amiable, neighborly spirit of
naive diplomats and "technological boys." Similarly, Jerry Conant's adultery is washed clean by the italicized rhapsodies that
bracket it; Rabbit Angstrom's desertion of wife and infant is made
heroic as the expression of a stubborn integrity.

All can be understood and explained, and no one is responsible.
Updike's novels, *The Coup* among them, are exercises in absolu-
tion that is unearned, because intention is never acknowledged,
guilt never assigned. The boy, having sated himself on the pie
cooling in the window, grins and says, "I couldn't help myself."
For all the failed boys who inhabit the level prairie of Updike's
fiction, we are asked to find this explanation enough.

THE SHORT STORIES

The author's deepest pride, as I have experienced it, is not in his incidental wisdom but in his ability to keep an organized mass of images moving forward, to feel life engendering itself under his hands. But no doubt fiction is also a mode of spying; we read it as we look in windows or listen to gossip, to learn what other people *do.* Insights of all kinds are welcome; but no wisdom will substitute for an instinct for action and pattern, and a perhaps savage wish to hold, through your voice, another soul in thrall.

UPDIKE
Picked-Up Pieces

The Same Door: Unexpected Gifts

by Robert Detweiler

The Same Door, published in 1959, is a collection of sixteen short stories written over a period of five years and originally published, some in different form, in *The New Yorker;* and they represent various stages of Updike's art. The first story, "Friends from Philadelphia," was also Updike's first commercially published fiction, written in 1954 after his graduation from Harvard. The others were composed during his 1955 scholarship year at Oxford, during his two-year tenure as *New Yorker* staff writer writer (1955-57), and during his first two years as an independent novelist. Consequently, the stories have little formal unity as a collection, and any attempt to generalize about them is confounded by exceptions.

Certain aspects of casual unity are created by a consistent authorial attitude toward life and by a recurrent structural technique. Updike himself articulates the attitude in the foreword to a later collection called *Olinger Stories.* Answering the complaint that one of those stories seems to have no point, he comments, "The point, to me, is plain, and is the point, more or less, of all these Olinger stories. *We are rewarded unexpectedly.* The muddled and inconsequent surface of things now and then parts to yield us a gift." This point is the one made as well, if sometimes negatively so, in the *The Same Door,* and it expresses a conviction of the author that becomes more determinative as the body of his fiction grows. Updike is a Christian, if not a "religious" writer in the accepted sense, and the centrality of grace in the Protestant experience finds its way into his art through the expression of the gift or the reward.

The particular unifying technique is similar to the construction of the Joycean "epiphany," at least according to the way in which that much-debated term has been generally understood. Somewhat as in Joyce's *Dubliners, The Same Door* stories, instead of attempting the brutal surprise or the psychological shock, concentrate on producing the gradual revelation—the culminating knowledge-plus-emotion that dawns upon the protagonist following his crucial experiences and upon the reader after he has finished the story. Also, as in Joyce's stories, Updike's epiphanies, while they do not depend upon an overt religious context (except in "Dentistry and Doubt"), translate fundamentally religious or at least moral experiences into artistic imagery and action. The revelatory moment does not result from any sensational conflicts or climactic scenes, for these are not stories of deep passion, violence, or death. They occur in the midst of daily life, mixing with the stuff of the mundane; and the insight slowly materializes through a fine fusion of memories, reflexes, and some subtle catalyst of the unexpected. Against the wonted beat of familial or vocational being, a counterpoint insinuates itself in these stories that at last upsets the rhythm and forces the characters and reader to pause and then to reconsider the whole composition.

The second narrative, "Ace in the Hole," could be a preliminary sketch for *Rabbit, Run.* Fred "Ace" Anderson, like Harry Angstrom, is a twenty-six-year-old ex-high school basketball star, married, father of a small child, and the sad product of maternal domination. On the particular day of the story, he has been fired from his job—not for the first time—as a used-car salesman; and he returns home to await the arrival of his working wife and to appease somehow her anticipated anger at his latest failure. The story is packed with the complications and baggage of young American marriage. Evey, the wife, is Roman Catholic; and Ace is Protestant—a sore point between them. Their life is saturated with TV, pop music, beer, and the omnipresent cigarettes. They appear to have married directly out of high school when they were too young and when they had developed no skills; and they survive in a precarious financial state. Evey has matured, but Ace has not. He lives in the illusion of his teenage glory and is a childish egotist. Updike describes in detail how Ace lovingly combs his long, sleek hair in front of the mirror; and he stresses that, while Ace has just lost his job—a reason for actual concern—he is really bothered because a mention of his high-scoring record in the local sports news that day has employed his name of Fred instead of Ace.

That evening Evey takes rather stoically the news of the firing (Ace's mother has already told her), but the irresponsible young husband soon irritates her into bitter recriminations. Then Ace turns on his charm. He distracts her by applauding their baby daughter's antics, then persuades her to dance with him to the sound of dinner music on the radio. The tale ends with the two of them, everything unresolved, dancing a quickening swing step in the isolation of the drab apartment, trying pathetically to relive the popularity of their carefree high school days.

Updike has, amazingly, already found his metier in "Ace in the Hole." The story offers less in terms of plot and action than "Friends from Philadelphia" but much more in terms of pure mood created out of sheer verbal craftsmanship. It is, much like *Rabbit, Run*, a sustained metaphor of nervous movement and a tension of opposites. Ace is always in motion: driving the car, smoking hastily, tapping a foot in rhythm, running home from his mother's house with the small daughter in his arms—still shifting restlessly on life's basketball court, trying to score and to be the hero again with the effortlessness of the natural. But Ace is not a natural in the workaday world. An indulgent mother and cheap early fame have spoiled him, and he is already a clearcut failure at the approaching prime of life. The antagonistic characters, his opposites, make his plight the more obvious. The prowling high school youths who insult him at the traffic light only show him (like the boys playing back-alley basketball at the start of *Rabbit, Run*) the reckless innocence that he has lost. His weary and dispirited wife, with her dogged common sense, makes him seem more of a loser.

Apart from a sexual innuendo, the title has a double sense. The protagonist is Ace "in the hole": jobless, unprepared to be a man, and threatened with a spouse nearly ready to leave him. But he also *has* his ace in the hole: his animal charm and his instincts that will help him to survive even if he ruins others in the process. The story is an inversion of the maturation pattern, for the events

that should jolt the initiate into growing up at last only cause him
to fight reality with a wasteful nervous energy. "Ace in the Hole"
seems authentic because it fashions a modern American type, the
teenage hero seduced by quick success into thinking that the adult
world is easy to conquer but who soon suffers disillusion and the
gradual degeneration into bumhood. Olinger can be too kind,
the family-community can be too generous, when it offers its
sons what they should strive a lifetime to deserve—and then permits grace to turn quickly into judgment. Updike has forced more
news about one dead end along the American way of life into one
brief story than many writers manage to report in a whole novel.
It is no wonder that he returned to the theme and the place and
expanded the microform into *Rabbit, Run.*

"Snowing in Greenwich Village," the seventh of *The Same
Door* series, is one of the most impressive performances in the
collection. It shifts from the Olinger setting to Manhattan and
introduces Richard and Joan Maple, a young married couple who
appear again, older and unhappier, in *The Music School* and in
four uncollected short stories. Very little actually happens in the
narration; instead, it shows the author absorbed in his persistent
but delicate probing of interacting personalities. Richard (in the
advertising trade) and Joan have just moved to West Thirteenth
Street in the Village and have invited an old acquaintance over
for the evening, Rebecca Cune, a girl with "a gift for odd things."
    The three drink sherry and converse, but the talk is dom-
inated by Rebecca's wry recollections of the strange people she
has known. Joan, who has a cold and has not been at all witty in
the conversation, is roused by the clatter of horses of mounted
policemen. She rushes to the window, sees snow falling outside,
and hugs her husband in a moment of unguarded intimacy while
their guest watches blandly. When Rebecca leaves, Richard walks
her home and follows her upstairs, aroused, to see her apartment.
At her door as he prepares to leave, they are poised to embrace;
but Richard destroys the critical moment with a joke that mis-
fires, and departs.
    The undertone of sexual competition pervades the tale. Joan
and Rebecca are at cautious odds from the start, and Updike
contrasts them graphically: Joan's angular "Modiglianiesque"
features give her an air of simplicity, but Rebecca is a da Vinci

type whose constant enigmatic smile reminds one of the mystery of the tantalizing Mona Lisa portrait. Beneath the purposefully casual conversation, one is made to feel the unnamed struggle. Richard is the prize, Joan the defender of her property, and Rebecca the predator. Joan's weapon is her defenselessness; Rebecca's, her cool and cryptic reserve that promises a hidden excitement. Richard is caught between loyalty toward his wife, who is put at a disadvantage by the off-beat discussion, and Rebecca's novel attractiveness. The chatting remains discreet, but the adultery motif accompanies it through the repeated references to beds: in the first paragraph, Richard lays Rebecca's coat and scarf on their marriage bed; Rebecca relaxes on the floor in the living room with her arm on the Hide-a-Bed (while Joan sits straightbacked on a chair); Rebecca tells about the bedroom troubles she had in sharing her apartment with a pair of lovers; and, when Richard at the end visits her apartment, he is surprised to see the double bed that dominates the room. The subtlety of the imagery matches the subtlety of the invitation to extramarital adventure.

But Rebecca's strength is also her weakness. Her knack for comic recitation gradually emerges as the extent of her substance. She achieves her unique personality at the expense of others, exaggerating their foibles to fit the style of her performance. That Rebecca is a predator in every way Richard suddenly grasps after his wife's impulsive embrace, as he sees Joan and himself from Rebecca's viewpoint. She will twist the moment of tenderness into a joke when she narrates the scene to other friends: the simple wife with the sniffles who hugs her husband in ludicrous joy because it happens to be snowing. But Richard's discovery does not make her less desirable; for when Richard escorts her home (at Joan's insistence—a smart if risky strategy, since it forces her opponent's move), they hold an embarrassed dialogue that masks the tension of pre-sexual encounter and that continues inside her apartment.

Updike produces the tension by allowing the inane comments to fill the void of anticipation. The crucial moment, exquisitely described, occurs at the door when Richard acts to leave; and the result could go either way. Rebecca, very close to him in the shadows, is waiting for him to make the move. If he does, he betrays his wife; if he doesn't, he becomes the ridiculous male.

He tries a joke and stutters; the timing and the situation are ruined. He is free but at the expense of his pride.

Since this is Richard Maple's story, one must inquire what unexpected gift he receives. It may be, in part, the thrill of the just-missed extra-marital adventure; but, more likely, it is that he does *not* become intimately involved. He has had the quick glance into the tantalizing maze of illicit romance but also the luck, or the grace, to avoid its penalties—emotional, social, and moral. The revelation of mutual attraction between a man and a woman is a joy not only because it reassures one of his desirability but also because it indicates an elementary kind of human communication. A fine line may exist between lust and love, but the libido need not always incite to sexual consummation; it can produce other kinds of knowledge as well. Lust can teach.

"The Happiest I've Been," the final story of the collection, returns with considerable nostalgia to the context of a fading moral innocence. John Nordholm (as Updike states it in the Foreword to *Olinger Stories*), having taken his turn as protagonist in "Friends from Philadelphia," narrates the story in the first person as a nineteen-year-old college student who is home in Olinger for the Christmas vacation. The tale is stylistically different from the others in *The Same Door*. It is essentially plotless and has the form of a reminiscence, a series of smoothly connected vignettes that one would guess to be transposed autobiography—Updike's personally experienced Shillington into the fictive Olinger of 1951. Yet the story evokes a mood that marks a transitional stage in one's maturing rather than a specific history and geography. It is a period of the end of youthful innocence, when one practices the rites of adulthood half-willingly to demonstrate sophistication, yet lingers with the more familiar and less complicated habits of late adolescence.

John is picked up in the evening by Neil, a friend of his, to drive to a girlfriend's New Year's party in Chicago, seventeen hours distant; but, once beyond parental ken, they decide to attend first in Olinger a party given by former high school classmates. They stay at the party until three in the morning and then take two girls home to nearby Riverside. Margaret, one of the girls, invites the others into her parents' home for early coffee; while Neil and the other girl pet in the darkened house, John and

Margaret sit and talk until she falls asleep in his arm. As dawn breaks, the two boys finally leave for Chicago. Neil has John drive the car and sleeps beside him as the trip begins.

Except for "A Gift from the City," this is the longest story of the collection and one of Updike's favorites—a fact that in itself does not necessarily insure its quality; but the author does achieve his artistic ends through control of narrative idiom, perspective, and manipulation of an efficient metaphoric pattern. John tells the story in a retrospective late-teenager style—one relatively free of Updike's now ripened elaborate diction—that infuses his experience with a simple, forthright authenticity. But the angle of vision is not therefore wholly a teenager's; it is a double view that tempers the precious hours of the youthful past with the increased wisdom of the present.

The result is a certain discrepancy of moods and tones that creates the sense of loss now beginning to invade Updike's fiction and appearing strongest in *The Centaur* and *The Music School.* This mood is indicated in the adverbial superlative of the title ("The *Happiest* I've Been") and in the shadow of sadness that lingers over the careful description. Updike quotes Henri Bergson in the preface to *The Same Door:* "How many of our present pleasures, were we to examine them closely, would shrink into nothing more than memories of past ones!" That realization, which applies exactly to this story, is also Wordsworthian: with increasing self-consciousness comes the loss of natural, spontaneous joy, so that the stylizing mind must reconstruct its pleasures artificially out of the past.

But even if that much of the romantic survives in Updike, he possesses the discipline to fashion a universally meaningful event out of a private memory and to create thereby sentiment instead of sentimentality. "The Happiest I've Been" broadens into a modern maturation ritual, replete with the archetypal accoutrements, that does not simply dress up the old forms of twentieth-century art but also adds a new interpretive dimension. The season, the party, and the trip embody and symbolize the transitional nature of the experience that introduces a new stage of maturity. It is nearly New Year (the classmates pretend that it *is* New Year's Eve), the time to begin formally a fresh kind of existence; and the trip has echoes of the *rite de passage.* John leaves the old farm and his gnarled grandmother and aging parents for young, robust Chicago and the girlfriend awaiting him there; and, of course, the actual journey begins at the pristine moment of dawn. It is an emphatic moment of separation from family and home and the start of the independent journey through adult life.

The party particularly has ritual elements. It is a last meeting in youthful irresponsibility; less a reunion than a final celebration of oneness; still held in a parental home, but in one from which the parents are absent. The games, the alcoholic drinks, the dancing, all combined with a constant awareness of *the time,* blend the playfulness of adolescence with the growing sophistication of impending adulthood. When at midnight "everyone" tries to kiss the only married girl of the group, the concentrated ritual duality becomes most apparent; it is an embracing of the new state of being attempted through a playful gesture.

The new relevance of the maturation pattern appears after the party among the privacy of the two couples. The movement is from the group to individuals, from the tribe to self-conscious formal structures. For John Nordholm, the revelation of beginning maturity that promises goodness for the future and that makes him the happiest he's been comes through the double incident of demonstrated faith that others have in him: "There was knowing that twice since midnight a person had trusted me enough to fall asleep beside me." The nostalgia for an irretrievable carefree past is balanced by a pride in the assumed responsibility of adult relationships. One trusts one's sexual being, one's safety, with the other person; and there is joy in accepting the burden of that faith.

Here once more, finally, is the theme of the unexpected gift that runs through all the stories. To be treated as an adult, and the ability to respond as one, are two of life's subtle presents; to be introduced to the challenges of manhood through the expressed new trust of old friends is a surprising graciousness of nature, or of fate. Indeed, Updike might interpret it as an extension of God's blessing into one's deepening self-conscious existence.

"The same door" as a metaphor of communication is physically or figuratively present in all of the stories of the collection. It can function literally, as with Richard and Rebecca frozen in the tension of sexual attraction at the door of her darkened walk-up, or the poor Negro waiting outside the Village apartment for help from strangers ["A Gift from the City"], or George Chandler entering timidly to intervene in the neighbors' marital battle ["His Finest Hour"]. Or it can be the symbolic door between husband and wife, between old friends, or between chance acquaintances. Some doors are opened quickly and gladly, others are opened only to be slammed shut, some are quietly closed, and some are never opened at all. The image of the door, a familiar object of ordinary life, is fitting and effective for Updike's purpose: to show that the formative events of one's being occur within the framework of the common, and that the common moments can be redeemed or lost through the quality of one's response to others.

Memory in *Pigeon Feathers*

by Arthur Mizener

Wordsworth might be talking about Updike rather than himself when he says in *The Prelude:*

> I am lost, but see
> In simple childhood something of the base
> On which thy greatness stands;... The days gone by
> Return upon me almost from the dawn
> Of life: the hiding places of man's power
> Open; I would approach them, but they close.
> I see by glimpses now; when age comes on,
> May scarcely see at all; and I would give,
> While yet we may, as far as words can give,
> Substance and life to what I feel, enshrining,
> Such is my hope, the spirit of the Past
> For future restoration.

This is a classic statement of the romantic attitude; it is also a precise description of Mr. Updike's almost irresistible impulse to go home again in memory to find himself. Most of his stories and his first three novels are about the same town. The rest of his stories are memories, too, but of the more recent past, of his own marriage, for instance, as is the opening story of *Pigeon Feathers,* called "Walter Briggs." This is a story in which a husband and wife, driving home with their sleeping child, play a memory game, trying to recall the names of all the particulars they can of the people they had known at the summer camp where they spent their honeymoon. There is one man whose name neither of them

Excerpted from "The American Hero as High-School Boy: Peter Caldwell," in *The Sense of Life in the Modern Novel,* by Arthur Mizener (Boston: Houghton Mifflin Co., 1964), pp. 247-66. Copyright © by Houghton Mifflin Co. and by William Heinemann Ltd. Reprinted by permission of Houghton Mifflin Co.

can remember. But as the husband is falling asleep that night, remembering exactly what his wife had been like and how much he had loved her on that honeymoon, he finds what he wants. He raises himself on his elbow and calls his wife's name, "softly, knowing he wouldn't wake her, and [says] 'Briggs. Walter Briggs.'"

Not that the past need be happy; what matters is that it is made real by the intensity of feeling that has accumulated around it, as nothing else is real. Thus, in a story called "Wife-Wooing" the hero remembers, in a moment of intense desire for his wife, another detail from that honeymoon, of how in the cabin where they slept a "great rose window was projected upward through the petal-shaped perforations in the top of the black kerosene stove, which we stood in the center of the floor. As the flame on the circular wick flickered, the wide soft star of interlocked penumbrae moved and waved as if printed on a silk cloth being gently tugged or slowly blown. Its color soft blurred blood. We pay dear in blood for our peaceful homes." Here we can catch a glimpse of why Updike is so deadly serious about his literary elaborations of homely experience; that red reflection cast by the kerosene stove on the simple cabin roof is the image of his deflowered wife and his cathedral's rose window, the image of the price we pay for our homes, here and in the eternity we know because it is here. In Shillington, Pennsylvania, as Peter Caldwell knows, "we lived in God's sight."

In this way the glow of joy and pain, of intensely felt experience, together with all its transcendent implications, gathers around the particulars of the past for Mr. Updike, whether he is writing about his childhood and parents or about his wife and their children, or about both, as he is in "Home." The epigraphs of his very first collection of stories, *The Same Door*, are a quotation from Bergson that discusses the importance of memory to desire ("What would there be left of many of our emotions, were we to reduce them to the exact quantum of pure feeling they contain by subtracting from them all that is merely reminiscence"), and a passage from T. S. Eliot about family love, "within the light of which/ All else is seen." Precise recollection, then, especially of family love, is vital to him; it is the actual experience in which the saving truth is incarnate, and it worries him to lose the least fragment of it, as he seems to feel he is gradually losing his understanding of the past; the epigraph of his latest book of stories is from Kafka, and begins: "In revenge, however, my memory of the past has closed the door against me more and more." This anxiety, if it is real, appears premature, for *Pigeon Feathers* is filled with prodigies of recollection from that time.

In "The Persistence of Desire," for example, a young man very like Peter Caldwell returns to Olinger to see his eye doctor, and finds himself in the doctor's waiting room with a girl very like Peter's girl Penny. They are both now married, but he cannot resist the desire that comes flooding back with memory, and he begins to woo her again. "Aren't you happy?" the girl says, and the young man replies "'I am, I am; but'—the rest was so purely inspired its utterance only grazed his lips—'happiness isn't everything.'" When he comes out of the doctor's office, his eyes dilated and unfocused from the drops the doctor has used in checking his vision, the girl is waiting for him. She slips a note into the pocket of his shirt. He cannot focus his eyes to read it, but in his shirt pocket it "made a shield for his heart. In this armor he stepped into the familiar street. The maples, macadam, houses, cement, were to his violated eyes as brilliant as a scene remembered; he became a child again in this town, where life was a distant adventure, a rumor, an always imminent joy."

The hero of "Flight" remembers with minute psychological realism a high-school love affair with a very similar girl and builds up around their story a world of remembered details of his grandmother and grandfather, his mother's shocking jealousy of the girl, the high-school debates and dances of his courting. It is a loving and meticulous re-creation of the past and Updike's mind probes it with the delicacy of a surgeon, seeking what makes it in memory so preternaturally alive and meaningful. Even the knowledge that the past is not a shelter from lifelessness, as it now seems to be, comes to him, in a story called "A Sense of Shelter," as a memory. What he remembers is how he achieved the courage to tell the most mature and mysterious of his high-school classmates that he loved her, only to discover that she was having a bitterly unhappy affair with an older man. "You never loved anybody," she said. "You don't know what it is." He knows now that she was right, knows enough to remember what he thought then with a schoolboy's uncertain insight—"after all, it was just a disposition of his heart, nothing permanent or expensive"—as true in a sense more terrible than he could then have imagined.

It always seems to Updike, as he says of his grandmother whom he recalls again and again, "necessary and holy, to tell how once there had been a woman who now was no more," to tell everything, "all set sequentially down with the bald simplicity of intrinsic blessing, thousands upon thousands of pages; ecstatically uneventful; divinely and defiantly dull." He feels this way because, in memory, the transcendental value of the people he loved as a child inheres in them, an intrinsic blessing. This motive comes out very clearly in one of the experimental stories in *Pigeon Feathers,* "Packed Dirt, Churchgoing, a Dying Cat, a Traded Car." In it the narrator brings together a series of ostensibly unconnected recollections, because in each he discovers some object that has been humanized and thus has acquired intrinsic blessing that he can, in memory, recognize. He opens the story with a statement of this point: "I...am always affected— reassured, nostalgically pleased, even, as a member of my animal species, made proud—by the sight of bare earth that has been smoothed and packed firm by the passage of human feet. ...the more matter is outwardly mastered, the more it overwhelms us in our hearts." Churchgoing is for him "to sit and stand in unison and sing and recite creeds and petitions that are like paths worn smooth in the raw terrain of our hearts," and "the expectantly hushed shelter of the church is like one of those spots worn bare by a softball game in a weed-filled vacant lot." The incident of the cat, as the narrator says, "had the signature: decisive but illegible." While he is wandering about waiting for his child to be born, he finds a dying cat in the street and puts it behind the hedge of the nearest house "to be safe," though he is sure it is dying. "It suffered my intrusion a trifle stiffly. It suggested I was making too much fuss, and seemed to say to me, *Run on Home.*" A few hours later he calls the hospital and, "after some rummaging in the records," they are able to tell him his daughter has been born. Something far more complicated gathers for him around the car he cannot bring himself to trade in—lust and love and all kinds of death. "Not only sand and candy wrappers accumulate in a car's interior, but heroisms and instants of communion." The packed dirt, the dying cat, the churchgoing, the car have become, each in its different way, a part of some heroism or some moment of communion; they have been mastered; they are intrinsically blessed. That is all that ever matters for Updike about any object or event. "The Blessed Man of Boston, My Grandmother's Thimble, and Fanning Island" is a similar collection of moments of intrinsic blessing, images that, if he could properly evoke them, would be full of joy, "just as a piece of turf torn from a meadow becomes a *gloria* when drawn by Dürer." But he despairs of ever realizing life that fully. "As it is," he says to his reader, "you, like me, must take it on faith."

This is a feeling for the sacredness of life itself, and it is accompanied by a real horror of death. The narrator of "Packed Dirt" has to wake his wife up in the middle of the night, so great is his horror of dying, and Updike deals with this horror at length in a much too brilliant symbolic story called "Lifeguard." The lifeguard is real enough, in his way; a divinity student during the winter, "in the summer," as he says, "I disguise myself in my skin and become a lifeguard." It is a disguise, the skin— real enough as far as it goes, but not the important reality. Walking around in our skins we are all to Updike what his lifeguard is, dying animals with the capacity to love. "Young as I am," the lifeguard remarks, "I can hear in myself the protein acids ticking; I wake at odd hours and in the shuddering dark and silence feel my death rushing toward me like an express train." The psychological process is like swimming: "We struggle and thrash, and drown; we succumb, even in despair, and float, and are saved"—by human love that, like the rest of life, walks around dressed in flesh and blood, or, as the lifeguard puts it, "our chivalric impulses go clanking in encumbering biological armor." It may be an awkward kind of equipment for a chivalric knight to wear while he is saving the princess, but we have to use it if we are going to guard life: "every seduction is a conversion." The story ends with an image of great ingenuity that catches up the whole significance of Updike's humanist parable. This lifeguard has never been called on to save a life, but "someday," he thinks, "my alertness will bear fruit; from near the horizon there will arise, delicious, translucent, like a green bell above the water, the call for help, the call, a call, it saddens me to confess, that I have yet to hear."

Updike's Quest for Liturgy

by Michael Novak

Though he is barely thirty, John Updike has already awakened themes dormant in American letters since Hawthorne and Melville. Surely many religious people feel their own childhood, their hopes and terrors, to the tips of their toes when they read him. Yet the established critics seem to miss what he is saying.

"The point to be made about John Updike," George Steiner wrote about *The Centaur,* "is tiresomely obvious. ... It is, of course, the gap between formal, technical virtuosity and the interest or originality of what is being said." Yet Updike is often writing about man's search for personal immortality. He sometimes takes Protestant Christianity with ruthless seriousness. He is willing to try to understand life in American small towns and suburbs as it is now lived; he is not a prophet of dangerous living, nor a preacher of meaninglessness. He regularly refuses the values, the starting-points, of the secular reformer. He does not take the lead in the causes the critics like to support; he sometimes takes a direction they fail to see.

To illustrate these points, I would like to invite close attention to the four-part story with which Updike closes *Pigeon Feathers:* "Packed Dirt, Churchgoing, A Dying Cat, A Traded Car." This story, I believe, is central to his work, and touches on nearly all his themes. It is also one of the most perfectly worked pieces of prose in the English language, perhaps even overworked, too elaborate. Through its four sections, the story ascends in a complex spiral. Updike begins with images of a path being destroyed by machines, and reflects on the interaction of men, machines, and nature; he next finds images for a contemplative view of the world; he confronts death; and last of all he confronts evil and finds an image for immortality. He seems to be struggling to find images, like Salinger in a more precious way, for that deep, serene, perennial way of looking at life which the secular, active West has lost.

"We in America need ceremonies, is I suppose, sailor, the point of what I have written"; so Updike concludes the present montage. *Why* do we in America need ceremonies? This is what Updike must show us. The first reason he suggests is that ceremonies are necessary, because through them we become human. But the second reason thrusts more sharply home: it is so that we will be able even to *conceive* what immortality is like, and therefore what we are like.

"Packed Dirt" concludes a cycle of stories. The title story, "Pigeon Feathers," catches the same hero, David Kern, in his more religious, small-town youth. Young David asks the minister at Sunday School (an experience like that of Philip Roth in "The Conversion of the Jews") "Where will Heaven be?" The minister replied in a forgiving tone: "David, you might think of Heaven this way: as the way the good that Abraham Lincoln did lives after him."

David is appalled. *That* means nothing. He is disgusted at this betrayal of Christianity, this ignorance compounded with a lie. His pseudo-religious mother tries to comfort him, and ensnares herself in worse ignorance, worse lies, worse sentiment.

" 'Mother, good grief. Don't you see'—he rasped away the roughness in his throat—'if when we die there's nothing, all your sun and fields and what not are all, ah, *horror?* It's just an ocean of horror.' " Young David "needed to begin to build his fortress against death. They none of them believed. He was alone. . . . All those sexy, perfumed people, wisecracking, chewing gum, all of them doomed to die, and none of them noticing," he alone recognizing that "we cannot, *cannot,* submit to death."

Now since Freud at least, it would be fashionable to think that something must be wrong with David: after all, people *don't* live forever and there's no need even for them to want to (his religious mother thinks he's greedy). But the young David Kern concludes his contemplation of the pigeons he has shot "robed in this certainty: that the God who had lavished such craft upon these worthless birds would not destroy His whole creation by refusing to let David live forever."

"Packed Dirt" opens with David Kern admitting that he is always "reassured, nostalgically pleased, even, as a member of my animal species made proud" by the sight of bare earth made firm by the passage of human feet. He is reassured, and that is the passive fruit of ceremony. He is made proud, for ceremony is an active victory won by his animal species.

Patches of packed dirt abound "in small towns"—not so much in cities. They are "unconsciously humanized intervals of clay," made by the quiet interaction of men with the earth. They remind him of his childhood, "when one communes with dirt down among the legs, as it were, of abiding fatherly presences. The earth is our playmate then, and the call to supper has a piercingly sweet eschatological ring." To become as a little child is to treat the earth as a playmate, unself-consciously commune with things, be aware of a fatherly presence, know that the piercingly sweet call of death bids one home.

But machines enter the neighborhood to make way for cars, making "our rooms shake with the curses of their labor." The littlest Kern, not yet two, is frightened by the gnawing, mashing machines. By the next morning, however, the children—children, mostly, make paths—had treaded a path up the cliff left by the machines. This "modest work of human erosion" is one of those things which make Kern proud. It is a ceremony which seems precious to him, "not only because it recalled" his own childhood, but above all because "it had been achieved accidentally, and had about it that repose of grace that is beyond willing."

The children are at home with nature, but we "in America have from the beginning been cleaving and baring the earth, attacking, reforming the enormity of nature we were given, which we took to be hostile." The theme of American history has been: Conquer this continent; exalt man over nature. But now Updike estimates our triumph: "We have explored, on behalf of all mankind, this paradox: the more matter is outwardly mastered, the more it overwhelms us in our hearts." The scientific attitude is not the attitude of men, but of artisans. For men the world is not so much an enemy as a playmate, and if the war is "incapable of ceasing," it is, at least, "good to know that now there are enough of us to exert a counter-force"—enough to favor man over artisan.

"Churchgoing" begins just where "Packed Dirt" leaves off: it takes churchgoing "purely as a human recreation." From the human point of view alone, whether one chooses "to listen, or not listen, as a poorly paid but resplendently robed man strives to console us with scraps of ancient epistles and halting accounts, hopelessly compromised by words," churchgoing gives us a chance to be ourselves, to observe, to think. It is "the most available democratic experience," where, as at the polls, we are "actually given our supposed value, the soul-unit of one, with its noumenal arithmetic of equality: one equals one equals one." Sitting and standing in unison, we "sing and recite creeds and petitions that are like paths worn smooth in the raw terrain of our hearts." But even to describe churchgoing, Kern admits, is to corrupt it: it sounds much too preachy and self-conscious.

As a child, David Kern felt "nothing in church but boredom and an oppressive futility." Only at fifteen, did he feel "a pleasant emotion in church," when on raw March nights during Lent he went in the family Chevrolet to usher with his father, while "the wind howled a nihilistic counterpoint beyond the black windows," and the "minority flock furtively gathered within the hostile enormity of a dying, sobbing empire." His restless father thought of church "as something he helped run," anxious for the moment to pass the plate. Young David felt like an initiate, smug, condescending, as he gallantly lowered the felt plate towards each pew of "The Others," and began to know the dangers of even the lowly honor of being usher.

He recalls, from later in his life, the "Second Century quality" of churches in the Village: "In Manhattan, Christianity is so feeble its future seems before it. . . . The expectantly hushed shelter of the church is like a spot worn bare by a softball game. . . . The presence of the city beats like wind at the glowing windows." He hurries home afterwards "to assume the disguise" of a nonchurchgoer. He alternates churches, so as not to become among the known, who can look condescendingly on "The Others." "We are the others. It is of the essence to be a stranger in church." For though community is crucial, so likewise is personality uncluttered and naked in the sight of God.

On an island in the Caribbean, Kern attends a church in which he stands white among the dark natives. "For windows the church possessed tall arched apertures filled not with stained glass but with air and outward vision," and outside little girls were playing on "the packed dirt around the church." Yet in this moving setting, the "service was fatiguingly long," and natives who could hardly speak English were led through "exhaustive petitionary prayers (for the Queen, the Prime Minister, Parliament) and many eight-versed hymns sung with a penetrating, lingering joy. ... Musical stress, the British accent, and Negro elision worked upon the words a triple harmony of distortion."

The church ceremony seems such a betrayal: Kern loses his place in the hymn — "without a visual key I was lost" — and, bored, turns from the restless deacons slipping in and out of the windows, towards "the earth's wide circle round." "The Caribbean seemed a steeply tilted blue plane to which the few fishing boats in the bay below had been attached like magnetized toys." The churches do not seem to understand symbol and ceremony any longer. They are as technological and dry as the cities of cement. They do not relate us to the earth. Updike concludes this section, too, with a philosopher: "God made the world, Aquinas says, in play." The Caribbean speaks with more eloquence than the church.

The third section, "A Dying Cat," begins with a brief meditation on the ambiguity of matter, but twists the spiral of the story upwards from inanimate nature to the question of life and death: "Matter has its radiance and its darkness; it lifts and it buries. Things compete; a life demands a life."

From an island in the Caribbean, the scene shifts to "another English island," England itself, where on a lonely road late at night David Kern encounters something frightening which he does not then understand. America is somehow stifling for the religious man; we receive our supernatural mail on foreign soil," and on the present incident the "signature" is "decisive but illegible."

For six years Kern was unable to talk to his wife about it. Yet in itself the incident could have been innocuous: while his wife lies "swathed in white, ready for nothing so much as a graduation ceremony" in anticipation of childbirth, Kern comes upon a dying cat. It seemed to be, in the shadows, "about the size of a baby"; and of course it is as the cat dies that, that night, his perfect daughter is born.

Kern is determined not to let the cat die without ceremony. He laid her—he "felt it was female"—behind the hedge, and went back to his car to write a note to leave with her. Palm and three of the fingers of his glove are dyed a sacramental "wine-brown." The cat suffered his return stiffly: "It suggested I was making too much fuss, and seemed to say to me, *Run on home.*" He went back home, read from Chesterton's *The Everlasting Man,* prayed for his wife, and finally fell asleep.

The fourth and last section, "A Traded Car," is too long to follow in detail; as in the earlier parts, nearly every prominent word and surely every incident sends echoes forward and backward through the story. It opens: "When we returned from England, we bought a car." Before the paragraph is out, we are led to see that the car, if anything in America, is going to have to bear the symbolism that might help us understand ourselves. "Not only sand and candy wrappers accumulate in a car's interior, but heroisms and instants of communion. We in America make love in our cars, and listen to ball games, and plot our wooing of the dollar: small wonder the landscape is sacrificed to these dreaming vehicles of our ideal and onrushing manhood."

The ugly bulldozers push aside our paths to make room for highways; losing the symbols of nature, we gain the car. Kern and his wife treat their new '55 Ford as if it were a "broad blue baby," and it is not until their baby daughter born in England is nearly six that Kern can bring himself to trade it in. However, before relinquishing it to Detroit (who will "devour her child"), Kern has a last crucial adventure in the Ford.

At a dance with a woman not his wife, Kern falls sickeningly in love. The sweet desire leads to no more than her stroking his erect thumbs, but Kern's Sunday school conscience tells him that "to lust after a woman in thought is the same as committing adultery."

Unable to distinguish between automatic attraction and interior consent, Kern lies awake that night in terror. "To feel a sin was to commit it; to touch the brink was to be on the bottom of the chasm." But the real terror was that the "universe that so easily permitted me to commit adultery became...a universe that would easily permit me to die. The enormities of cosmic space, the maddening distension of time, history's forgotten slaughters, the child smothered in the dumped icebox, the recent breakdown of the molecular life-spiral, the proven physiological roots of the mind, the presence in our midst of idiots, Eichmanns, animals, and bacteria—all this evidence piled on, and I seemed already eternally forgotten...I prayed...prayed, prayed for a sign, any glimmer at all. ... Each second my agony went unanswered justified it more certainly: the God who permitted me this fear was unworthy of existence."

Intensely moved, Kern awakens his wife to tell her he is frightened; pragmatically, a little bored, she gives him the Stoic answer; he falls asleep as on the night of that other encounter with death. A phone call the next day tells him his father is dying. "Instantly I was relieved. The weight on me rolled away. All day death had been advancing under cover and now it had struck, declared its position."

A visit to church that night, and next day he begins his drive to Pennsylvania: *"Run on home."* He picks up a hitchhiking sailor, one of those "docile Titans—guileless, competent, mildly earnest —that we have fattened, an ocean removed from the slimming Latin passions and Nordic anxieties of Europe."

The writer, Kern, and the nameless sailor have little to talk about; yet their relationship is not at all that of brilliant isolated artist and the beautiful blond beast that Thomas Mann describes in the stories of the *Death in Venice* cycle. Updike is not after the Platonic distinction in types of men, the elite and the herd; he is after the incomprehension, the shallowness, the easy adjustment, the lack of life in our scientized environment, our "abundance of milk and honey, vitamins and protein." It sometimes seems that natural wealth, science, and pragmatic adjustment are enough; and in this environment, how can one hear of God or immortality?

A little later, the sailor gone, Kern stops at a Howard Johnson's in the Mennonite country; they remind him of an earlier time, of "that Pennsylvania knowingness—of knowing, that is, that the truth is good." At home, his mother pours him a glass of wine: "Wine had a ceremonial significance in our family; we

drank it seldom." His mother tells him his father has "lost his
faith": "He never was much of one for faith," she adds. "He was
strictly a works man."

The next day, mother and son visit the family doctor; Kern has
time to reminisce about the order, delight, and hope of childhood. Knowing his own faith gone, too, he follows his mother into
the hospital. Leading him, she is already exercising the responsibilities of widowhood.

In the ensuing conversation with the older Kern, David finds
his father talking mostly of how he'll miss his car. Just as David
begins to feel the coming separation with his father (and cannot
speak of it for "There were no words, no form of words available
in our tradition"), and as his mother is already weeping, a girl
from the Lutheran Home Missions comes to visit, notebook in
hand. Young Kern is afraid she'll be made fun of; far from it, the
older Kern tells her after a warm conversation, "You're a wonderful woman to be doing what you're doing." The woman leaves
"transformed into just that. As a star shines in our heaven though
it has vanished from the universe, so my father continued to shed
faith upon others." A cat's dying balanced a baby's birth: a law of
continuity, a kind of permanence.

For the first time, David realizes that when he says "home" he
means "a far place, where I had a wife and children." His father is
not going to die just yet and, though it comes as a disappointment
to the bedridden man, David tells him he must return home. In
an instant during which his face was blank, the older Kern "was
swallowing the realization that he was no longer the center of even
his son's universe." As David is about to drive north, his mother
reminds him of the night he was born, when his father drove
north from Wheeling: "the story of his all-night ride was the first
myth in which I was a character."

Driving home in the sunset, Kern enters a new myth. Pennsylvania again reminds him of repose, of "the certainty that the
truth is good." "It seemed to me for this sunset hour that the world
is our bride, given us to love, and the terror and joy of the marriage is that we bring to it a nature not our bride's." But if the
world is not of our nature, what shall we find to symbolize for us
what our nature is like?

Like Kern's nighttime fall through an empty universe, the car ride begins to seem "meaninglessly coquettish," then "maddeningly obstinate," then "frighteningly empty." A "stellar infinity of explosive sparks" is needed to drive the effortlessly moving car, and these pass into his body. He stops for coffee and "the hallucinatory comfort of human faces"; the music on the radio obliterated time; it "began to seem a miracle that the car could gather speed" from his numb foot.

Gradually, the car becomes David Kern's soul, as little by little he leaves his body. "We climbed through a space fretted by scattered brilliance and bathed in a monotonous wind. I had been driving forever, furniture, earth, churches, women, were all things I had innocently dreamed. And through those aeons my car, beginning as a mechanical spiral of molecules, evolved into something soft and organic and consciously brave. I lost, first, heart, then head, and finally any sense of my body. In the last hour of the trip I ceased to care or feel or in any real sense see, but the car, though its soul the driver had died, maintained steady forward motion, and completed the endless journey safely."

Out of flux, Updike fashions a symbol of permanence, of spirit, in which we might at last be able even to *understand* immortality. But the very car which furnishes him this symbol, that six-year-old Ford, is soon to be traded in for a new one: "when he returned the car would be new, and the old one was gone, gone, utterly dissolved back into the mineral world from which it was conjured, dismissed without a blessing, a kiss, a testament, or any ceremony of farewell."

In a pragmatic, secular America, it is almost impossible for faith to take intelligent root, and men, though having ears, cannot hear; for there are almost no correlates in our experience for what the Word of God says. Even though he is so far limiting himself to his own experience, John Updike is beginning to make religion intelligible in America, and to fashion symbols whereby it can be understood. It is not surprising if the critics see only the dazzling words, and do not grasp what they mean. "We in America need ceremonies," is, I suppose, the point of a great many of the words he has written.

The Music School: A Place of Resonance

by Charles Thomas Samuels

The Music School contains nearly all the stories John Updike has published in the past four years. As before, there are too many trifles: unfortunately, chronological arrangement places too many of them at the beginning of the book. Nevertheless, *The Music School* is Updike's best collection, with superior examples of every sort of story that he writes.

"Lifeguard" in *Pigeon Feathers* was a consideration of the ambiguities of secular life through the reverie of a divinity student who is earning tuition on the beach. With a contrapuntal technique that plays on its title, "The Music School" treats the same theme with greater poise. Though more audacious than the earlier tale, which managed to turn bathers into theological terms, this story does not mock its speaker's pain with a brazen virtuosity.

Other stories, formally less innovating, comprise Updike's clever portrayals of marital tension. Cleverness, however, is sometimes evasive here. As Updike showed in *Of the Farm,* a quarrel has its own rhythm. Artificially composed, the notes sound shriller than they need to be, frequently false. The short-story form, particularly as practiced in *The New Yorker,* forces Updike to impose structural neatness upon materials that seem authentic only when free from external restraint. So, in "Giving Blood," the precise oscillation of the Maples' love is cut short arbitrarily. In a restaurant where they go to share the moment of camaraderie, born while they donated blood, the husband finds he lacks money to pay for his affectionate invitation; and the wife, obviously punning, replies: "We'll both pay." Surfeited with cleverness, the reader now disdains the pun implicit in the whole story: what could have been a moving glimpse at familiar despair blinds us with a glossy surface to its underlying truth.

Two tales in *The Music School* manage to make slickness a virtue. "Avec La Bébé-Sitter" and "The Rescue" don't strain for outsize responses. The couples in them are either past the Maples' danger or their troubles are unreal. The first story is a sardonic anecdote about two people on the rocks who hope to cement their foundation by moving to Antibes. One afternoon while the wife is gone, the husband, manfully learning French from their baby-sitter-maid, blurts out the house's secret. Ironically, his confession creates an emotional order on these shifty Mediterranean sands which the family lacked back home. In the second story, a young woman who suspects her husband is unfaithful decides not to yield to disruptive anger. Faced with a fortuitous image of divorced self-righteousness, spread-eagled on an icy ski slope, she becomes certain that her husband must be innocent. Cleverness can capture only small ironies in human affairs, but it is the merit of both stories that their ironies precisely suit their treatment.

Updike's art is more polished in this volume than in his earlier collections, but *The Music School* would be a less resonant place were it not for one group of stories representing an advance in scope. One of these, Updike's best story to date, is another of those doctrinal debates which he presents as ordinary encounters, like Hook and Conner discussing the nature of virtue in the poorhouse sitting room, or Rabbit and Eccles defining grace on the golf course. In "The Christian Roommates" the essential Updike meeting of pharisee and would-be saint occurs at Harvard, an institution designed to train adolescents—thus, a perfect setting for Updike's theme. Not even Salinger has created so touching a display of that mixture of fear and bravado with which the college student approaches an adult role. The background of "The Christian Roommates" is crowded with young souls fixed in brittle postures of self-defensiveness, like the homesick colored boy who warms himself in the unfamiliar New England cold with nightly blowing on a trumpet mouthpiece, or the witty roommates who mask their enmity by collaborating on improvised musical comedies at the expense of all outsiders.

Against this background, Updike presents the engagement of

Orson Zeigler, lanky, Midwestern, athletic valedictorian, who has mapped out his future as town physician and pillar of society, with Hub Palamountain, maddeningly arrogant, vegetarian, boor and yogi. Each moment of their conflict is finely rendered. When Orson first enters the room which will become their battleground, Hub dazzles him with those personal details—divorced parents, unpopularity, conscientious objecting to the draft, and arcane religious zeal—which give Zeigler his first glimpse of depths hidden in his own life. In the midst of this recital, Hub accounts rather solemnly for his summer job as gluer in a plywood mill. "It's a kind of excessive introspection," he intones, "you've read *Hamlet?*" Fresh scrubbed Orson feels his soul challenged. "Just *Macbeth* and *The Merchant of Venice,*" he pleads.

Definitive as it is, their contention is never expressed in moments less natural than this one. In his best work, Updike infuses his story with meaning not by commenting on the action but by always finding the right gesture or word for his people so that their significance is the satisfying accumulation of all they have said or done. Thus, for the final impact of Hub's god-lust on Orson's shallow correctness, Updike finds the perfect measured fact: when the boy becomes the man he had envisioned, he carries "a kind of scar...without pain and without any clear memory of the amputation. ... He never prays."

Though "The Christian Roommates" is typical, it suggests the author's willingness to break the essentially domestic walls of his universe, a willingness best realized in two other stories: "At a Bar in Charlotte Amalie" and "The Bulgarian Poetess." The first tale is a rigidly controlled description of events witnessed at a bar in the Virgin Islands. The tableau is formed by the slightest shift in the arrangement of its components: a prim schoolteacher who by entering the bar starts the story is subtly drawn into its languid corruption as a finale. Nothing much happens, but we know this bar down to the last cloying drop of rum with which its inhabitants assuage their aimlessness.

"The Bulgarian Poetess" is the volume's emotive triumph just as "The Christian Roommates" is its triumph in human understanding. There is little fulfilled love in Updike's fiction: he is too aware of its contingency. But "The Bulgarian Poetess" creates a moment of love which is all the more precious for being fugitive. Its hero is an American novelist whose best work is behind him and whose life has dried for want of affection. On a feckless red-taped journey to Bulgaria, he meets a fellow writer whose female grace and tenderness give him sustaining proof of what he has had to live without.

In the course of this story, Updike needs to provide some informed literary chatter for his writers and cultural hangers-on. What he makes them say is intrinsically interesting. How many of our writers can demonstrate a character's intelligence? How many can find the right words for two adolescents who are taking each other's measure? How many can describe the exact sensation of feeling blood drained from your arm or the gradations of shadow as the sky darkens?

Updike's range of experience is both common and confined; he avoids those upheavals in which many of us like to think we find our true reflection. Some readers will persist in finding him trivial; they will miss separable and obtrusive "ideas"; even fervent admirers must admit that his situations are often too slight. But within the ordinary moments he selects, his precisely expressive language always embeds an insight authenticated by gesture, a truth extensively portrayed. No one has ever denied his skill. But we ought to remember that in art skill is not a dispensable adjunct to seriousness: it *is* seriousness: proof that the artist esteems his craft, his subject, his readers. Updike's reverence for life won't disdain small moments and won't compromise itself with inflated or pretentious language. His seriousness is chastened by modesty, his nostalgia is both joyful and unillusioned his precision is both linguistic and dramatic. Is there another new American novelist who gives such continuous proof of the power of art?

Keeping Up with Updike: *Bech: A Book*

by Jack Richardson

How can a contemporary novelist confront experience? How, knowing that art has worn out so many of the details of life, can one still fix a narrative of a novel's length into a world made up of "things" and "characters"? How can one make the selection of events or the color of an eye without arousing disquieting feelings about old-fashioned literary calculation? Or again, how to make those eyes and the events they witness not seem examples of a self-indulgent modernism or a coy eccentricity? When excess is tolerated, indeed sought after, by the public and its critics, how can one keep those first tentative ideas for a novel from serving an easy, *étonne-moi* aesthetic?

Finally, how simply to describe, how to hang qualifiers, metaphors, and images onto events without making the language seem obstructive or cloying, without bringing on oneself the charge of naïveté, of writing as if the objects of the world had not already been heavily described by those masters who made the novel an exploration in naming the particulars of experience? More primitive still: How to move a character across a furniture-stuffed room and not create the deadening sense that words once again are bustling us through a moment that seems somehow perfunctory and that writer and reader are being held by an effete convention?

These questions nowadays hover around the novel. One does not need to believe in a non-linear theory of art, or in progress, or in the artist as a conquistador of new forms, to wonder if this ritual exchange between a single imagination and a loose gather-

"Keeping Up with Updike," by Jack Richardson. Reprinted with permission from *The New York Review of Books*, 15 (October 22, 1970), 46-48. Copyright © 1970 NYREV, Inc.

ing of receptive readers has not become an empty, formal agree-
ment—a matter of cultural manners rather than a spontaneous
and enjoyable common trust. Fortunately, of course, these questions do not intrude each time someone with a literate memory
reads, or for that matter writes, the first sentence of a novel. Just
as we do not inhibit our daily actions by constantly justifying
them with ethical principles, so also we do not read for pleasure
only after assuring ourselves that the novel, as an expressive form
in the last third of the twentieth century, still vindicates itself.
Nevertheless, there are moments—at a sudden break in the narrative, for instance, when we see a cloudburst of fine writing coming on; or when punctuation begins to fade, words couple with
their neighbors, and we know that we are off into another neatly
planned simulation of unguarded thought—when all the paraphernalia of the novel seem like polite rituals.

If the novels of John Updike occasion such speculations, it is
because they are more nakedly traditional than the works of most
of our readable contemporaries. By traditional I do not mean
that they are simply put together with a debt to a certain historical
style, but rather that they present fragments of life without the
constant imposition of extraneous attitude, without, that is to say,
making the self-conscious and fashionable gestures to irony. *The
Centaur, Rabbit, Run, Of the Farm, Couples* are all works that
unfold stories which seem to have no large aesthetic or philo-
sophical frame from which the reader is meant to derive their
meaning. Here and there, one may sniff out in these novels some
genteel religiosity or notion of a guiltless nature that is a witness
to, and absorbant of, human passion; but most of the incidents
unfold in Updike's work without metaphysical coercion or for-
malist tricks.[1]

Then, too, to narrow the idea of tradition, Updike's works have
generally come to us without the fashionable patina of creative
self-consciousness. They do not writhe over the problem of their

[1] The one exception to Updike's general lack of literary guile is, of course,
the mythological overlay of *The Centaur*. Those Greek intrusions into the
Americana of a small-town high school seem so mistaken and so at variance with
the usual fine integration of his novels, that, in speaking generally of his work,
I would prefer to set them aside as a collective instance of simple absence of
mind.

own composition; in their margins there is ˏno apperceptive author whispering dicta on what fiction can and cannot do. In a time of anti-novels, epistemological novels, novels as reportage, novels as history, novels as games, etc., Updike accepts the old principles of the form. He does not torture, analyze, or make fun of the novel so that it will not seem a quaint and out-of-date curio. From this assurance comes, I assume, his belief in the novel of characters and his narrator's trust in their plain predicaments.

Here, of course, he is heir to a specific Anglo-American legacy; namely, that the writer is esteemed not for his powers to fabricate examples of the outlandish, but rather for his ability to uncover unusual patterns and shadings where an ungifted eye sees only a single, quotidian tone. Often this means that he must examine with exhausting effort the unassuming and commonplace so that he can make the truths about them self-evident and impressive. To do this today argues great faith in the slow, hard-won revelations of novels and in the absolute value of imaginary men and women whose claim to our attention is predicated on the value of their author's insights and on how smoothly he forces us to make the transition from his tidy world of language to our rough, disordered one of experience.

To read Updike, then, is to come to the heart of a form that has seen a lot of hard service in the past. *Rabbit, Run* and *The Centaur,* to me his most successful works, do not try to disguise their heritage. Indeed, they insist upon it. At every page they reveal themselves as artifices, as *written,* as a display of observation. The celebrated Updike style, that often wearisome struggle for the most precise yet extensive metaphor, is like those Dickensian asides that unabashedly remind us that a writer is present. This reminder, however, is not meant to unsettle our belief in the experience of fiction. On the contrary, it is rather an attempt to re-enforce it, to make certain that the reader attains a certain emotional intensity, that he will see and feel as the author wants him to.

Sometimes, as when Rabbit takes flight at the beginning of his story, there is a tense balance kept between the packed, unremitting lyricism of Updike's prose and the action it surrounds; from image to image, one can almost catch the language breathing in rapid unison with Rabbit. The details of the impromptu basketball court, the apartment, the town, and the labyrinthian turnpike at night are described in a way that suggests that they are charged with secrets vital to Rabbit's life, secrets that might be uncovered if analogies were pushed further and further to the resolution of a final metaphor. Rabbit's spasmic escape sustains all this in the way that the leisurely scope of the Victorian novel permitted an author time to sigh and moralize in his own voice without breaking the rhythms of his art and causing the reader to stumble out of a psychic sympathy with him.

Similarly, in *The Centaur,* Caldwell, a teacher moving half gratefully toward death after a lifetime of trying to kindle in his students an interest in the universe, is caught at such a heightened point in his life and in such extremes of self-abnegation that one appreciates Updike's intention to hold him firmly within the finely described details of a small town, to fix him, as it were, on a proper level of reality.

Caldwell is an eccentrically powerful character, and it is interesting to see Updike work so hard, not only to surround his protagonist with mystery, but also to ensure that this high-school teacher will not carry a meaning beyond himself. Whereas in *Rabbit, Run,* the "writing" is meant to approximate the inarticulate awareness that is driving Rabbit, in *The Centaur* it serves the opposite purpose; to counteract ironically Caldwell's slightly mysterious, evocative behavior. Even in this ambitious book, Updike wants to stay within the boundaries of the traditional novel, to convince us of the common actuality of what is presented.

Sometimes, however, as in *Couples,* Updike merely convinces us that his lyrical moments are little more than escapes from the novel itself. In such a work, one sees why there exists a certain impatience with the old assumptions of the novel. For *Couples* is almost a case study in the effects of literary decadence, if such a phrase is taken to mean purposeless ornamentation, formalized passions, and a joyless candor about sex that tries to disguise the lack of any real life in all those swooning copulations.

For all his gifts and intelligence, Updike seems as lost as the reader in this saga of suburban *Angst.* Here all his traditional weapons have let him down: he has observed keenly, each of his characters carries his own portmanteau of telling peculiarities, events glide together neatly and engender enough agitation to keep the couples of Tarbox moving through their abortions, wifeswappings, community intrigues, and graceless aging. Yet every-thing seems frozen and all of Updike's ingenious evocations of seascapes or prose illuminations of the orgasm cannot animate a book that is so formally dead.

It would be simple to say that *Couples* is merely a stillborn effort, a good writer's failure. However, I think that there is some-thing more portentous in this collapse, something that almost suggests the exhaustion of the genre itself. For it is not so much that this novel is bad as that it is worn out. Reading it, one feels more and more constricted by the limits Updike has set. When a good writer makes all the right choices and still comes up with a four-hundred-page stretch of tedium artificially stimulated by an occasional, anxious lyricism, one may very well wonder if some mistake has not been made that runs far deeper than miscalcula-tion. One could conclude that the form itself no longer sustains our interest and that, like the modes of allegory, it has had its time.

From this dark hypothesis it is easy to come to Updike's most recent work, *Bech: A Book,* for of all the many things Bech is, he is mainly a beguiling embodiment of the novelist's problem. Bech is a blocked writer. The author of a reputation-making first novel, a reputation-bolstering *novella,* and a long "noble failure," Bech has, in his middle forties, fallen on barren times. He now writes, we are told, a review or two and some "subjective reportage" for *Esquire.* Apart from these, his muse is silent and he is gradually fading into a literary "personality," an object to be dispatched on cultural exchanges and lecture tours.

He is indeed a harried man, and we see him at cross monologues with his Iron Curtain colleagues, being used for a week by a pretty gossip columnist in London, fighting the tedium of his mistress and the vacuities of a former student while vacationing at a place resembling Martha's Vineyard, and sensing death and the break-down of his art while on the fecund campus of a Southern college for girls. Throughout, Bech keeps a keen, melancholy, and ironic eye on his absurdities, and gradually becomes that rarity in mod-ern fiction: a real portrait of a writer that is appositely agonizing and justifiably humorous.

In the book's Foreword, a benediction from Bech himself, Updike has anticipated the *roman á clef* games by admitting that

Bech is something of a Jewish pastiche. To me, because his mus-
ings are so Herzogian, there is more Bellow in Bech than Mailer,
Roth, Malamud, et al., but this is only a dutiful conjecture. Bech
is a way of literary life that has in part absorbed many writers, a
way of life that presents slightly tawdry but comforting alterna-
tives to the work they feel guilty for not doing. But it is really not
Bech's career that interests or the fact that, as he says, he has
become his own creation. Rather, it is his darker battle to hold
onto his faith in art itself that keeps Bech from being simply a
clever conceit. The battle is fought on all levels: from the vapid-
ness and willful misunderstanding of an interviewer to Bech's
own disquieting night thoughts. But his worst moments come
when he is surrounded by intensely literary Southern belles at a
dinner table. First, they give him a classic case of existential
upset:

> Their massed fertility was overwhelming: their bodies were being
> broadened and readied to generate from their own cells a new body
> to be pushed from the old, and in time to push bodies from itself,
> and so on into eternity, an ocean of doubling and redoubling cells
> within which his own conscious moment was soon to wink out. He
> had had no child. He had spilled his seed upon the ground. Yet we
> are all seed spilled upon the ground. These thoughts, as Valery had
> predicted, did not come neatly, in chiming packets of language, but
> as slithering, overlapping sensations, microorganisms of thoughts
> setting up in sum a panicked sweat on Bech's palms and a palpable
> nausea behind his belt.
>
> [Rpt. New York: Fawcett World Library, pp. 127-28]

And the defense and consolation of art?

> He looked around the ring of munching females and saw their bod-
> ies as a Martian or a mollusc might see them, as pulpy stalks of
> bundled nerves oddly pinched to a bud of concentration in the
> head, a hairy bone nob holding some pounds of jelly in which a
> trillion circuits, mostly dead, kept records, coded motor operations,
> and generated an excess of electricity that pressed into the hairless
> side of the head and leaked through the orifices, in the form of
> pained, hopeful noises and a simian dance of wrinkles. Impossible
> mirage! A blot on nothingness. And to think that all the efforts of
> his life—his preening, his lovemaking, his typing—boiled down to
> the attempt to displace a few sparks, to bias a few circuits, within
> some random other scoops of jelly that would, in less time than it

takes the Andreas Fault to shrug or the tail-tip of Scorpio to crawl
an inch across the map of Heaven, be utterly dissolved. The widest
fame and most enduring excellence shrank to nothing in this
perspective.   [p. 131]

Have such thoughts stultified Bech, or has his block created
convenient, apocalyptic visions of human insignificance? It really
doesn't matter, for Bech loses either way. Pinioned by his own
fears, trapped, as he again tells us, in a naturalistic style, there is
nothing left for him but to accept the honors of his society as
though they were post-mortem testaments.

Updike could have had many intentions in writing *Bech:* as a
rejoinder to a competing style, as a parody of fashionable attitudes, as a sympathetic act of imagination, as an attempt to state
the American writer's case in the broadest terms possible. However, whatever the impetus, he has written a book quite unlike
any of his previous works, a book that does not seem to struggle
with the obligations of convention, that does not have to wrest its
excellence from eroded soil. Everything about *Bech* is lean, antic,
and to the point, and it has a daring that is supported, rather than
encumbered, by the lessons of tradition. With its intelligence and
verve, *Bech* reaffirms that writing is still our most subtle way of
telling things. Perhaps also it hints that, in finally stultifying
Bech, Updike has propitiously somewhat liberated himself.

At the Flashpoint: *Museums and Women*

By Rosemary Dinnage

Museums and women: what is cunning Mr. Updike up to, in the title of his new book of short stories? Museums and women, for him, both are intersection points for the forces that tug apart his brilliant, cloven universe: time and eternity, passion and guilt, death and permanence, the natural and the moral order. Museums and women both touch impermanence with order and survival (of past objects, future beings): both oppose death, arrest time, crystallize a longing for its debris.

Of that longing he has said in an essay on courtly love:

> what is it but love for that part of ourselves which is in Heaven, forever removed from change and corruption? A woman, loved, momentarily eases the pain of time by localizing nostalgia. ... The images we hoard in wait for the woman who will seem to body them forth include the inhuman—a certain slant of sunshine, a delicate flavour of dust, a kind of rasping tune that is reborn in her voice; they are nameless, these elusive glints of original goodness that a man's memory stores toward an erotic commitment.
>
> ["More Love in the Western World," *Assorted Prose*]

This corrupt, histrionic, artistically exciting version of sexual love was already foreseen in Mr. Updike's first novel, *The Poorhouse Fair*. In it an old and virtuous male world ushered in the fallen, contemporary one that gives him so much scope:

> Thus pronouncing, Hook had a very clear inner apprehension of what virtue was: An austerity of the hunt, a manliness from which

comes all life, so that it can be written that the woman takes her
life from the man. As the Indian once served the elusive deer he
hunted, men once served invisible goals, and grew hard in such
services and pursuit, and lent their society an invisible temper. Impotent to provide this tempering salt, men would sink lower than
women, as indeed they had.

[Rpt. New York: Fawcett World Library, p. 111]

In this lapsed world where discarded women carry the onus of
masculine failure of nerve, "momentarily ease the pain of time"
for them, and suffer, as metaphysical objects, the worship and
curses due to gods, Mr. Updike's Don Juan figure—it might be
Piet Hanema of *Couples,* or Rabbit, or the narrator in many of
these stories—insatiably pursues the "elusive glints of original
goodness":

> I looked back, and it came to me that nothing about museums is as
> splendid as their entrances—the sudden vault, the shapely cornices,
> the motionless uniformed guard like a wittily disguised archangel,
> the broad stairs leading upward into heaven knows what mansions
> of expectantly hushed treasure. And it appeared to me that now I
> was condemned, in my search for the radiance that had faded be-
> hind me, to enter more and more museums, and to be a little less
> exalted by each new entrance, and a little more quickly disen-
> chanted by the familiar contents beyond.
>
> ["Museums and Women"]

Original goodness, original sin, and woman have not had such a
press since Genesis and John Donne. If this is Christianity's posi-
tively last appearance in serious English or American literature,
it leaves the stage with panache; if sexual drama is disappearing
with permissiveness, Mr. Updike at least is still loading every
rift of it (so to speak) with awe.

By writing almost as much in the short story as in the novel
form he is wisely ignoring a current literary trend. In his stories,
some no longer than a couple of pages, his exuberance is compressed as strictly and efficiently as liquid in an aerosol; his
subject always being the flashpoint, the explosion of dark against
light, the arrested moment when mortality illuminates life, this
compressive form disciplines him admirably. To achieve his sudden wanings, he takes the opposite course from Beckett's in approaching the same area (to the next generation perhaps the two

may seem two sides of an authentic twentieth-century coin). Where Beckett goes straight to dread and emptiness and sparsely reproduces them, Updike surrounds them with life and movement and then stops the action; so that suddenly we hear the silence and see the dark. There is a click, a stillness, and all the energy that poured into a representation of liveliness outlines its absence. "I can hear the catcher snicker," says his baseball player,

> and for a second of reflex there I can see it like it used to be, continents and cities and every green tree distinct as a stitch, and the hickory sweetens in my hands, and I feel the good old sure hunger. Then something happens. It blurs, skips, fades, I don't know. It's not caring enough, is what it probably is, it's knowing that none of it—the stadium, the averages—is really there, just *you* are there, and it's not enough.   ["The Slump," *Museums and Women*]

But what other writer is able to surround the split second of mortality with so many varieties of life—speaking in the voices of an archangel, a used-car salesman, Queen Iseult; packing a potential novel into a psychoanalytic session, a party, a car drive; seeing on a ball "the Spalding guarantee in ten-point sans-serif," in the shadow of a vine leaf "innumerable barbaric suggestions of scimitars, flanged spears, prongs, and menacing helmets"; comparing a nervous couple at a family gathering to one of "those isolated corners of interjections and foreign syllables in a poorly planned crossword puzzle"; following Kierkegaard "as, crippled, agonized by distinctions he scribbled on and on, heaping irony on irony, curse on curse, gnashing, sneering, praising Jehovah in the privacy of his empty home in Copenhagen"; with a girl's bare shoulder bones in the supermarket "like a dented sheet of metal tilted in the light"?

Another writer, perhaps, might have pursued a legend that Christ escaped the Cross to settle in a remote Japanese island; might have given him the stoop of an elderly kimonoed Japanese, and blue eyes—but would the eyelids have been wrinkled "like the armpits of a salamander"? Who else would include, in the memories of a thesis-writing Nonconformist clergyman experiencing mystical rapture in a dentist's surgery in Oxford, "Max Beerbohm's sentence about there always being a slight shock in seeing an envelope of one's own after it has gone through the post"? Mr. Updike's style is itself a museum, a great apparently

uncatalogued collection of rarities preserved against extinction,
as here [in the story "Archangel"] in *Pigeon Feathers:*

> The white arms of girls dancing, taffeta, white arms violet in the
> hollows music its ecstasies praise the white wrists of praise the
> white arms and the white paper trimmed the Euclidean proof of
> Pythagoras' theorem its tightening beauty the iridescence of an old
> copper found in the salt sand. The microscopic glitter in the ink of
> the letters of words that are your own. Certain moments, remem-
> bered or imagined, of childhood. Three-handed pinochle by the
> brown glow of the stained-glass lampshade, your parents out of
> their godliness silently wishing you to win. The Brancusi room,
> silent. *Pines and Rocks* by Cézanne; and *The Lace-Maker* in the
> Louvre hardly bigger than your spread hand.

Even his grotesqueries—the choked bottlenecks of fantasy, the
ham-handed rhetorical questions, the superfluous fireworky
crackle—seem, in a writer who could eat half a dozen of his literary contemporaries for breakfast, voluntary: as though, for-
swearing the cosmopolitanism of "The Bulgarian Poetess," the
poker-faced parody of "One of My Generation," the outrageous
jeux d'esprit (cocktail party for Jurassic fauna—"we had an
amphibious babysitter who had to be back in the water by one"),
he swears—honest John, farm-bred in Shillington, Penn.—to
abdicate all foreign sophistication and become as a little child, as
an all-American sophomore majoring in Creative Writing and
Great Philosophies of the World. But his most willed naiveties
become, in spite of himself, subtle, for he is inescapably metaphysical, a wit in the full sense of the word. In a world seeming
more and more drained of supernatural tension, his exuberant
guilt, his magnificent, cunning despair, his sharpening of needle-
points for more and more angels to dance on, make a fine, resonant stir.

Disengagement in *Museums and Women*

by Richard Todd

Recall if you can the 1950s and try to retrieve a feeling that existed then. It's common now to remember those as silently anguished years, all of us mute with rage at the banality of the culture, and there is some truth to that memory—there was rage, including much that didn't know its name—but the feeling I have in mind is different. It began with the odd and not altogether unpleasant sense that the world had recently ended.

The world was *about* to end, of course, in "nuclear holocaust," but it had ended already in terms of the possibilities for human behavior that remained alive. Everyone knew that large gestures, heroic intentions, a full-throated voice were no longer available. Everyone knew that the only acceptable mode of speech and vision was irony. "Everyone" was, of course, not everyone, but it was many: this sensibility flourished (often in mutually contemptuous forms) in English departments and advertising agencies, fraternity houses and "converted barns." The twentieth-century malaise that had belonged to what used to be called "bohemia" had moved in a gentled form to the suburbs. The suburbs were one symbol of the compromised quality of life. Another was the curious Bomb. It surely traumatized not nearly so many people as it was fashionable to claim, but it probably did alter the scale on which we thought of human life: it contributed to the sense that human beings had become a toy breed.

"A smug conviction that the world was doomed," John Updike remembers (in the voice of a character who is "in securities") in a story from his new collection, *Museums and Women*. The story works to re-create another emotion of the years, simultaneous "fear and gratitude. Young people now are many things, but they aren't afraid, and aren't grateful." If anyone so young—this is the year he is forty—is entitled to nostalgia for those years, it is John Updike, who was the poet of their precarious coziness. The "fifties," I suppose, extended into the early sixties; although the Kennedy inauguration could have been said to end them on time, a dedicated "privatist" could easily enough dissociate himself from the cadences of Theodore Sorensen; the civil rights movement drew the line. If you were, as I was, in college at the end of the decade, Updike, still in his twenties, was a figure to reckon with, his stories appearing regularly in Friday's welcome mail, the *New Yorker*.

In 1959 Updike wrote what was then his richest, most accomplished story, called "The Happiest I've Been." It recounted the last night at home for a young man about to return to college from the Christmas holidays. Not much really happened. There was a New Year's party. A girl fell asleep on his shoulder. A friend driving with him fell asleep on the seat. Dawn occurred, as he drove safely over slick roads, and further into the trip the young man had his happiest moment, which consisted of an expansive feeling for the landscape, the trip, and, in no small part, the pleasure that two people had trusted him enough to fall asleep at his side. I struggle to say how wonderful a story this seemed. Its power lay initially—as always in Updike—in the perfectly rendered detail. Beyond that there was the paradoxical daring of the story, its defeat of conventional expectations concerning what the passage to adulthood (which was, after all, the subject) ought to be about. Updike was making a story out of stuff trivial enough to be the stuff of one's life. This is all there was, he said, and all there would be; the implication was that life would hold no more exalted moment than the instant the story recorded. (The antiheroic impulse was strong; Updike was moved by the success of Jack Kerouac to parody his book's claims for the beat life with an account of a boy on a tricycle—"On the Sidewalk.")

Thinking of "The Happiest I've Been" I find that a phrase from its last paragraph comes back: "the moment of which each following moment was a slight diminution." As the assistant professors used to say: *Just so.* A diminution. Updike's stories even then were often about a sense of loss. So are they still. Most of the stories in *Museums and Women* were written in the past five years, but they evoke the time of Updike's earliest success. They are, of course, "minor" work; even as Updike was writing them he had his mind on more ambitious things, particularly *Rabbit Redux,* which included vastly more various sexual, social, and political content than do the stories. But his short fiction isn't to be dismissed; I'd maintain that his most fully realized novel is the one most like a short story: *Of the Farm.*

In the title story of *Museums and Women,* the narrator, musing on his marriage and on his affairs, some of whose trysts have occurred in museums, is moved to the realization (in a shamelessly elaborate metaphor) that what is most "splendid" about museums is not their content but their entrances. "And it appeared to me that now I was condemned, in my search for the radiance that had faded behind me, to enter more and more museums, and to be a little less exalted by each new entrance, and a little more quickly disenchanted by the familiar contents beyond."

Loss upon loss, and loss itself becomes a diminution. What is lost is nothing very extraordinary; only a moment of happiness, or a moment when the possibility of happiness might be glimpsed. Another story describes a day on which the hero has some bridge-work done, goes to a party, gets drunk, skids his car off the road, as his patronizing wife predicts ("Darley, you know you're coming to that terrible curve?"), and a woman (divorced, seductive) riding with them suffers a minor injury to her leg. He quickly sobers: "Never again, never ever, would his car be new, would he chew on his own enamel, would she kick so high with vivid long legs."

Implicit in most of these stories is an awareness of two sorts of time: one's own and social time, and the stories often play off the ironic contrast between history and the present moment. "The Carol Sing" in the new volume describes a community at church at Christmastime, preoccupied with small tragedies, and remarks on the music—"these antiquities that if you listened to the words would break your heart." Another finds the transience of our lives in a contemplation of the enduring pipes in an old house.

The smallness of Updike's subject matter (in, at least, his short fiction) is of course accompanied by his celebrated, lushly intricate descriptive style. The title story of the collection begins: "Set together, the two words are seen to be mutually transparent:

the E's, the M's blend—the M's framing and squaring the structure lend resonance and a curious formal weight to the M central in the creature, which it dominates like a dark core winged with flitting syllables." Words at moments become objects and organic things, larger and more real than what they denote. First and last sentences are particular repositories for cleverness: look from one to the other and more often than not you will find them punning against one another, tying a bow around the story.

These habits produce a certain response in Updike's critics. From the start of his career it has been usual to speak of him in wistful tones. If only he weren't so precious. If only he'd write about something important. If only he wouldn't waste his talent.

I imagine that this criticism has rankled. Like a girl accused of coyness, Updike must have wanted to say: But whether you know it or not that is what you like about me. The delicacy of Updike's style derives from the sense that you had better keep your eyes on the small task at hand: look around the room and you'll see pointlessness. "Better, I suppose, to sing," it is said at the end of "The Carol Sing," "than to listen."

Though so many of the stories are chronicles of melancholy, there is at their heart a kind of assurance. A considerable distance exists between the cool contemplative voice of the stories and the experience it describes. Whether in "Museums and Women" the M's and E's perform the sort of architectural and anatomical functions that the narrator claims is, as you enter the story, beside the point. You are affected by the detached voice, which, it becomes clear, has the most magic control over its perceptions, but remains strangely remote from the life of which it speaks.

There is this difficulty in Updike's stories: for all their recognitions of the religious impulse, their honoring of tarnished values, they are not stories in which moral choice occurs. Instead, they render modes of reconciliation and acceptance: values in themselves, of course, but not ones to arrive at easily. I only reluctantly uncrate the central word of a fifties' critical vocabulary: the stories are sentimental, in the sense that they invite us to value an unearned emotion.

A certain moral paralysis afflicts Updike's fiction (though it is a problem from which Harry Angstrom tries to free himself in

Rabbit Redux). It becomes more visible now, as Updike's shorter fiction loses its exact grip on the present moment. The stories address themselves to a cultural situation that held sway most strongly when Updike began his career; they provide a way of feeling good about a world whose language continually suggested that life had become a diminished thing.

Chronology of Important Dates

1932   Updike born at Shillington, Pennsylvania, on March 18, son of Wesley R. and Linda Grace (Hoyer) Updike.

1937   Begins attending public schools in Shillington, fictionalized as Olinger in Updike's stories and novels.

1945   The family moves to a farmhouse in the country near Plowville, Pennsylvania, eleven miles from Shillington. Updike continues in the Shillington public schools, where his father teaches high-school mathematics.

1950   Enters Harvard on a tuition scholarship. Begins to write for the *Harvard Lampoon,* a humor magazine.

1953   Elected president of the *Lampoon.* Majors in English literature. Marries Mary E. Pennington, a fine arts major from Radcliffe, on June 26.

1954   Writes his senior essay on Robert Herrick, the seventeenth-century English poet. Graduates *summa cum laude* from Harvard. Sells first short story ("Friends from Philadelphia") to *The New Yorker.* Travels to England on a Knox Fellowship and enrolls in the Ruskin School of Drawing and Fine Art at Oxford.

1955   Daughter Elizabeth born. Returns from England and joins the staff of *The New Yorker* as a reporter for the "Talk of the Town" column.

1957   Son David born. Leaves *The New Yorker* staff in March to concentrate on his poetry and fiction, and moves with his family to Ipswich, Massachusetts.

1958   *The Carpentered Hen* (poems) published.

1959   Publication of *The Poorhouse Fair* (novel) and *The Same Door* (stories). Son Michael born. Receives a Guggenheim Fellowship.

1960   *Rabbit, Run* (novel) published. Receives the Rosenthal Award of the National Institute of Arts and Letters for *The Poorhouse Fair.* Daughter Miranda born.

1962   *Pigeon Feathers* (stories) and *The Magic Flute* (adaptation for children of Mozart's opera) published.

1963   Publication of *The Centaur* (novel) and *Telephone Poles and Other Poems.*

1964   *Olinger Stories: A Selection* and *The Ring* (adaptation for children of Wagner's opera) published. Receives National Book Award for *The Centaur.* Elected a member of the National Institute of Arts and Letters. At the invitation of the State Department, visits Russia, Rumania, Bulgaria, and Czechoslovakia as part of a U.S.-U.S.S.R. Cultural Exchange Program.

1965   Publication of *Of the Farm* (novel), *Assorted Prose* (literary parodies, sketches, and reviews), and *Verse* (a paperback volume containing *The Carpentered Hen* and *Telephone Poles).* For children: *A Child's Calendar.* Receives *Le prix du meilleur livre étranger* for *The Centaur.*

1966   *The Music School* (stories) published.

1968   *Couples* (novel) published. Updike appears on the cover of *Time* magazine. Moves with his family to London for a year.

1969   *Midpoint and Other Poems* and *Bottom's Dream* (adaptation for children of *A Midsummer Night's Dream*) published.

1970   *Bech: A Book* (linked stories) published.

1971   *Rabbit Redux* (novel) published. Receives Signet Society Medal for Achievement in the Arts.

1972   *Museums and Women and Other Stories* published.

1973   Travels in five African countries as a Fulbright Lecturer.

1974   *Buchanan Dying* (drama with autobiographical Afterword) published. The Updikes separate and John moves to Boston.

1975   *A Month of Sundays* (novel) and *Picked-Up Pieces* (criticism) published.

1976   *Marry Me* (novel) published. The Updikes file for divorce.

1977   *Tossing and Turning* (poems) published. Updike elected to the fifty-member American Academy of Arts and Letters. Marries Martha R. Bernhard on September 30 and lives in Georgetown, Massachusetts, with her three sons.

1978   *The Coup* (novel) published.

1979   *Too Far To Go* (a collection of the Maples stories) and *Problems and Other Stories* published.

Notes on the Editors and Contributors

ROBERT ALTER is professor of comparative literature at the University of California, Berkeley. His books include *Fielding and the Nature of the Novel, After the Tradition: Essays on Modern Jewish Writing, Partial Magic: The Novel as a Self-Conscious Genre,* and *Defenses of the Imagination.*

ROBERT DETWEILER teaches at Emory University. In addition to his book on Updike, he has published *Saul Bellow: A Critical Study.*

ROSEMARY DINNAGE, an English critic, is on the editorial staff of the *Times Literary Supplement.*

DEAN DONER is academic vice-president of Boston University and a wri er of stories and criticism. He edits the newsletter of the John Updi Society.

HOWARD EILAND, coeditor of this volume, teaches English at Bost College.

RICHARD GILMAN taught until recently in the Yale School of Drama. books include *The Confusion of Realms, Common and Uncomm Masks,* and *The Making of Modern Drama.*

JOSEPHINE HENDIN is the author of *The World of Flannery O'Connor Vulnerable People: A View of American Fiction since 1945.* She tea contemporary fiction at the New School for Social Research.

RICHARD LOCKE publishes regularly on contemporary fiction and editor of *The New York Times Book Review.*

DAVID LODGE is senior lecturer in English at the University of Birm ham, England. He has published studies of Evelyn Waugh and Gra Greene as well as *The Language of Fiction, The British Museu Falling Down,* and *The Novelist at the Crossroads.*

JOYCE MARKLE has taught English at Loyola University. A found the John Updike Society, she was a consultant in the filming of Up story "The Music School," which was televised nationally by the P Broadcasting System in 1977.

DEBORAH MCGILL is an assistant editor of *Harper's*.

ARTHUR MIZENER, professor emeritus of English at Cornell University, has written many studies of modern literature, including biographies of F. Scott Fitzgerald and Ford Madox Ford. He is the editor of a Twentieth Century Views volume on Fitzgerald.

MICHAEL NOVAK is Ledden Watson Distinguished Professor of Religion at Syracuse University. His books include *Belief and Unbelief, Choosing Our King, The Rise of the Unmeltable Ethnics,* and *The Joy of Sports.*

JOYCE CAROL OATES, the novelist and story writer, has also published two books of literary criticism: *The Edge of Impossibility: Tragic Forms in Literature* and *New Heaven, New Earth: The Visionary Experience in Literature.*

MARTIN PRICE is Thomas E. Donnelley Professor of English at Yale and the author of *Swift's Rhetorical Art* and *To the Palace of Wisdom.* He has edited the Dickens volume in the Twentieth Century Views series.

JACK RICHARDSON is the theater critic for *Commentary* and the author of a number of plays, including *The Prodigal, Gallows Humor,* and *Xmas in Las Vegas.*

The late CHARLES THOMAS SAMUELS taught English at Williams College and was the author of *The Ambiguity of Henry James, Encountering Directors,* and *John Updike.*

GEORGE STEINER is Extraordinary Fellow at Churchill College, Cambridge. His recent books include *Language and Silence, Extraterritorial: Papers on Literature and the Language Revolution, In Bluebeard's Castle: Some Notes Toward the Redefinition of Culture,* and *On Difficulty.* He is also coeditor of the Twentieth Century Views volume on Homer.

LARRY E. TAYLOR teaches at Southern Illinois University.

DAVID THORBURN, coeditor of this volume, is a professor of literature at MIT and the author of *Conrad's Romanticism.*

RICHARD TODD reviews fiction for various magazines, including *The Atlantic,* of which he is an editor.

ROBERT TOWERS is the author of two novels, *The Necklace of Kali* and *The Monkey Watcher.* He teaches English at Queens College in New York City.

EDWARD P. VARGO is a Roman Catholic priest and former chairman of the Department of Language and Literature at Divine Word College in Iowa. He is currently a professor of English at Fu Jen University in Taiwan.

Selected Bibliography

There are three volumes devoted to primary and secondary bibliographical material:

Olivas, Michael. *An Annotated Bibliography of Updike Criticism, 1967-1973, and a Checklist of his Work*. New York: Garland Publishing Co., 1975.

Sokoloff, B. A., and David E. Arnason. *John Updike: A Comprehensive Bibliography*. Darby, Pa.: Darby Press, 1970; Folcroft, Pa.: Folcroft Press, 1971; Norwood, Pa.: Norwood Press, 1973. Limited editions.

Taylor, C. Clarke. *John Updike: A Bibliography*. Kent, Ohio: Kent State University Press, 1968.

These volumes should be supplemented by the useful listings of critical articles contained in the John Updike number of *Modern Fiction Studies* (Spring, 1974), in the annual bibliographical numbers of *PMLA*, and in the *Newsletter* of the John Updike Society (issued irregularly several times a year from the Office of the Academic Vice President, Boston University).

Books and Monographs

Burchard, Rachel C. *John Updike: Yea Sayings*. Carbondale, Ill.: Southern Illinois University Press, 1971.

Detweiler, Robert. *John Updike*. New York: Twayne Publishers, 1972.

Hamilton, Alice, and Kenneth Hamilton. *The Elements of John Updike*. Grand Rapids, Mich.: William B. Eerdmans, 1970.

Hamilton, Kenneth. *John Updike: A Critical Essay*. Grand Rapids, Mich.: William B. Eerdmans, 1967.

Markle, Joyce B. *Fighters and Lovers: Theme in the Novels of John Updike*. New York: New York University Press, 1973.

Samuels, Charles Thomas. *John Updike.* University of Minnesota Pamphlets on American Writers, No. 79. Minneapolis: University of Minnesota Press, 1969.

Taylor, Larry E. *Pastoral and Anti-Pastoral Patterns in John Updike's Fiction.* Carbondale, Ill.: Southern Illinois University Press, 1971.

Vargo, Edward P. *Rainstorms and Fire: Ritual in the Novels of John Updike.* Port Washington, N.Y.: Kennikat Press, 1973.

Essays and Reviews

Adler, Renata. "Arcadia, Pa." *New Yorker,* 39 (April 13, 1963), 182-88. On *The Centaur.*

Atlas, James. "John Updike Breaks Out of Suburbia," *The New York Times Magazine,* December 10, 1978, 60-64, 68-76. Valuable biographical article, drawing on interviews with Updike's friends and family.

Brenner, Gerry. "*Rabbit, Run:* John Updike's Criticism of the 'Return to Nature,'" *Twentieth Century Literature,* 12 (April, 1966), 3-14. Among the most influential academic essays on Updike.

Burgess, Anthony. "Language, Myth, and Mr. Updike," *Commonweal,* 83 (February 11, 1966), 557-59. On *Of the Farm* and Updike as stylist.

Gass, William H. "Cock-a-doodle-doo," *Fiction and the Figures of Life.* New York: Knopf, 1970. Pp. 206-11. Hostile, mocking account of *Couples* as "the suburbanite entry in the porno pageant."

Gill, Brendan. "A Special Case," *New Yorker,* 47 (January 8, 1972), 83-84. On *Rabbit Redux* and the autobiographical strain in Updike.

Harper, Howard M., Jr. "John Updike: The Intrinsic Problem of Human Existence," *Desperate Faith: A Study of Bellow, Salinger, Mailer, Baldwin, and Updike.* Chapel Hill: University of North Carolina Press, 1967. Pp. 162-90. On Pascalian and existential themes in *Rabbit, Run.*

Hunt, George. "John Updike's 'Sunday Sort of Book.'" *America,* 132 (June 21, 1975), 477-80. Valuable concise summary of Updike's career through *A Month of Sundays,* stressing his religious themes.

Kermode, Frank. "Shuttlecock," *The Listener,* 7 November 1968, p. 619. Suggestive comparison of *Couples* with Ford's *The Good Soldier.*

McGill, Deborah. "Promises Made and Broken," *Durham* (N.C.) *Morning Herald,* January 2, 1977, p. 3D. On *Marry Me.*

Novak, Michael, "Son of the Group," *The Critic,* 26 (June-July, 1968), 72-74. Eloquent defense of Updike's middle-class themes and sexual explicitness, focusing on *Couples.*

Ricks, Christopher. "Flopsy Bunny," *New York Review of Books,* 17 (December 16, 1971), 7-9. Thoughtful negative review of *Rabbit Redux,* claiming Updike is overprotective toward his characters.

Samuels, Charles Thomas. "Updike on the Present," *New Republic,* 165 (November 20, 1971), 29-30. Incisive review-essay on the relations between the Rabbit books and the limits of Updike's psychological realism.

Sissman, L. E. "John Updike: Midpoint and After," *Atlantic,* 226 (August, 1970), 102-4. On *Bech* and the vagaries of Updike's reputation among the critics.

Vickery, John. *"The Centaur:* Myth, History, and Narrative," *Modern Fiction Studies,* 20 (Spring, 1974), 29-43. An academic defense of the mythical method in Updike's third novel.

"View from the Catacombs," *Time,* 91 (April 26, 1968), 66-75. Useful cover story, profiling Updike at the time of *Couples.*

Wood, Michael. "Great American Fragments," *New York Review of Books,* 19 (December 14, 1972), 12-18. On *Museums and Women.*

Index

TWENTIETH CENTURY VIEWS

TWENTIETH CENTURY VIEWS

TWENTIETH CENTURY VIEWS